Eating NAFTA

The publisher and the University of California Press Foundation gratefully acknowledge the generous support of the Anne G. Lipow Endowment Fund in Social Justice and Human Rights.

Eating NAFTA

TRADE, FOOD POLICIES, AND THE DESTRUCTION OF MEXICO

Alyshia Gálvez

UNIVERSITY OF CALIFORNIA PRESS

University of California Press, one of the most distinguished university presses in the United States, enriches lives around the world by advancing scholarship in the humanities, social sciences, and natural sciences. Its activities are supported by the UC Press Foundation and by philanthropic contributions from individuals and institutions. For more information, visit www.ucpress.edu.

University of California Press
Oakland, California

Library of Congress Cataloging-in-Publication Data

Names: Gálvez, Alyshia, author.
Title: Eating NAFTA: trade, food policies, and the destruction of Mexico / Alyshia Gálvez.
Description: Oakland, California: University of California Press, [2018] | Includes bibliographical references and index. | Description based on print version record and CIP data provided by publisher; resource not viewed.
Identifiers: LCCN 2018009975 (print) | LCCN 2018014744 (ebook) | ISBN 9780520965447 (E-book) | ISBN 9780520291805 (cloth : alk. paper) | ISBN 9780520291812 (pbk. : alk. paper)
Subjects: LCSH: Food industry and trade—Mexico. | Nutritionally induced diseases—Mexico. | North American Free Trade Agreement (1992 December 17) | Free trade—Economic aspects—Mexico. | Free trade—Social aspects—Mexico. | Agriculture and state—Mexico.
Classification: LCC HD9014.M62 (ebook) | LCC HD9014.M62 G355 2018 (print) | DDC 338.1/972—dc23
LC record available at https://lccn.loc.gov/2018009975

Manufactured in the United States of America

26 25 24 23 22 21 20 19 18
10 9 8 7 6 5 4 3 2 1

For Lázaro, Elías, and Carlos. Always.

Antes, las personas podían vivir del campo, de la tierra tan fructífera que tenemos en México. . . . Vivíamos de una manera humilde, quizás, pero era buena, con principios y valores. Ahora, sin embargo, las cosas son muy diferentes. Creemos que más que avanzar, hemos ido en retroceso. Porque la idea del progreso sustentada en aprovecharse de las necesidades de los que menos tienen, no puede ser más que una violación a sus derechos humanos.

In the past, people could live from the land, from the fertile earth that we have in Mexico. . . . We lived in a humble way, perhaps, but in a good way, with principles and values. Now, however, things are very different. We believe that more than advancing, we are actually moving backwards. Because an idea of progress that is based on taking advantage of the needs of those who have the least, cannot be anything but a violation of their human rights.

—Norma Romero Vásquez, coordinator of Las Patronas and winner of Mexico's 2013 National Human Rights Prize

Slow death, or the structurally motivated attrition of persons notably because of their membership in certain populations, is neither a state of exception nor the opposite, mere banality, but a domain of revelation where an upsetting scene of living that has been muffled in ordinary consciousness is revealed to be interwoven with ordinary life after all, like ants revealed scurrying under a thoughtlessly lifted rock.

—Berlant 2007, 761

Contents

Illustrations

Preface

When Aura left her town of Santo Tomás Tlalpa, in the state of Puebla, Mexico, for New York City in 1999, she was so thin that the raindrops missed her on the way down from the clouds.[1] She was accustomed to the strenuous life of a *campesina*—working hard, and eating humbly: beans, tortillas, eggs, squash, herbs, and occasionally meat or chicken. Her hardiness helped her cross the border on foot, enduring days of walking in the desert with little to sustain her. It helped her to adapt to life as a laundry attendant in New York City. During her ten years in el Norte, she learned to like foods that people in her hometown had heard of on television and from other migrants: Chinese take-out, Southern fried chicken, and New York–style pizza. She found it tricky to cook in the small, crowded apartment she shared with compatriots, and later her husband and son, in the South Bronx. But, since even eating fast food out was more expensive than cooking, she would always find a way to make stews and salsas, tortillas and beans. She was shocked to discover that meat was cheaper by the pound than some of the squash and herbs she was used to cooking back home, so she never skimped on protein. Having more cash in her pocket meant she indulged her family's taste for soda, juice, and treats. After weathering the 2008 recession in the United States, and saving as much as they could, she and her husband have now returned to Mexico and are living in their hometown. In Santo Tomás Tlalpa, they own a home and upon returning, they opened a business. Aura is the proprietor of Mini-Tienda Manhattan, a small convenience store specializing mostly in snacks and soda. But, what comes next is clouded by a new reality. Aura's family's aspirations and savings may need to be dedicated to maintaining her own and her family members' health: Aura has been diagnosed with diabetes and her son is classified as "at risk" because he is overweight. They are not alone. About eighty thousand Mexicans die of type 2 diabetes each year, and the number of diabetics has increased by about 2 percent per year every year for the last two decades, making the disease the leading cause of death in Mexico.[2]

Mexico's public health crisis, accompanied by crippling health care costs, requires a big response, and it is getting one. A soda tax, a prohibition on junk food sales in schools, and a ban on marketing to children are touted in national and multinational contexts as an exemplary state response. But others are conspiring just as energetically to ensure that these efforts fail. It remains to be seen whether Mexico will manage to reverse one of the most precipitous increases in chronic disease in human history. We must also think about who is to blame. Is it Aura, and others like her, who have given up rural ways of life and adapted to a sedentary lifestyle, consuming more processed food and beverages? Or is there a larger culprit? Perhaps the same economic and social forces that took Aura to New York are also to blame for her illness.

"Whatever ails Mexico, the United States is going to catch. We are a system. We're intertwined and inseparable." These were the words of Father Alejandro Solalinde, outspoken priest and director of a migrant shelter in Ixtepec, Oaxaca, on a visit to New York City in May 2015. Even though many people in the United States seem to believe that when it comes to Mexico, "good fences make good neighbors," history and contemporary life show us that what happens in Mexico and other parts of Latin America reverberates in the United States, and vice versa.

Although trade and foreign investment are framed as a means for countries to achieve mutual prosperity, they are also, arguably, a space in which more powerful countries exert their will over less powerful ones.

History is rife with examples of the United States using military, economic, and political tools to advance its own aims.[3] Latin America has long served as a laboratory for social and economic experiments that are rehearsed, refined, and ultimately implemented elsewhere.[4] This has been so since the Monroe Doctrine, in which the United States declared its intention to stand up for its neighbors while maintaining exclusive rights to intervention in the region. It continued with the early twentieth-century approach of President Theodore Roosevelt, who claimed to "walk softly and carry a big stick" while reinforcing his objectives with gunboat diplomacy in Latin America and the Caribbean. This continued and intensified in the Cold War with the mid-twentieth-century interventions, overt and covert, in the Dominican Republic, Guatemala, Nicaragua, El Salvador, and Chile, among other places. The United States has not frequently imposed military force on its neighbors in recent years, but since the 1980s, trade has become an ever more common and important way that it influences other countries.

Trade partnerships also set the terms for private entities to operate globally. Global trade constitutes an arena involving deep collaboration between corporate interests and governments to advance specific geopolitical, social, and economic aims.[5] We can see this with the words of US president Bill Clinton on the signing of the supplemental agreements of the North American Free Trade Agreement (NAFTA) between Canada, Mexico, and the United States: "We have to create a new world economy . . . This is our opportunity to provide an impetus to freedom and democracy in Latin America and create new jobs for America as well. It's a good deal, and we ought to take it."[6]

More than twenty years later, Donald Trump railed against trade deals as a presidential candidate, claiming that NAFTA has moved manufacturing jobs to Mexico and hurt the American middle class; as president he has threatened to undo such deals. He argues that Mexico is "winning" at the expense of US workers as a result of NAFTA. Trump's anti-trade stance is one of his most popular positions among his supporters. He has also promoted derogatory stereotypes and racist views about Mexicans and Mexico that go well beyond a critique of trade arrangements. Trump's open promise to undo or renegotiate all US trade deals has moved trade negotiations out from the back rooms where congressional aides traditionally chugged coffee and haggled over phrasing. While historically such deals escaped the interest of most of the general public, today trade has become an important issue for the electorate on the right and left.

It is ironic that twenty years after its activation, NAFTA is suddenly on the front page of newspapers. Many critics of NAFTA's impact in the United States focus on how the agreement hurts American workers and pushes manufacturing jobs south of the border.[7] Indeed, the US trade deficit with Mexico is close to $60 billion.[8] On this issue, some politicians on both the right and the left in the United States are in agreement, including Trump and Vermont senator and former Democratic primary candidate Bernie Sanders. The impact of globalized trade on US workers is not a new concern: US presidential candidate Ross Perot famously warned in the early 1990s of a "giant sucking sound of jobs going south" if NAFTA was passed.[9] But the trade agreement's impact goes far beyond jobs.

I argue that the dominant pro- and anti-trade arguments provide an incomplete picture. The middle and working classes in each country are navigating a transforming and globalizing economy that might best be seen as producing common threats. Characterizations of NAFTA as an encroachment by Mexico on US prosperity obscure the fact that the working classes in both countries have been victimized by shifts in their respective economies.

If we assess the two decades since the implementation of NAFTA, which went into effect January 1, 1994, we can see many reasons to be concerned. While business is booming, the economic gains have not been equitably distributed in the population. According to a 2017 report assessing twenty-three years of NAFTA by the nonpartisan think tank Center for Economic and Policy Research, Mexico ranked fifteenth of twenty Latin American countries in growth of real GDP per person from 1994 to 2016, a rate of growth much lower than the average for the region.[10] If Mexico had retained its pre-1980 growth rate, it would today be qualified as a high-income country, but instead, 20.5 million more Mexicans were poor in 2014 than in 1994, a rate of 55.1 percent. Some counter that the rise in the number of poor is attributable to population growth, pointing to a decline in poverty of 3.9 percent. But Mexico's Latin American neighbors saw a drop of poverty in the same period more than five times greater, an average of 25 percent. Moreover, inflation-adjusted wages rose only 4.1 percent in twenty years, and unemployment is today 3.8 percent compared to 3.1 percent in 1994.[11]

While NAFTA resulted in many new jobs in Mexico in automotive industries and manufacturing, the growth, based heavily on high-tech automation of production, has not been enough to absorb all of the workers who come of age each year.[12] Industrial export agriculture is booming, but in ways that do not create high-paying jobs with upward mobility; further, it contributes to income divergence, or inequality.[13] The oft-mentioned US trade deficit with Mexico includes all agricultural products, such as the berries, limes, mangoes, peppers, and cucumbers that people in the US enjoy year round, but does not take into consideration that the success of large-scale commercial agricultural producers in Mexico has not translated into gains for most Mexican farmers, workers, and consumers. Mexico has become a vibrant manufacturing center for aeronautics, cars, and electronic components, but the vast majority of the Mexican people have not experienced the prosperity promised them as part of a globalizing economy.[14] And some of the improvements to the Mexican economy that can be attributed to NAFTA-era policies have had consequences that few anticipated or would celebrate: a rise in diet-related illness, a loss of access to traditional foods, and a decline in the viability of rural ways of life.

Likewise, many activists and analysts believe that NAFTA led to a massive, two-decade migration of Mexicans to the United Sates, which peaked at 12.8 million Mexicans residing in the United States in 2007.[15] The flow of migrants slowed and reversed after the recession of 2008. With migration today at net zero, there are as many people returning to Mexico as entering the United States.[16] Migration is no longer channeling workers out of the economy, but this is not because there are enough jobs and opportunities to incorporate them and the millions coming into the workforce each year. A rise in organized crime, drug and human trafficking, and violence perpetrated by state, paramilitary, and criminal organizations has shaken Mexican civil society.[17]

While Mexicans anticipated that expanded trade through NAFTA would bring greater access to consumer goods at lower prices, higher wages, and a modernization of the economy, they surely did not expect to see the countryside decimated, subsistence strategies hindered, and poverty increased. Some have described the impact of NAFTA as a full-frontal assault on the poor. As the Bishop of Coahuila and 2012 nominee for the Nobel Peace Prize Raúl Vera explained, "We are no longer talking about the marginalization of people, but their elimination."[18] Anthropologist Linda Green refers to those most at risk in the post-NAFTA economy as "nobodies," "redundant" and "disposable" people who "fit into a system in which violence, fear and impunity are crucial components."[19]

Surplus people, those who do not have a place in the Mexican economy, are colloquially referred to as "*ni-nis*" (short for *ni estudiando, ni trabajando*, people who are neither working nor studying). Many people today find economic survival to be precarious and contingent on a reorienting of their lives, obliging them to commute long distances, migrate to other regions within Mexico, or cobble together multiple part-time and contingent occupations. While some of these shifts are common to contemporary life in neoliberal economies, there are aspects of the Mexican experience that have been underacknowledged. The reorganization of Mexico's economy since NAFTA has transformed family life. Many people are no longer able to maintain multigenerational households, as they did in the past, in which resources and efforts are pooled for mutual benefit. While small-scale farming and barter may have previously softened the need for cash in rural communities with high levels of self-sufficiency, today's labor and economic arrangements make cash king. The jobs that are available often take people far from their families, and away from the land.[20] Instead, people increasingly attune their living arrangements and rhythms of life to the demands of precarious employment, housing, and transportation. As we will explore later, shifts in the Mexican federal government's policies for addressing poverty have recently shifted to a model based on financial inclusion, emphasizing an expansion of market participation and credit that promotes consumption over other kinds of economic activity. Even while we can characterize the present moment in Mexico as one in which citizens are less able to find productive work, escape poverty, or migrate to the United States, consumption has risen, particularly that of goods that flooded Mexican markets following the implementation of neoliberal trade policies.

Mainstream discussions of NAFTA fail to assess the ways that the fates and futures of people in the US and Mexico are locked together—for better or for worse. While workers displaced from US manufacturing worry about the effects of trade on jobs, the effects for Mexicans have included troubling health trends. A pernicious consequence of NAFTA's changed economic landscape is a rise in noncommunicable diseases. In Mexico, the top three causes of death and disability are now diet-related chronic diseases: diabetes mellitus, ischemic heart disease, and chronic kidney disease.[21] These noncommunicable diseases have surpassed infectious diseases as the primary causes of death and disabling disease.[22] Data from 1990, before NAFTA, and 2013, nearly twenty years after it took effect, reveal the consequences: chronic kidney disease increased 276 percent, diabetes 41 percent, and ischemic heart disease 52 percent.[23] Chronic disease and disability rob "productive days" from workers, taking them out of the workforce temporarily or permanently.

Mexico's partners in NAFTA, and indeed countries around the world, have seen a rise in chronic disease, but in Mexico the shift in the public health outlook is particularly disturbing. While most globalizing nations have seen what is called an epidemiological transition—rising life expectancy along with a shift from infectious to noncommunicable diseases as the primary causes of death—in Mexico the transition has been abrupt and "dissonant," with chronic disease claiming lives faster than rising life expectancy can lengthen them.[24] To illustrate this we can look at deaths from diabetes. Today, diabetes is the number one killer in Mexico. If we contrast this with the other NAFTA signatory nations, diabetes is not among the top five causes of death for the United States and Canada. In Mexico, diabetes is both more prevalent (15.8 percent of adults in Mexico versus 10.8 percent in the United States and 7 percent in Canada) and more deadly; a diagnosis of diabetes in Mexico is more likely to be fatal than in the United States or Canada.[25] The rate of increase in Mexico is also higher than in the other countries.[26] Both the United States and Mexico had about eighty thousand diabetes-related deaths in 2014. However, the US population is more than twice the size of Mexico's, so the risk of dying of diabetes in Mexico is roughly twice as high. In contrast, for Canada, there is about a tenth the risk as in the US.

This book is about the rapid transformation of the Mexican food system and its connection to the policies implemented under NAFTA. The government's rearrangement of the national economy has costs—costs for the health of Mexican citizens and for the maintenance of traditional ways of eating. Paradoxically, as Mexican people have faced a transformation of their foodways since NAFTA, the way they used to eat has become highly fashionable. As traditional Mexican cuisine has fallen out of the reach of average Mexican people, it has become available as a luxury product for global foodie elites. In this book, I explore how the Mexican public health crisis caused by the increased consumption of industrial foods since NAFTA has coincided with the elevation of Mexican ways of eating as a global cuisine. We examine the health consequences of NAFTA and how the Mexican government has begun to address them. Finally, we explore the ways that diet-related illness has been framed as an issue of personal responsibility in ways that deflect societal responsibility for restructuring economic, political, and food systems.

1 Introduction

In 2008 I visited my friend María's mother in Santo Tomás Tlalpa, in a rural part of the state of Puebla. She asked me how her daughter, son-in-law, and grandchildren were doing in New York City. She had not seen her daughter in a dozen years, and had met her grandchildren only once when they visited during school vacation. While she talked, she charred chiles, onion, tomatoes, and garlic on the open flame of her gas stove. She combined them by hand in a stone *molcajete,* making a last-minute salsa to serve with the meat, stewed vegetables, and tortillas she made for lunch.

Eight years later, I sit in the same kitchen. María's mother died two years ago. Now Elena, María's sister-in-law, makes a quick stew of zucchini and tomatoes to take to her two younger children for a midmorning meal at the elementary school down the street, served with warm tortillas from the vendor nearby. While she cooks, a neighbor drops off a stalk of *cacallas,* small buds that grow on a tall stalk and are the fruit of the maguey cactus, which are savored here during their short season of availability. Elena tells me we will sauté them in a little oil and eat them later.

Later that day, Elena and her husband Samuel host a group of college students from New York that I've brought to town as part of a documentary film course. Relying on help from several older women in the neighborhood, they build a fire in ventilated metal barrels in the courtyard outside the kitchen. They cover the fire with a pair of large disc-shaped *comales*, or griddles, and make quesadillas, hand-pressing the tortillas as they go, filling each with squash blossoms and stringy fresh queso Oaxaca. We eat the quesadillas along with the sautéed cacallas.

A few days later, I am invited to eat with María's husband's family, a short walk down the street. I stand with the matriarch of the family in her outdoor kitchen behind the house. Protected from the intense sun by a three-sided wooden shelter, she tends a wood fire and hand shapes *memelas*, sometimes called *sopes*. They start as a slightly thick tortilla, flattened with a tortilla press from a ball of freshly ground corn *masa*. As they come off the comal, she pinches the border of the disc to create a raised edge, seemingly not feeling the heat that burns me when I try. She applies a quick brush of *asiento*, pork lard, and places the memelas back on the comal to toast a bit more. Finally, they are dressed with a thin coat of mashed black beans, a drizzle of red or green salsa, a sprinkling of *cotija* cheese or *queso fresco*, or a bit of chorizo, and a sprinkle of chopped cilantro.

The quesadillas and sopes I enjoyed in Mexico are part of what I identify in this book as *milpa*-based cuisine. Far from what is often sold as "Mexican food" globally, this is a style of cooking with great regional variation, that across regions shares a core set of ingredients and cooking techniques. Milpa-based cuisine depends on ground corn, fresh vegetables, and a series of distinct steps to prepare the corn masa and salsas. While not all of the people I describe grow their own corn now, or did so in the past, their diet relied heavily on the products that are traditionally grown in a rural milpa, an intercropped field that includes corn and also other plants such as squash, beans, tomatoes, tomatillos, and chiles. The core of milpa-based cuisine is corn that is grown locally, then dried, removed from the cob, and stored in sacks. When it is used, it is nixtamalized (soaked in mineral lime and water) before being ground into masa. Tortillas, quesadillas, and memelas are examples of some of the foods made with corn that many families eat daily and that are made fresh for each meal. Freshly made stews and salsas are another mainstay, using the other vegetables that happily grow intercropped in the same field with corn. Cheese, eggs, and potatoes provide easy and varied substance to meals. Meat, seafood, chicken, and sausage play minor roles, not appearing at every meal and often in small quantities when they do.

If we look at more than five centuries of foodways in Mexico, we see that people have changed the way they eat with shifts in the food system over several rough periods: the era preceding European contact; the period of conquest and colonization, the phase of urbanization and industrialization, and the turn outward with NAFTA and globalization. Each of these periods coincided with significant changes in the political and economic structure of the region and influenced the ways people ate, and the ideas each social sector had about the food, health, and morality of their own and other groups. While each wave after the conquest period represented a threat to and significant alterations of milpa-based cuisine, only the most recent phase of post-NAFTA alterations to the food system have really threatened its viability. Milpa-based cuisine requires access to ingredients, labor, and rhythms of life and mealtimes that are not as feasible today. For some, that is a story of liberation, since milpa-based food systems historically depend on rural household and labor arrangements that were dependent on relentless female domestic labor, and are not easily compatible with formal labor force participation. Those who no longer work the land or spend hours a day grinding corn and shaping masa into tortillas may or may not desire to go back to that kind of lifestyle, but I wish to point out that the transition away from this way of eating has costs, many of which are not widely acknowledged or well known. Further, those who wish to maintain or restore rural ways of living arguably should have the possibility of doing so.

NAFTA eliminated tariffs and barriers to trade between Mexico, the United States, and Canada, uniting them in a single market and facilitating direct investment and the flow of goods across borders. Globalization has the effect of distributing consumption of industrial products far and wide. It has been both praised and criticized for leveling difference, making it possible for people at all income levels to consume the kinds of goods that used to be more readily available in wealthier nations. Mexico is not alone in having seen dramatic shifts in the availability, affordability, and distribution of industrialized products, including foods and beverages. It is also not alone in seeing health consequences from the rise in consumption of foods and beverages associated with diet-related illness. That

Mexico's chronic disease burden is especially high does not make the outline of what has happened in Mexico's dietary transition very different from what has happened in so many places as food systems have become industrialized and globalized. How is the Mexican story unique?

In the story of the transformation of Mexico's food system and foodways, we see a convergence of economic trends and policy decisions that have taken ancestral ways of eating out of the reach of the average Mexican citizen, while making traditional foods available as a high-value, high-status commodity to be "elevated" and reinterpreted by global elite chefs. For many Mexicans today, processed and packaged food is easier, cheaper, and more readily available than milpa-based cuisine. Even in rural areas, consumption of sodas, snacks, and candy has increased dramatically, while tortilla consumption is down. Preferences have changed, of course, as more people have access to the kinds of foods advertised in the media, but the food system has brought some things within reach while distancing others.

Food systems are complex webs of food production, distribution, sales, marketing, processing, and preparation that shape what we eat, where it comes from, and how much it costs. Most of the food system, like the cables that bring us electricity, is invisible to the consumer and is often taken for granted. In heavily industrialized urban places like Manhattan, where I live—an island that produces almost no food—it can be difficult to visualize or understand the many pathways by which food comes to sit on the supermarket shelf. Even when we buy fruits and vegetables at a farmers' market, where we can imagine a direct path from field to market stall, we do not necessarily know the regulatory, commercial, social, and other networks by which that particular farmer came to be selling those particular potatoes or apples in that location. Large-scale, multinational food systems depend even more on a complex web of policies and networks of private and public actors and entities that may not be perceptible to us as consumers.

Food systems influence and shape foodways, and vice versa. Historically, foodways in most places have depended primarily on foodstuffs produced locally and regionally. While some trade in spices, teas, oils, coffee, and other products goes back thousands of years in some regions, most food did not travel very far before being consumed. Innovations in refrigeration, transportation, food packaging and preservatives, and mass production of food contributed to new possibilities for food to travel from one area to another before being consumed.[1] For many kinds of food, especially in cities, this became the norm rather than the exception. Today, an apple in my local supermarket in New York City is as likely to have been grown in New Zealand or Chile as in the apple orchards a hundred miles away in Upstate New York.[2]

This development has expanded what we have available to us, making it possible for us to exercise a great deal of choice in the foods we eat. But increasingly in the United States, consumers find it problematic that we do not know where so much of our food came from and we have begun to ask about the conditions in which our food is produced. We demand reforms to our heavily industrialized food system. Nutrition, health, consumer advocacy, and environmental activists have found common cause and won some victories: Walmart now sells organic products; McDonald's now uses poultry and dairy products raised without antibiotics or hormones. In response to controversies about their funding of research on the health effects of soda consumption and marketing campaigns that target children, Coca-Cola and Pepsi have joined efforts to combat childhood obesity and offer more low- or no-calorie beverage options than before.[3]

But what does the industry do, faced with a growing awareness about the harm of industrialized food and beverage production and consumption? Issue a mea culpa and stop peddling products that scientists increasingly link to chronic disease? No, they have increasingly set their sights on new markets in the developing world. Declining consumption in industrialized countries doesn't matter to shareholders when there is a whole world of new consumers to be targeted. Along with their counterparts in other countries, rural and low-income Mexicans have provided a market for producers of industrial foods to offset declining sales in the United States. Mexicans' increased consumption has propped up economic arrangements like NAFTA and produced a vibrant regional economy, but it is impacting their health.

Chronic, noncommunicable, diet-related illness is different from other kinds of public health concerns in that its etiology—the way people understand the pathways for becoming sick—is firmly rooted in personal behavior.[4] Even though public health research indicates that personal behavior is not the main factor contributing to chronic disease, this idea is persistent.[5] In fact, overwhelming evidence indicates that structural factors such as social and economic disparities; food distribution, availability, and regulations; and access to preventive care play the biggest roles in rates of chronic disease. Nevertheless, commonsense understandings of diet-related disease in popular discourse and public policy continue to put the individual at the center. Obesity, diabetes, heart disease, and other conditions are imagined to rest within the control and power of the individual. These diseases are described, often even by those who suffer from them, as a "failure" of knowledge, habits, self-control, diet, and exercise.

Many argue that Mexican waistlines have expanded faster than others in human history because Mexico has a legendary sweet tooth, not because its political leaders and their economic advisers have sold off shares of their compatriots' stomachs as surely as a retailer negotiates shelf space. The massive effort by transnational food corporations working in the spaces carved by trade deals to expand the global reach of their products and ensure the purchase and consumption of larger quantities of calories by people all over the world is forgotten or ignored. Lowering the barriers to global marketing and distribution of their products, trade deals accelerate the processes by which ultraprocessed foods and beverages become available the world over. They also provide a way for transnational corporations to delay an anticipated day of reckoning in which their products come to be universally understood as harmful to health, even while in many places, that information has already prompted declines in consumption and policies to further curb marketing and sales. This is not to say that responsibility for rising rates of chronic disease rests exclusively or primarily with corporations or policy makers who seek to boost trade. Chronic diseases are multifactorial, as we explore in later chapters. But the correlation between the rise in chronic disease and globalizing trade accords begs an analysis of the ways that business practices, trade policy, anti-poverty, and public health campaigns converge and propel some kinds of consumption over others and also some ways of thinking about and addressing chronic disease.

As long as so many people understand diet-related chronic diseases to be rooted in knowledge and behavior, we will continue to think they fall outside of the realm of politics and economic development. I propose that we instead consider the massive proliferation of diet-related illness as a kind of structural violence—a result of policy decisions and priorities. Structural violence is defined by anthropologist and medical doctor Paul Farmer as "a way of describing social arrangements that put individuals and populations in harm's way."[6] Farmer argues that structural violence distributes and determines suffering in a population, revealing "symptoms of deeper pathologies of power" closely tied to the social conditions that group people and expose them to differing degrees to harm.[7] This concept offers us a way to understand epidemics, especially when they are accompanied by events, such as an earthquake or war, that differentially impact the rich and the poor, the powerful and the marginalized. We can deploy this theory to think not only about infectious diseases and abrupt causes of death such as accidents, violence, and disasters, but also about chronic disease. Chronic disease is, essentially, a slow-moving disaster, more deadly than earthquakes and infectious outbreaks, and especially insidious for its slow and sometimes invisible work. It is not indiscriminate, as those with the greatest wealth and social status are not as vulnerable as the socioeconomically disadvantaged. I argue that the methodical, aggressive, and intentional reorienting of Mexico's economy away from small-scale agriculture and toward foreign direct investment and global trade has had worrisome consequences: the sickening of the population and the neutralization of demands they can make—on their political leaders and the economy.

At the same time that diet-related illness is on the rise, we can see that Mexican food is having a moment as a world-renowned cuisine. The global rise in price, popularity, and appreciation of Mexican cuisine is the other side of the coin of Mexico's epidemic of diet-related illness. With Mexican cuisine newly vaunted as a sophisticated and complex tradition with global reach and popularity, sincere appreciation for Mexican food has never been more widespread. This popularity has driven an interest in "authenticity" and generated a market for high-end interpretations of what was traditionally a peasant, milpa-based cuisine built around a "trinity" of ingredients: corn, beans, and squash.[8] Specialists in Mexican food outside of Mexico have been freed from having to modify their dishes for the palates of non-Mexicans: by toning down spiciness or loading up on melted cheese and sour cream, as was typical in the past.[9] Instead, "foodies" around the world today demand ingredients such as handmade tortillas, fresh vegetables and herbs, and a broad palette of chiles and salsas. It seems every food magazine and cooking show on television includes at least one recipe for tacos, tortilla soup, or fresh salsa. Gone from ingredients lists are hard "taco shells," "taco seasoning" packets, and shredded orange cheese (except

well known as it spreads

to their liking

when they are occasionally used ironically). The lines between "high" and "low" have been blurred, and not only for Mexican food, with culinary school graduates turning to ethnic cuisines more broadly, often "elevating," "reimagining," or "reinventing" emblematic dishes, whether they serve them from a food truck or on a white tablecloth.

All of this has brought "Mexican food" (a misnomer referring to an endless array of regional and subregional cuisines and cooking styles) to its apex. Food means a lot more than what we put into our mouths: it is an object of our aspirations and our memories. It is a vehicle for nostalgia, and also for prestige. It is a way that people communicate who they are, the group to which they belong, and who they desire to become. Even though food has always played an outsized role in Mexico's imagining of itself as a nation, today, more than ever, food is a site of contention where we can observe debates and struggles over identity and status, rights and responsibilities, and individual and collective well-being.

This book looks at both sides of the coin together. In it, I trace the paradoxical rise of Mexican food as a global cuisine at the same time that average citizens in Mexico find traditional foods increasingly out of reach or out of step with their lifestyles. Corn, the most basic element of Mexican food, exemplifies larger trends in the economy, as small-scale farmers find they can no longer afford to grow it, and as it is becoming more common for it to be eaten and drunk in highly processed forms in chips, sweets, and sodas, rather than in tortillas, *tamales,* and *atole.* Consumption of soda and processed foods has risen while the availability and affordability of ancestral foods and even water have declined. While NAFTA was an engine for this shift, it is just one part of a constellation of ways that the Mexican government has changed its orientation to its citizens' needs, especially those related to anti-obesity, anti-poverty, health, development, and education policies, in ways that drive Mexican families even further away from traditional livelihoods and eating habits.

These policies and programs, and the overall restructuring of Mexico's food system, have health consequences. They also generate ripples across borders: the rise and subsequent leveling of rates of migration, and the connection to Mexican migrant workers in the United States who sustain food production and preparation industries, while often experiencing a decline in their own health.

This book examines the ways that the binational relationship between the United States and Mexico, and specifically trade policy, have shattered foodways in Mexico—changing what is on plates, how it gets there, what we think about it, and how it impacts our neighbors' bodies. While economists and business elites celebrate the linking of North American markets as a success, there is another story to tell. As intimate and basic as food is in its relation to human life, it is a lens by which to see how our world is changing and becoming ever more connected across borders. What we see is globalization gone wild. The winners, large corporations and industrial farms, have achieved a level of unprecedented prosperity and power at great human cost. This leads us to ask whether traditional Mexican foodways will be reduced to an elite, luxury experience for a few, or preserved for everyone. We must consider whether human-scaled food systems are compatible with trends toward globalization and neoliberal economic policy. When we examine what is gained and what is lost in the transformation of ways of producing, distributing, and eating food, we might ask, can ancestral methods be restored with benefits for health and prosperity for all?

Our story largely focuses on the period since the 1994 implementation of NAFTA. Over two decades, Mexico's median educational level, income, and labor force participation all rose after it went into effect. The country's emergence as a global leader in automobile and aircraft manufacturing, export agriculture, among other sectors, is celebrated by its leaders. While NAFTA is hailed as a success by some economists and political scientists, it has produced many negative consequences for Mexico's population.[10] On the heels of NAFTA's passage, Mexican migration rapidly accelerated, as did the expense and risk involved with border crossing.[11] Moreover, the number of those living in poverty rose according to the government's own statistics and think tank calculations.[12] In addition, obesity and diabetes rose dramatically in Mexico in the same period: 71.3 percent of the population has come to be classified as overweight, and 32.8 percent obese, while obesity among women has increased 270 percent.[13] By 2017, the rate of diabetics in Mexico had reached the rate of almost 16 percent of the population.[14]

I imagine that as a reader who has picked up this book, you might already be one of the many people concerned about the industrialization of food production, the decline of the small family farm, and the rise of diet-related illnesses in the United States, but you may not be aware of the health consequences of these trends across our borders. While awareness about the industrialized food system and the health problems associated with processed foods and beverages has risen dramatically in the United States, few know about how these trends are playing out across borders and in markets that are adopting our foodways. Trade policies that promote the exchange of goods, including food, also change ways of eating. When we look at these ripple effects, it seems that the food and beverage industry is taking advantage of the lag time in popular awareness of the long-term risks of processed foods and beverages to sell them as broadly as possible in developing markets, no matter the consequences. But we must ask whether the health and human costs of diet-related illness are simply collateral damage along the path to the milestones of economic development established by Mexico's politicians as well as global financial institutions. If more Mexicans adopt an "American" way of eating and its related health effects, is a higher risk of death from chronic disease the cost of Mexico's trade and economic policies?

Twenty years after the passage of NAFTA, the small-scale farming of corn, traditional ways of eating, and the health of Mexican communities are threatened. Today, Mexico imports 42 percent of its food and has a persistently high rate of poverty, at 55.1 percent.[15] The current state of affairs sometimes sounds like dystopian science fiction: a post-migration Mexico where social engineering has resulted in a low birth rate and the death of the family farm, while the poor receive cash incentives for conforming to certain kinds of middle-class behavior that distance them further from rural ways of life. Local green markets have been replaced with supermarkets overflowing with processed food and soda. "Gringos" clamor for handmade tortillas, while Mexicans have become the world's top consumers of instant noodles.[16]

CHANGES IN MEXICO'S ECONOMY

Although multinational trade has many critics, many insist that the future lies in global collaboration for mutual benefit and prosperity. They tell us that a rising tide lifts all boats, and that protectionism and isolationism are unwise in an ever more globalized economy. Goods, commodities, and capital rocket between countries at unprecedented speeds. The products that circulate—cell phones, televisions, and blue jeans—are likely to have been manufactured with components made in multiple countries. Those who are troubled by these flows are cast as attempting to slow or stop a rising tide. Those who fear that globalized trade threatens labor standards and the environment are advised to work for the inclusion of humanitarian or environmental aims in trade deals that might raise wages or provide labor protections. For those worried about US manufacturing jobs, trade proponents argue that jobs can be better preserved by modernizing the workforce through training and education. In these formulations, both proponents and critics of the changes brought by globalization see them as inevitable.

Politics, by necessity, entails compromise and concessions. Every great "deal" made by a party or politician throughout history has involved a certain degree of compromise. Purity is a luxury of the activist, because governing, we are told, involves being willing to give up some of what we are fighting for in order to get a deal done. NAFTA, like all trade agreements, involved a certain amount of nose holding on all sides. There were people and collective interest groups in Mexico, Canada, and the United States that opposed various parts of the deal for any number of reasons, including the perceived threat to US workers and to small-scale Mexican producers (of food, goods, cultural products, and more).[17] But even the most ardent opponents of NAFTA did not articulate a concern about the possibilities for radical transformation of almost every aspect of life, including the physical well-being of the Mexican people.

The likely consequences of the planned shift to global free trade were alarming enough for NAFTA opponents; they did not also anticipate the far-reaching destabilization of the countryside and the health consequences the trade agreement would produce. Furthermore, research connecting nutritional and epidemiological transitions to global trade was still nascent, while the food and beverage industry made significant efforts to cast doubt on the relationship between their products and diet-related illness.

Twenty years hence, while it was understood that NAFTA had initiated a process of economic and political transformation, we can see unanticipated consequences for the health of the Mexican people. It is as if the trade deal meant Mexican bodies, and to a certain extent those of people in the United States and Canada, too, were put up for sale like any other market good. The expansion of markets would be accomplished by the expansion of waistlines.[18] Multinational food and beverage corporations seek to increase consumption of their products in ways that encourage us to consume beyond what we need and to leave aside other ways of eating that take more time, effort, and skill. Mounting scientific evidence demonstrates that one kind of calories is not the same as another—that these products chemically alter bodies with the consequences being not simply weight gain, but also diabetes, cancer, metabolic syndrome, and other ailments.[19]

Hyperpalatable, ultraprocessed foods are products that are engineered to activate cravings and override cues of satiety.[20] They are marketed to appeal to ideas about modern and cosmopolitan lifestyles, and priced and sold in ways that preempt and dislocate other kinds of consumption. They are products that scientists have proven have negative health consequences—and not simply when people eat them in large quantities. As we will explore later, some of the ingredients used in processed food and beverages can produce metabolic changes and alter the function of organs, leading to cascading health effects that go beyond caloric intake.[21] When such ill effects begin to manifest, more products are proffered as solutions—lower fat, lower sugar, smaller portions, "diet," "lite" or "light," "natural," and "healthy" processed foods as a solution to other processed foods. And when that is not enough, the sister industries that produce pharmaceuticals and medical devices promise uninhibited lifestyles, health "solutions" that are convenient, affordable, easy, even "fun," putting a happy face on the real-life problems of diabetes and metabolic disorders.[22]

What is more, and perhaps most important of all, the negative consequences of consumption of such products can be completely externalized by their manufacturers, framed as a problem of overconsumption and insufficient physical activity. Scholars, investigative journalists, and consumer advocates have begun to reveal the tremendous investments in sponsored research and marketing made by corporations precisely to generate an aura of confusion about what causes weight gain and diet-related illness.[23] People who become sick are made to bear the brunt of responsibility for their ill health because they should know better than to consume in excess. Thus, even as "diet-related" illnesses assume epidemic proportions, killing and sickening people more than any other cause, it is individual responsibility and behavior that are to blame and greater "culture" and "education" that are presented as solutions. Corporations join hands with public health officials to address the "obesity epidemic" by promoting "moderation" in consumption, as well as nutrition education and exercise, without addressing changes in the food system. As we will see later, such an approach centered on behavioral change is promoted not only by the corporations but also by many nutritionists, dietitians, medical doctors, and public health officials.

NAFTA marked a dramatic change in the orientation of the Mexican economy. The agreement was just one piece of a larger project to "modernize" Mexico's economy and link its market to the United States and Canada. Politicians from more than one political party supported the country's transition from a subsistence agriculture–based economy to one based on manufacturing. They saw particular promise in the kind of manufacturing associated with *maquiladoras*, the factories that produce a single component in a long production chain spanning across borders and flexibly responding to changes in materials, transportation, and labor costs. The new economy was made to order by multinational corporations seeking lower labor costs and new markets. This required massive economic, social, and political transformations, including even a revision of the Mexican Constitution.[24] In theory, NAFTA would enable Mexico to compete with US firms, receive US products cheaply, export more goods, and enable millions of *campesinos* (peasants) to transition to urban, industrial livelihoods. For the United States, the trade deal would expand markets for US goods, protect US industries, lower the costs of imported goods for US consumers, and enable the country to shift away from manufacturing and toward high-tech and knowledge-based industries.

To understand the trade agreement's urgency for Mexico, we must look back a decade earlier, to 1982, when Mexico defaulted on its foreign debt and entered into a series of structural adjustment programs imposed by the International Monetary Fund and World Bank in exchange for servicing its debt.[25] In a prescribed package of reforms, structural adjustment was imposed on nations seeking loans, development aid, and sometimes even emergency aid. In return for debt rescheduling, indebted countries were required to reform their governments, cut welfare expenditures, strip labor protections, and allow for the privatization of all sectors, ostensibly for the purpose of developing and "streamlining" their economies.[26] Although these reforms were promoted by multinational development agencies like the World Bank and the International Monetary Fund, the US influence over these institutions is so strong that the prescription advocated for borrowing nations to reform their economies in the 1980s and 1990s is commonly referred to as "the Washington Consensus."[27] Mexico became an early laboratory for this type of program, and there, structural adjustment meant an end to Mexico's history of energetic intervention in its national economy through price supports and subsidies of staple crops, import substitution, and long-standing policies of protectionism and tariffs in trade.[28]

In 1990, then Mexican president Carlos Salinas de Gortari (1988–1994) went on a networking campaign, seeking foreign investment by Europe to solve Mexico's debt problems. He was unsuccessful with European countries, but was somewhat unexpectedly able to generate interest in a trade agreement between Mexico, Canada, and the United States.[29] Mexico was predisposed to a large-scale restructuring and liberalization of its economy, and the United States encouraged it to reform even further the basic premises of its contract with its citizens. At the same time, according to Cameron and Tomlin's detailed account of the deal, the US negotiators made it clear to their Mexican counterparts throughout the process that the trade deal was not a high priority for them; they delayed negotiations, sometimes failed to show up at them, threatened to walk away, and made demands so unreasonable they could only be seen as an effort to make the deal fall apart. For the United States, the potential impact of NAFTA was seen as relatively insignificant both economically and politically. Mexico, as a weaker player in the negotiation, had more to lose, and had to promise more to get the deal done.[30] Mexican negotiators did not perceive the repeated US threats to walk away as an idle bluff, but rather assumed that any inflexibility on their part would cause the deal to crumble. For Mexico, the stakes were seen as too high to lose the chance for a deal, or even to try to negotiate for better terms.

The transition sought by Salinas and his team, comprised largely of Harvard- and University of Chicago–educated economists, was not imagined to be painless. While it was widely understood that the relationship between the United States and Mexico needed to include terms governing the flow of goods, capital, and people, the United States refused to allow migration to be on the table. To remove one leg of what had been envisioned as a three-legged stool made the entire deal wobbly from the start. I learned in a conversation with a former foreign minister who was at the negotiating table that the Mexican government anticipated that a half-million campesinos would be displaced before a place could be found for them in the new economy, a process some called "de-peasantization."[31] What they did not expect, or account for in the deal, was that a half-million people *per year* would emigrate for the next decade and a half. Even as Mexico urbanized and industrialized, it expelled millions, leading to 10 percent of the Mexican population living in the United States by 2006.[32]

Many of those who migrated were small-scale farmers whose livelihood was threatened by NAFTA. They found that new trade policies did not open fresh opportunities for the products they were growing. Instead, they closed existing markets and came with protections for US agricultural industries that hindered Mexican farmers' ability to compete. At the same time, Mexico was obliged to eliminate most of its supports of corn—its most important and iconic crop—while subsidized corn from the United States soon flooded its market. Further, customary reciprocity, barter, and complementarity in agricultural production within and between small farms was challenged by various factors, including an exodus of laborers, high input costs, and an ill-timed drought.

Rising poverty and changing economic conditions began to prompt a popular backlash against the ruling party's economic policies. In its efforts to respond to popular demands, the government developed innovative social programs, including the much discussed "Progresa" program, later called "Oportunidades," and now called "Prospera."[33] These programs to address poverty sought to exchange cash, given directly to mothers, for behavioral change. Women enrolled in the program were incentivized to fulfill benchmarks, such as taking their children for immunizations and medical exams, attending parent-teacher conferences, and keeping children in school until they completed compulsory education in the eighth grade. These anti-poverty programs increased the availability of cash in communities previously marginalized by formal consumer markets. More cash enabled different kinds of consumption than the more local, reciprocity-based economy for basic foods and goods that had predominated before. As cash became king, the "supermarketization" of even small cities began in earnest.[34]

For some, this is economic development. With NAFTA, Mexico had promised its citizens greater opportunities in higher skilled jobs. If these gains were anticipated to lead to a rise in obesity, and even diabetes and heart disease, the framers of the economic reforms might have thought them a small price to pay. Such "first world" problems could have been seen as preferable to the "third world" problems Mexico had in the 1980s: a demographic crisis of too many youth and not enough jobs or educational opportunities for them, coupled with volatile economic booms and busts.

But for others, like opposition party leader and presidential candidate Andrés Manuel López Obrador, it was "the biggest pillage in history."[35] NAFTA undid the promise of the Mexican Revolution to ensure an equitable and just distribution of the nation's wealth to its people by rolling back Article 27 of the constitution, which administered land holdings after the Mexican Revolution. The trade agreement entailed a restructuring of the economy and the political system—but arguably most significant of all—a reorientation of everyday life to market logics. The economy was no longer to be centered on production, subsistence, or self-sufficiency, the guiding principles of earlier eras. Instead, comparative advantage, foreign direct investment, free trade, and security would be the mantra of Mexico approaching the twenty-first century. But such ambitious projects of change do not happen overnight and they come with unintended consequences. Some of the most severe consequences have been seen in the bodies of Mexicans themselves.

A NOTE ON OBESITY

> "Obesity" is a medicalized term that does violence to fat people.
>
> —Guthman 2009, 188

Before continuing, I must specify how I use the term "obesity" in this book. There are complications and problems with the way obesity is defined and measured, and the ways that it is sometimes bundled with noncommunicable chronic diseases as though it were itself a disease and not a correlated risk factor. Many scholars have critiqued the metrics used to define overweight and obesity, such as body mass index, or BMI,[36] as well as the conceptualization of obesity itself as a disease.[37] The construction of risk factors, and calculations of risk, too, have been critiqued in productive ways.[38]

More insidious than the conceptual problems with metrics themselves is the way the categories that emerge from those metrics classify people as "overweight" or "obese," categories that can spill over into characterizations of people as undisciplined, careless, reckless, unproductive, and a drain on the nation's productivity.[39] Fat studies scholar Wann writes that "American culture is engaged in a pervasive witch hunt targeting fatness and fat people (a project that is rapidly being exported worldwide)."[40] In the same volume, Weismantel argues that there are racialized aspects to the denigration of people who are deemed overweight or obese: "An ugly stew of hatreds come together in the abhorrence with which we regard fleshy bodies, especially if they are dark-skinned, ineptly groomed, or cheaply dressed."[41]

Since I am sympathetic to the fat studies perspective that fat talk is "bio-abuse" that does little more than to mistakenly blame individuals for their perceived failure to comply with what Greenhalgh calls "the healthist expectations of bio-citizenship," I asked myself early on whether the story I tell in this book can be told without reference to obesity at all.[42] Convinced as to the complete inadequacy of common measures like BMI, I wondered whether we can we even know with precision if the scandalous claims regarding Mexico's obesity epidemic are true, or if they are relevant as a measure of health. Have public health scholars, policy makers, and citizens' groups simply jumped on the bandwagon that girth is a public health menace?

As a result, I considered writing this book about changing food practices in the two countries and their public health consequences without even referencing obesity. The rise in the prevalence of diabetes is certainly as good a measuring stick as any for the ominous consequences of changing diets. I decided I needed to engage directly with the discussion about rising rates of obesity for two reasons. First and foremost, it is the anchoring idea for discussions about the public health consequences of changing food systems and food practices in Mexico. While food sovereignty, discussed later, is an essential part of certain social movements in Mexico that intersect with indigenous rights, environmental sustainability, economic equality, and more, it has not achieved the mainstream currency that obesity has. Mexico's federal government issued its call to action under the title of the National Strategy for the Prevention and Control of Overweight, Obesity, and Diabetes. Second, as in the United States, concerns about the health of the Mexican nation have focused on overweight and obesity, not on the shift in recent decades toward a dramatically different system for the production, provision, and consumption of food. For this book to be intelligible within these binational discussions, I must engage the debates about obesity and overweight, while continuing to question how these are defined, what metrics are used, and most importantly how the obsessive attention to obesity and overweight inappropriately associate the burden of blame with the individual rather than the social contexts of health.

STUDY METHODS

When I began this project, I struggled to identify appropriate research methodologies for accessing the information I thought would be necessary to answer my main questions: How has NAFTA impacted the ways that people in Mexico and the United States eat? What are the health consequences of that shift?

I followed the rise in diet-related illness in Mexico for a few years before starting to research it, but I followed the rise in popularity and sophistication of Mexican food—as a home cook and as an avid eater—for quite a bit longer. When I moved to New York City to attend college in 1991, my mother routinely express-mailed me tortillas from my home state of California because they were not yet widely available and I couldn't imagine living without them. Today, in New York, it seems like a new high-end Mexican restaurant launches every week, while New Yorkers, Mexican and non-Mexican, queue up happily outside a growing number of taco trucks, *tamal* vendors, and *paleta* stands.[43]

I was curious about why my friends' families in Mexico seemed plagued by diabetes, and also why in the United States many seemed to so facilely link obesity to diabetes and to Mexican Americans. In a previous study focused on birth outcomes among Mexican immigrant women in New

York City, I found that they boasted better than expected health and birth outcomes in spite of socioeconomic disadvantage, what researchers have called the "immigrant paradox." I wondered if there was a paradox to be found here, too, where a closer look at the data might reveal that more recent Mexican immigrants have superior health outcomes in diet-related illness than their counterparts who have lived longer in the United States.

Once I began systematically following the public health and epidemiological research tracing the recent rise in noncommunicable chronic disease, what I found was alarming. In the United States, Mexican populations suffer in disproportionate numbers from diet-related illness. In Mexico, too, in both urban and rural areas, diet-related illness was rising precipitously. I asked whether we might we see instead an unraveling of the immigrant health paradox, with new waves of immigrants actually as sick as or sicker than people born in the United States, as more people around the world adopt US eating practices.

Around the same time, I also realized that the fact that Mexican migration has leveled off, and in fact reversed since the economic crisis of 2008, is not widely known by the general public in either country. Politicians (led by the current president of the United States) and anti-immigrant groups continue to talk about migration as though it were "out of control," a "flood" perpetuated by a "porous" border. I could see in visits to people I knew in rural areas of Mexico that people were no longer migrating in large numbers, at the same time that the healthy lifestyles that protected their family members when they migrated were changing rapidly. I wondered how all of this information could be reconciled and also be better understood. I also asked myself how those of us who study these things could get this information out and provide the best evidence to account for these trends.

As a cultural anthropologist, my training inclines me to always look to the micro, for what is happening *on the ground* that illustrates larger social, economic, and political trends. So, I had to ask myself if it was possible to conduct an ethnography of NAFTA. If so, where should I situate myself? To whom should I speak? Having conducted research in Mexico and with Mexican populations in the United States for almost two decades, and frequently traveling to and around Mexico for research, other academic work, and pleasure, I knew that the story I was interested in telling could be told from anywhere—everywhere, really. Part of the insidious nature of the transformation of Mexico's food system was its generality. Even remote rural communities formerly left out of many economic and social policies, marginalized by many of the trends toward urbanization and modernization, were being aggressively incorporated into consumer markets, like their city-dwelling counterparts. While geographic isolation once insulated many rural communities from both the positive and negative factors of city living, today those differences have become blurred.

I pondered whether it would be enough to tell this story from one place, using it as a metonym for other places, and for the larger story, or whether it would be better to "follow the policies" and conduct a multi-sited research project that would enable me to trace the ideas and the discourses that lead to food and trade policy and the ways they play out in the lives of individuals and communities.[44] Alternatively, I thought I could choose to primarily study up, examining the ideas of policy makers at the top levels of government who design trade policy, health campaigns, and social welfare programs.

In the end, I decided I had to do all of these. As such, this book uses ethnographic fieldwork along with discourse analysis, policy analysis, and other methodologies.[45] While I have long-standing relationships with communities in the state of Puebla and returned to them for short fieldwork stints throughout this project, I also continued to communicate with many of the people in Mexican communities in New York City with whom I've been working, conducting research, and eventually becoming close to as friends since graduate school. I also conducted new fieldwork in Mexico City and in Quintana Roo state, places where I have spent a lot of time over the years. I traveled to Mexico for short-term research stays of one to four weeks seven times in the 2014–2015 academic year with this project, in addition to multiple trips for research and other purposes before and since that period. Further, my five-year tenure as founding director of the Jaime Lucero Mexican Studies Institute at the City University of New York from 2011 to 2016 gave me very high-level contacts in ministries of the Mexican government that I probably would never have gained access to otherwise. I learned in my first graduate ethnographic methods class at New York University with Bambi Schieffelin that "everything is data," and this helped me be attuned to the evidence for Mexico's response to the "obesity epidemic" in all kinds of governmental programs and forms of public engagement.

The story told here has no particular place; diet-related illness and responses to it can be seen everywhere one looks in Mexico. The issue is astoundingly pervasive and seems, even in a time of political conflict, civil society unrest, and profound economic and education reforms, to be a topic on everyone's minds. In the United States, it is almost impossible to avoid discussions of immigration, health care, and trade policy, and perhaps even more difficult to ignore the incredible popularity of Mexican food (as if anyone would want to!). So, what I have done here is combine data gathered in both countries from different scales, ranging from micro to macro. I looked at the ways that individuals produce, purchase, prepare, and consume food. I talked to people about how their ways of eating changed over time and about how diet-related illnesses affect their lives. I paid attention to the messages about health, diet, and lifestyle that people say they have received from the media, advertising, the government, and medical professionals, as well as the ways they decide what to do with those messages. I examined the structural issues that shape the contexts in which we all live our lives—the government policies and regulations that govern food and trade, as well as public health and social welfare. I analyzed the underlying attitudes and ideas that are implicit in some of those policies and the ways that they aim blame and accountability. I noticed and analyzed how the policies are shaped by attitudes about the poor and Mexico's indigenous population that have a very long history. In this way, this book is interdisciplinary, while building on insights drawn particularly from medical and cultural anthropology, immigration studies, and Latin American and Latinx Studies.

Using a Latin American studies frame, we can see that ever since the European conquest, ideas about citizenship, responsibility, and capability in the hemisphere have been viewed through lenses of racialization, class, and gender. The same social groups viewed in the colonial and early independence periods as incapable of assuming the responsibilities of citizenship happen to be the same people now blamed for their own susceptibility to diet-related illness. There is a constant transmission of the message that if they only had sufficient discipline and education, they would be able to emulate the models of thin, fit biocitizenship modeled for them by the educated, elite, white, urban sophisticates who have continuously inherited Latin America's prosperity and power. Transnational food marketers and their lobbies have exploited those attitudes in order to shape the possible range of responses to the key questions that diet-related illness poses: whose fault is it and what can be done about it? As such, some of those attitudes and ideas about chronically marginalized sectors of Mexico's population have insinuated themselves into public policy, been reproduced, and taken on a reinvigorated life of their own.

In this book, I connect dots that have not been linked before between trade and food policy, migration, health, and foodways in both the United States and Mexico. This book does not answer once and for all what causes or what can be done about diet-related illnesses. Instead, I unpack some of the assumptions at work in the policies designed to address them and the flaws in reasoning on which those policies rest. While I fully participate in and am thoroughly enjoying the "moment" Mexican cuisine is having, I argue that the stories some are telling about it are inaccurate and have been appropriated and retold at the expense of others whose protagonism always seems to go unnoticed. I argue that Mexican food may in part be so popular at this moment precisely because it is falling out of reach for so many Mexican people. This is not to give a bitter taste to our tacos, but to look for ways to enjoy these rich and delicious food traditions while also respecting and protecting those to whom they have historically belonged.

By focusing on changes in Mexico's food system and food habits in the period since the passage of NAFTA, I reveal the ways that policy decisions made in both the United States and Mexico have dramatic consequences not only for the ways people eat, but also for their health. While US citizens elect representatives to create legislation governing domestic and foreign affairs, probably most of us are not aware of the ripple effects of US trade policy for our neighbors in Mexico, and beyond. Our conceptualization and understanding of democracy may not presently be big enough to account for the role corporate lobbying plays in establishing the regulatory and policy environment that increasingly governs not only this country but also all of our trading partners. Our ideas about food justice may need to be expanded beyond the local and the national levels.

Already, any gains for Mexico's economy from twenty years of increased orientation toward foreign direct investment and global trade are endangered by the massive public health costs of a sick population. The knowledge, methods, and technologies of small-scale agriculture cannot easily be recovered if lost. The destruction of ancestral methods of producing and consuming food will not easily be reversed. The milpa-based diet largely withstood—albeit with many modifications—the arrival of the Spanish, conquest, colonization, and countless waves of urbanization, industrialization, and modernization. However, today, it might become a relic, reconstructed for tourists and in elite restaurants, but out of reach of the average person.

PLAN OF THE BOOK

To tell this story, I work to dismantle some of the ideas that have framed causes and solutions for Mexico's persistent poverty and underdevelopment. I debunk the idea that small-scale agriculture is inefficient and always has been in Mexico. I show that the myth of the unproductive countryside has fueled various strategies to "de-peasantize" the nation's economy as a path for achieving development and prosperity. These programs for modernity build on ideas about indigenous and poor rural communities that date back to the conquest but are being revived in new ways to criticize those communities' uptake of processed foods and sugar-sweetened beverages. These ideas help obscure the causes for a rise in diet-related illness concurrent with globalized trade and foreign direct investment. While many middle-income nations have seen a rise in chronic disease with foreign direct investment and industrialization of food systems, the implementation of NAFTA provides a particularly neat frame with which to see the alterations of Mexico's economy, food system, and health outlook.

The next chapter, "People of the Corn," explores Mexico's ancestral cuisine and the ways that it has come to enjoy a moment of high prestige and appreciation in the global food marketplace in the last few years. I discuss the question of ownership over the food traditions of Mexico and the ways that Mexican food has come to occupy a prominent place in elite, global food circles.

The third chapter, "Laying the Groundwork for NAFTA," explores the political and economic context preceding NAFTA, and the ways that

Mexico's elected officials and business interests paved the way for the agreement and have benefited from it. I explore the concepts of food sovereignty and food security, and the ways that a push toward food security has generated the possibility of a Mexico that no longer produces food.

In the fourth chapter, "NAFTA: Free Trade in the Body," I describe the magnitude and characteristics of Mexico's so-called obesity and diabetes epidemic and the current hypotheses about the causes and treatment of obesity for individuals and at the population level. I point out some of the lesser known hypotheses for the abrupt rise in obesity and diet-related chronic diseases in the last few decades. Far from linking the rise of obesity to increased appetites for snacks and sodas, some of these hypotheses focus on ways that the production and consumption of processed foods and beverages have increased people's exposure to chemicals with metabolic and endocrinologic properties that produce weight gain and alter organ function.

In "Deflecting the Blame," the fifth chapter, I critique some of the assumptions about the causes and solutions for obesity using anthropological and historical understandings of class and ethnic differences in Mexico. I unpack Mexico's policy response to obesity and diabetes and demonstrate the ways that a progressive and aggressive policy response has been stunted in ways that favor transnational food corporations, while deflecting the blame for diet-related illness onto individuals and historically marginalized poor and indigenous populations. I address the idea that better health and wellness can be achieved for the Mexican population through greater education and socialization into healthful ingredients and cooking styles, narrowly defined.

In "Diabetes: The Disease of the Migrant?" I examine alternative etiologies for diabetes, including the syndemic connection drawn by some researchers between diabetes and emotional trauma. I explore how this theory is supported by many of the vernacular etiologies of diabetes in Mexican communities. In this chapter, I also raise the possibility that a "slow death" from diet-related illness has sinister ramifications in defusing and postponing calls for more just economic, trade, and migration policies.[46]

In "Nostalgia, Prestige, and a Party Every Day," I examine how food marketers and producers have manipulated cultural associations between food, status, identity, and ideas about the past to boost market reach. Processed food alternately imitates and provides a counterpoint to ideas about "traditional" foods. At the same time, many people make efforts to retain habits and knowledge associated with milpa-based cuisine. I acknowledge the inherent destructiveness of nostalgia in the variety that anthropologist Renato Rosaldo calls "imperialist nostalgia," mourning that which one has destroyed, in ways that further displace and destabilize historically dominant ways of preparing food.

In the conclusion, I attempt to "connect the dots" by linking changing food systems, policies and foodways, and diet-related illness to larger trends in Mexico and the United States: the militarization of security forces at the border and beyond, the drug war, and the widening gap between these two countries that share a long border. I also look for bright spots: food cultivators, producers, and artisans who defy the trends toward industrialization and provide alternative and utopian visions of a different kind of world where health, joy, food, and the interpersonal relationships that food preparation and enjoyment produce are not so heavily shaped by transnational food corporations, or even by immigration, health, social, and food policies. I argue that in addition to calls to "think globally, and act locally," responsible citizenship also requires us to see the ways that trade policies act globally in our name and raise our voices against policies that promote profits over health, even far from home.

Mexicans at home and in the diaspora and non-Mexican scholars, who, like me, have spent their lives studying Mexico and Mexican communities abroad, have resoundingly said to me in the last couple of years that they have never been more worried about Mexico. Confidence in institutions, in the ability of civil society to effect change, in the chances for democracy, are at an all-time low. Every day, new evidence emerges of a decades-old dirty war against social movements that has resulted in clandestine graves and tens of thousands of missing people. Optimism about the health, well-being, and intellectual and social engagement of the population is at its nadir. At the same time, in the United States, too, optimism is hard to find. The election of Donald Trump has set back struggles for immigrant rights and justice, food and health policy, and civil discourse in ways many people and communities are still struggling to assess and respond to.

ok is a love letter, but the object of my affection is not easy to e some of my friends and family secretly suspect this book was excuse for me to indulge my adoration of Mexican food, it is not just my love for the food and anger over its constant misrepresentation as unhealthy, but my love for Mexico and the Mexican people, among whom I've had the privilege to labor and live, that brought me to write this book. If the questions that arise from this inquiry are controversial and even polemical, they are raised with love and hope for a more just and sustainable future in which Mexicans can live with health, mobility, and prosperity, where and how they wish.

2 People of the Corn

COPENHAGEN AND TULUM, VIA NEW YORK

Standing in a spare, minimalist room lit softly by the Nordic sun, René Redzepi, celebrated Danish chef and owner of Noma, the Copenhagen restaurant ranked one of the World's 50 Best Restaurants, tells us how to make a tortilla.[1] In a video filmed for the *New York Times,* he works in what is probably one of Noma's famed kitchen labs, where his chefs explore fermenting, burning, rotting, and otherwise experimenting with locally foraged ingredients and what some would consider nonfoods (such as bark, lichen, hay, and musk ox skin). He introduces his assistant, Rosío Sánchez, a Mexican chef on his staff who is, he announces, planning to open her own taquería in Denmark.[2] He says that for three months Rosío has been "investigating tortilla and how to make it." He points to the hard, dried kernels of corn, in a small clay bowl. The next step, he narrates, is to add "calc." Rosío flinches ever so slightly at the mispronunciation of the key ingredient, *cal,* slaked mineral lime, but does not correct the boss. Redzepi lets the viewer know the corn was boiled in a mixture of water and lime, left to sit for half a day, and then it was ground. He shows a *molcajete* (a rounded, bowl-shaped mortar and pestle, more typically used for spices or wet ingredients like salsa or guacamole), even though a *metate* (a larger, flat, table-shaped slab of stone and a cylindrical, rolling-pin like grinder) is historically used for grinding corn in Mexico. He highlights these traditional tools, though it's worth noting that mechanical corn grinders have been widely used for decades all over Mexico. He shows a nice, fat ball of masa, the dough that is the final product of the grinding and kneading of the nixtamalized corn, so generously proportioned that it's unlikely to have been ground on the molcajete he shows.

After Redzepi gives the authoritative overview, it is Rosío who pats the masa into little balls, presses them flat with a tortilla press (which Redzepi jokingly refers to as "a new technical marvel"), and then places them on diminutive cast iron griddles on a seamless, knobless electric cooktop. No flame, no firewood, no battered *comal,* a griddle that is often made of clay, with room enough for a half dozen tortillas. It is almost as though Redzepi is a food archivist broadcasting from the future, working out of some post-apocalyptic kitchen lab in space, documenting long-lost cooking traditions dug up from earth's past. He turns to Rosío. "When are they ready?"

"When they soufflé," she replies.

The first one fails. He tosses it across the room. The second one soufflés like a pro. As Rosío works, he bends over the tortilla on the griddle, inhaling the aroma of toasting corn, and remarks:

> You can have Italian chefs talking about the difficulties in creating the right pasta. You'll pay 30, 40, 50 euros for a bowl of spaghetti because it tells the right story. But a tortilla can only cost, you know, 50 cents? For one, you know what I mean? Maybe the story-telling has been wrong. And therefore also their appreciation for it. That's what I believe. But once you have the right consistency, and the right quality of the tortilla, well, then it's like the perfect food.[3]

A lengthy article in the *New York Times* style magazine, *T,* accompanies the video and chronicles Redzepi's quest for the "perfect taco": "Over the years there have been pilgrims who have traveled to Mexico to experience mind alteration with buttons of peyote, but for Redzepi, a man who is often referred to as the greatest chef in the world, transcendence comes in the form of *enfrijoladas*":

> "You think you know what it's going to taste like," Redzepi says. "This to me is the best mouthful I've had in Mexico. I can't believe the flavor of this leaf. Wow. I'm getting chills."
>
> "I never take pictures of food, but I have to," mutters Danny Bowien, an American chef who has come along for the ride. "I have to, man."[4]

The magical leaf atop a tortilla with mashed black beans that sends Redzepi and Bowien into a reverie is avocado leaf, an example of the kind of core ingredient, along with wild greens like *verdolaga,* used by humble rural cooks for millennia in Mexico. He goes on, "That first mouthful. Soft. Tasty. Acidic. Spicy . . . I couldn't believe it. My virginity was taken. In the best possible way."

The article details a bro-fest of discovery between Redzepi, his friends, and a rotating cast of earnest Mexican chefs who specialize in creating newly reinterpreted staples of "Mexican peasant food," or what they often call "Modern Mexican": Enrique Olvera, Alejandro Ruiz, Roberto Solís. Redzepi's mission to forage for and celebrate such ingredients is referred to in the article as a "crusade." A friend and fellow traveler of Redzepi, Eric Werner, has opened a restaurant named Hartwood, in Tulum, on the Caribbean coast of the Yucatán peninsula, premised on the simple notion of charring, using only a wood-burning oven and a grill. "'It's like a whole new energy enters your body when you come out to these parts,' says [Werner]. As he says this, that energy is being delivered in the form of thunderous jolts to the spinal column. We're in a jeep heading into the humid thickets of the Yucatán jungle, and the red-dirt road is turning into a thumping riot of dips and jags."[5]

It is clear from Redzepi and his friends' exclamations, as much as the description of the *New York Times* reporter sent to follow them, that the trip is, even more than a crusade, a conquest. Ready for adventure in the "jungle," they "discover" and collect native ingredients and knowledge to take back to Europe and the United States, celebrating at the same time as they appropriate them. Paradoxically, he frames his mission as an anticolonialist one: "For many years in fine dining in Mexico, you had the cathedral on top of the pyramid. With chefs like Enrique Olvera, the pyramid starts to become visible again." Trying to shrug off the conquistador mantle, he suggests that it is his "virginity" that is taken, even while he characterizes this millennial and at the same time global and transnational cuisine as undiscovered.

In this chapter, we will explore the stratospheric rise in global availability and price of Mexican cuisine, the ways that certain narratives have propelled that ascent among certain global food elites, and how it coincides with a decline in consumption of tortillas and other traditional applications for freshly ground corn by people in Mexico. We will examine this process as a kind of social alchemy, in which specific arbiters of taste have taken it upon themselves to "elevate" Mexican food and charge astronomical prices for it, while for others those same kinds of foods have come to symbolize an old-fashioned and impractical way of cooking and eating that is increasingly unavailable and out of step with their circumstances and pace of life. This is not a simple case of cultural appropriation—although that is one aspect of it. Instead we see a simultaneous push and pull in which corn-based cuisine is taken up by foreign and Mexican elite chefs and moved into a global foodie sphere, and is also less accessible to low-income people in the places it originated. I posit that the kind of food that Redzepi celebrates can only attain such a high value globally by being lost to those who customarily ate it. While moving something from one geographic or cultural space to another is a feasible business strategy—setting up a taco truck near hipster bars, for example—to raise the price on a product like a tortilla to many times its customary monetary value requires it to have become scarce in those original spaces. We examine the role of narrative capital in telling certain kinds of stories that simultaneously romanticize specific elements of cuisine (like hand-ground landrace corn), while cleaving them from the historical conditions of their production and the people responsible for their development and custodianship over millennia. Separated from context, specific cooking methods, styles, and ingredients are "up for grabs" for whoever "tells the best story," with those from whom these traditions have been taken, the story goes, having insufficiently preserved or appreciated them.

Selling hand-ground tortillas with a market value of about a dollar per kilo for 30, 40, or 50 euros, the way some Italian chefs have done with their handmade pastas, may not have occurred to Mexican cooks, but it is occurring to Redzepi and the other celebrity chefs "reinterpreting" and "reviving" the taco in the rarefied world of trendy restaurants, including interpretations by his friends Danny Bowien and Alex Stupak.

In December 2016, Redzepi announced a seven-week "residency" in Tulum, Mexico, a "pop-up" restaurant where he and his team of chefs would travel in late spring 2017 to cook a multicourse tasting menu. The website announcing the project described it as follows: "The outdoor open-air restaurant will sit nestled between the jungle and the Caribbean Sea in Tulum. Exposed to the climate, it will be hot, steaming and unpredictable. Billowing smoke and the orange glow of flames will define us as all cooking will take place over the fire. It will be wild like the Mexican landscape as we share our interpretation of the tastes from one of the most beautiful countries we've come to know." The price to partake in this adventure, which, remember, is a single meal? A cool $600 US, *plus* another $150 US in taxes and fees.[6] All available seats sold out in two hours, six months before the pop-up would open, and the money went through the cloud, probably to a bank in Denmark, bypassing Mexico altogether.

Even as Redzepi calls Tulum "his adopted home," he continues to insist on using the language of discovery and conquest. While he and his entourage plunge into the "humid thickets of the Yucatán jungle," they do not notice, it seems, that they are in Quintana Roo, one of the most developed states in Mexico. Tulum, now the trendiest spot on Mexico's Riviera Maya for travelers like Redzepi, is home to yoga studios and temazcal-spas. It is where expectant diners queue up each evening before Hartwood's rustic dining room opens for business, even while the state is categorized as "almost completely developed."[7] While a few international travelers found the fishing villages and white sand beaches of the Yucatán peninsula in the 1960s, Tulum's distinction as an elite site for sustainable and wellness-based travel is recent. But Quintana Roo state is also home, eighty miles north, to Cancún, a city of high-rise hotels and US-style chain bars and restaurants, famed as a site for the worst excesses of scorched-earth tourism development. Already in the 1970s, proposals for ecotourism were emerging in the region as a corrective to hyperdevelopment that literally bulldozed forests and denuded the sea.[8] Anthropologist Thomas Leatherman writes, "Quintana Roo has experienced a transformation from one of the most economically marginal areas of Mexico into a tourist bonanza, an unqualified economic success for the Mexican government and foreign investors."[9] It also happens to be the region that best epitomizes the "coca-colonization" and "dietary delocalization" of its residents' typical diet: an abrupt rise in calories consumed, accompanied by persistent childhood malnutrition, adult obesity, and a lack of essential micronutrients plentiful in traditional foods but lacking in manufactured foods.[10] For locals, it does not matter if they work in or around ecotourism or mass-market commercial tourism; both have spelled a restructuring of their region and their lifestyles. Greater market dependency has meant a decline in dietary diversity and nutritional status in low-income communities. While Redzepi bounces in a jeep seeking culinary inspiration in the jungle, residents of the region have been experiencing an almost complete transformation of their food supply.

Famed for their resistance to Spanish conquest and "stubborn" retention of their language and lifeways, Yucatec Maya-speaking locals are now largely employed in the tourism industry as gardeners, hotel maids, kitchen workers, and more. They no longer participate in the slash-and-burn style of *milpa* agriculture of their parents and grandparents. Historically the most essential component of a meal, tortillas now provide 20 percent fewer calories in the coastal communities that are most integrated in the tourist economy than in rural inland communities that are less embedded in wage labor.[11]

In today's topsy-turvy world, Mexico's "peasant food" is shunned and made obsolete by an economic model built on food security, becoming increasingly inaccessible and even undesirable to the average citizen, but suddenly lionized by a celebrity chef and his pals.[12] At Enrique Olvera's New York City restaurant Cosme, where freshly ground corn masa is the star of the menu, diners can easily rack up a bill of $300 for dinner for two with drinks.[13] The establishment was named one of the world's best restaurants in 2017 by Bloomberg News.[14] At Pujol, Olvera's Mexico City restaurant, he put high-end Mexican food on the capital's map—offering a $96 six-course tasting menu that begins with "street snacks" and reaches its climax with a duet of "*mole madre,*" a mole sauce that has been built upon for, at the time of this writing, 1,325 days, paired with a "new" mole—on a plate, with nothing else. Another New York City chef/restaurateur, Alex Stupak, achieved momentary notoriety for the high prices at his restaurant, Empellón Cocina, and his four-hundred-word essay about his refusal to serve tacos and the "culinary racism" of diners who demand them. He was later quoted saying of Mexican cuisine, “I like that it’s an underdog . . . I like that it’s undervalued.”[15]

We can see that many different people and institutions are involved in promoting and profiting from the boom in Mexican cuisine globally. It is not uncommon of late to see the Mexican tourism board engaged in actively celebrating and marketing Mexico’s “authentic” cuisine. Mexico’s gastronomy is viewed as a draw for top tourism dollars. The three-part finale of the Food Network’s 2015 Top Chef competition was filmed in San Miguel de Allende, in Guanajuato state, and the Mexican tourism board was plastered all over the credits in every episode. The challenges posed to the finalists highlighted unusual ingredients unique to Mexican cuisine: *xoconostle* (prickly pear fruit), *escamoles* (ant larvae), Mexican chocolate, *mezcal,* and *huitlacoche* (a corn fungus, sometimes called in English “corn smut” or “truffle”).[16]

For Redzepi, who presumably is not up to date on Mexico’s centuries-old culinary, economic, social, and political battles over corn, the price and availability of maize flour, and land rights, it’s simply that tortillas have yet to have their story properly told: “Maybe the story-telling has been wrong. And therefore also their appreciation for it.”[17] We can only wonder who “they” are, those who do not appreciate the sublime tortilla. Perhaps Redzepi refers to Mexicans, who no longer eat as many tortillas, or he might mean the diners willing to spend obscene amounts of money for hand-rolled pasta and potentially also for corn tortillas. Redzepi and his friends have ventured into the heart of darkness, identified an underappreciated treasure, and brought it back, to elevate it, pay homage to it, and change its narrative, but it is not clear that his project benefits those who consider tortillas their own.

FORAGING IN QUINTANA ROO

While Redzepi took a *New York Times* reporter foraging in the jungle outside of Tulum, my foraging experience in the same state occurred in the middle of a resort city. Isabel told me to meet her in the street in an older section of town that has mature trees and narrow streets that intersect each other unpredictably. Playa del Carmen, known mainly as a beach destination for tourists, has grown exponentially over the last three decades. In spite of a hurricane that threatened the viability of the local beaches and resorts a decade ago, rapid growth has continued with a core of hotels, resorts, discos, restaurants, and bars flanked by an expanding ring of housing for middle- and low-income workers who serve the tourists in town, and also all along the Riviera Maya, from Tulum to Cancún, the entire coast of white sand beaches facing the Caribbean Sea.

Isabel moved to Playa del Carmen, like so many people, because that is where the jobs are. She does not work directly in the tourist industry. She is a single mom of three, and the hours and commute would be too rigid to allow her to take care of her children. She grew up in a small municipality in neighboring Campeche state, a four-hour, two-bus journey from Playa del Carmen. Her parents and siblings still live there. At home, she speaks Yucatec Maya, but part of the reason she is in Playa del Carmen is so her children can develop their fluency and literacy in Spanish and English, and thus improve their employability when they become adults. When I ask her about her hometown, she describes the plants growing on her family's land or their neighbors' and the everyday borrowing and giving of resources between neighbors.

While she does not work directly in the tourism industry, her work is in an auxiliary role: she works for a woman who sells breakfast to resort employees as they make their way to work each morning. She drags her two younger children out of bed each day at 2:30 a.m. and takes them to her employer's house, where together the two women make tamales and two kinds of cornmeal-based drinks commonly consumed for breakfast: *atole* and *champurrado,* flavored with chocolate. Their morning rush starts at 6:30 a.m. By midday, she is finished. Her younger children start their day from her workplace, groggily eating some of their mom's tamales before heading to school.

She wants to show me where to find *chaya,* an edible wild plant used for many different purposes in the region. Walking around this part of town (mostly homes of European and Mexican retirees who purchased or built their homes when Playa del Carmen was still a quiet fishing village), she points to what I would have guessed were "weeds" growing in the sidewalks and along the sides of houses. Chaya has a massive leaf that improbably extends horizontally off of the stem, not weighed down by its heft.

She says to be careful: there is a rash one can get touching or picking the leaves without protection. She uses a plastic bag over her hands to handle the leaves. She says this is one of the best plants endemic to the area—delicious, versatile, and known to have many beneficial properties, such as soothing an upset stomach. In local cafés and juice bars, chaya is commonly seen in beverages (such as *agua de limón con chaya*, a green-spiked lemonade, and other green juices) and also cooked into scrambled eggs. She points to other leaves, bark, and flowers all around us. Suddenly what appeared to my untrained eyes as a random jumble of untended plants begins to take on the appearance of an herbolary, full of a rich variety of plants used in food and medicine.

When we get back to the kitchen in the apartment I am renting, Isabel continues her lesson by cooking. She washes the chaya leaves and then layers them in a pot, one by one, filling the entire pot with a dense stack of leaves. She pours bottled water on top and allows the pot to come to a boil. Over more than an hour, she occasionally stirs, salts, adds more water, and tastes the resulting broth. When it comes time to eat the broth, she serves it in bowls, filled to the brim. The broth is complex and delicious even though it has only two ingredients aside from water: chaya and salt. We top it with toasted ground pumpkin seed powder and a fresh squeeze of lime, and sip it with spoons.[18]

IMPERIALIST NOSTALGIA AND *INDIGENISMO*

The growing acknowledgment of traditional Mexican cuisine as an element of cultural heritage that merits preservation and recognition is perhaps an example of "imperialist nostalgia," defined by anthropologist Renato Rosaldo as "where people mourn the passing of what they themselves have transformed."[19] This is a recurring theme in the Americas. Nostalgia is a feeling that helps fill in the gaps created by change and loss. While it does not allow for recovery or recuperation and does not argue for the wheels of change to halt, it provides a means of acknowledging the inevitable feelings of loss that change brings. We see that nostalgia has played an important role in phases of rapid destruction of cultural practices and of communities themselves.

In Latin American history, we can see that the powerful have at each stage taken time and energy to record and remember that which they are busy trying to eliminate. One example of this are periodic waves of *indigenismo*, a school of thought that celebrates First Peoples' cultural traditions, often coinciding with systematic efforts to dismantle them or assimilate them into the "mainstream." Following the Mexican Revolution (1910–1917), the progressive and energetic minister of education of the new government, José Vasconcelos, set the tone for Mexico's official approach to culture and decades of cultural work in the early twentieth century, not only by educators in the public schools, but by artists, bureaucrats, and the self-styled *científicos* who sought to chart Mexico's path to a progressive modernity. Painter Diego Rivera's iconic celebrations of indigenous imagery are perhaps the most notable example, but there was a whole generation of like-minded creative producers who dominated Mexico's official cultural industry and subscribed to shared ideals. Vasconcelos's influential book *The Cosmic Race* celebrated "the bronze race," produced in Mexico by the fusion of indigenous and European cultures.[20] This idea represented a sea change for the elites of Latin America, whose wars of independence were premised largely on a transfer of power and citizenship from European-born whites to American-born whites, with little consideration of the rights or cultural wealth of nonwhite majorities, including native peoples. However, what is sometimes overlooked in celebrations of Vasconcelos's manifesto is the notion that indigenous contributions to the formulation of the bronze race are framed as valuable only insofar as they are blended with European contributions—indigenous culture is celebrated at the same time as it is slated for assimilation. Likewise, today, while Mexican cuisine is elevated and celebrated, the food system in Mexico today is structured so that Mexico's ancestral foodways may not survive, except as a relic.

In 2010, Mexico's cuisine was inducted into UNESCO's Lists of Intangible Cultural Heritage, one of eight items on the list corresponding to the country:

> Traditional Mexican cuisine is a comprehensive cultural model comprising farming, ritual practices, age-old skills, culinary techniques and ancestral community customs and manners. It is made possible by collective participation in the entire traditional food chain: from planting and harvesting to cooking and

> eating. The basis of the system is founded on corn, beans and chili [*sic*]; unique farming methods such as rain-fed *milpas* (rotating swidden fields of corn and other crops) and *chinampas* (man-made farming islets in lake areas); cooking processes such as *nixtamalization* (lime-hulling maize, which increases its nutritional value); and singular utensils including grinding stones and stone mortars. Native ingredients such as varieties of tomatoes, squashes, avocados, cocoa and vanilla augment the basic staples. Mexican cuisine is elaborate and symbol-laden, with everyday tortillas and tamales, both made of corn, forming an integral part of Day of the Dead offerings. Collectives of female cooks and other practitioners devoted to raising crops and traditional cuisine are found . . . across Mexico. Their knowledge and techniques express community identity, reinforce social bonds, and build stronger local, regional and national identities. Those efforts . . . also underline the importance of traditional cuisine as a means of sustainable development.[21]

This acknowledgment by UNESCO sets the stage for preservation of Mexican cuisine. Although it is celebrated as an intangible and also living heritage, official recognition does not come with official structural support for people to sustain their ways of life. Using the term "traditional" no fewer than four times, and also using the present tense, the UNESCO description of Mexican cuisine implies a timelessness and continuity for this cuisine and its makers.[22] Left out are the ways that the styles of food preparation referred to here have accommodated multiple technological and cultural changes over the centuries, from manual metates and molcajetes to electric corn grinders and blenders. Also left out is the fact that the features of Mexican food preparation described have retained many basic characteristics since before European contact, but arguably are under greater assault today than during the conquest.

The UN description of Mexico's cuisine acknowledges the continuum between food production, preparation, and consumption that anthropologist Roberto González, in his book *Zapotec Science*, describes as *mantenimiento,* literally "maintenance," "the entire gamut of activities related to food production and consumption." He writes that many campesinos do not make a sharp distinction between agriculture, food preparation, and consumption, but see them all as a continual effort to sustain households over time and generations.[23]

These concepts importantly point to a "food system" more than a cuisine, the latter a term commonly used to refer to that which is already cooked, as well as styles of cooking. The people of Talea, among whom González conducted research, refer to the food they grow and eat as "clean." One of his informants noted, "Even though we only have our little beans, they are legitimate, and we can eat them with pleasure because we know they're clean." The people of Talea strongly prefer the food they produce locally, and "knowing where food comes from" is a critical measure of food quality. González analyzes this as a "civilizational assessment" by which people in Talea consider themselves to have a discerning sense of good quality food, as opposed to people in the cities, who "appear animal-like, since they eat anything, at any hour."[24]

Rural foodways in Mexico at present are often framed as having continuity with the foodways of the preconquest era in the same region. While many aspects of lifeways among the people of the region before Columbus are difficult to know with certainty due to the magnitude of the genocide of native people, authors of conquest-era codices and Spanish chronicles paid a great deal of attention to food and foodways, and thus we know some of their characteristics in Central Mexico, particularly the ways they differed from Spanish ways of eating at the time. The Spanish introduced major alterations of diet, including the addition of meat, lard, milk, and cheese from large domesticated livestock (cattle, pigs, goats, sheep).[25] While the people of what is today Central Mexico ate a lot of animal products—mostly smaller animals and insects—these were a relatively small portion of the overall dietary intake and complemented by a heavy emphasis on beans, corn, squash, and chiles. The Spanish also introduced wheat cultivation and harvest, and promoted the consumption of bread, especially in urban areas. For centuries after the conquest, foods associated with Europe were accorded higher status and carried higher prices in Mexico, with elite dining an emulation of European noble tables. Today, in contrast, Redzepi and like-minded chefs have made foraging and cooking with fealty to "origins," in ingredients and preparations methods, coveted ways for elites to eat around the world. While Redzepi seems more interested in peeling away than in understanding history, for many, this is a noble effort in which Mexico throws off the stifling burden of eurocentrism. It seems logical, then, that corn would be at the center of efforts to honor autochthonous cuisine.

COSME

It is a cold winter night and after some wrangling to get a reservation, my husband and I arrive at Cosme for dinner.[26] The *New York Times* restaurant critic, Pete Wells, had just named Cosme number one among the top New York restaurants in 2015.[27] Wells is intellectual heir and successor to Craig Claiborne, the *Times* original restaurant critic and kingmaker of chefs in New York for a generation, including one of the pioneers of high-end Mexican dining, Zarela Martínez, whose restaurant Zarela enjoyed rave reviews in the newspaper at its peak.[28] Claiborne was one of the most powerful and early US advocates for Mexican food's consideration as *cuisine.* He is credited with encouraging Diana Kennedy to write her first Mexican cookbook, *The Cuisines of Mexico,* published in 1972, which he then used as his platform at the *Times* to help make a classic for readers in the United States. In the preface to her book, he wrote that he shared with her the view that Mexican food was "peasant food raised to the level of high and sophisticated art."[29] Wells followed in Claiborne's footsteps when he declared that Cosme deserved the top spot for the year: "Most of all, the cooking is a thrill, largely because it sails right over ideas like tradition, authenticity and modernity. Many underpinnings come from Mexico, while a lot of the ingredients were bought locally. The flavors are here and now, though; you connect with the dishes right away."[30]

What about the food? My husband and I followed the server's suggestion to order a few dishes from each section of the menu: appetizers, vegetables, and proteins. Scallop *aguachile, cobia al pastor,* mushroom and squash *barbacoa,* and crispy octopus. Each course came with its own tortillas—different colors and thicknesses, made from different kinds of maize—as well as an *amuse bouche* before the first course of puree of pumpkin seeds to be dipped with "ash tortillas." The final touch on the meal: a meringue flavored by corn silk filled with corn mousse. The dessert was earthy and funky—the first and only time I have felt that a dish called to mind the words "manna" and "ambrosia." It tasted like life itself.

Cosme is all about corn. One of the arguments Olvera makes most powerfully with the menu and his cooking is that corn *is* life. Indeed, rumors have it he grows his own corn in Mexico for the restaurant, and it is shipped to New York City, where he nixtamalizes and grinds it for each day's tortillas. Even though it turns out that his demand for corn has spawned other businesses to supply him with it, as I ate, I imagined that monks whispered to it as it was planted and abuelitas sang to it as it was harvested. This is precious corn, with a whopping price tag to show for it.

How much are price and prestige related? We can look to the liquor industry for insight. When Grey Goose vodka was first released on the market, the beverage company decided to charge more for it than the market price of any other vodka on the market at the time.[31] Why charge more for a liquor that, arguably, does not have a taste? Because you can, and because its high price tag could be enough to generate prestige and interest, if only for its cheekiness. Its roaring success (including, ultimately, its sale to Bacardi in 2004 for $2 billion) is testament to this philosophy and since then, hundreds of "artisanal" and small-batch vodkas along with mass-produced vodkas with big marketing and design budgets have driven the average vodka price ever higher. Sidney Frank Importing Company, the firm that launched Grey Goose, later turned its attention to "superpremium" tequila, launching its namesake founder onto the Forbes list of richest billionaires.[32] Premium liquors continue to climb to stratospheric heights: recently actor George Clooney's tequila brand Casamigos was sold for about $1 billion US.

Is corn in the same category? Can certain foods be priced over others because they "tell a story," as Redzepi asserts? Indeed, "tell a good story" was what Grey Goose's mastermind Frank said was the secret to getting customers to pay more. What does it mean for certain people to tell the kinds of stories that elevate the price tag and the prestige of certain products? Is that construction of social capital the yin to the yang of the metastatic growth of automation and processing of the food industry? Different colors of maize—grown, harvested, nixtamalized, ground, and patted into tortillas or tamales by hand—were dietary staples in Mesoamerica for millennia. Today, precisely when it has become impossible for many poor and largely indigenous communities to continue living from the land, these foods are having a "moment" in the world of haute cuisine.

Mexico has been the origin place of thousands of varieties of corn and forty-one defined landraces, or types. The influx of US corn, the growth of industrial corn production and processing, and the withdrawal of support from the Mexican government have meant that many small-scale corn growers can no longer make a living from the land. In 2007, 70 percent of the tortillas and cornmeal consumed in Mexico were produced by a single company, Gruma, owned by the "Tortilla King," Roberto González Barrera, a *Forbes* billionaire whose family enjoyed very close ties, and some say, nepotistic favoritism, with the family of former Mexican president Carlos Salinas.[33] Gruma, parent company to GIMSA corn flour and Mission Foods, is the largest producer of tortillas and cornmeal in Mexico and in the United States, with as much as 90 percent of California's market share. Older methods for processing and distributing corn are no longer practical or the norm for most people. This has made hand-grown and ground corn available to a different crowd.

Recently, a few corn farmers have found a new partner willing to buy their corn to sell it to chefs seeking high-quality corn for their restaurants in Mexico, the United States, and Europe. Jorge Gaviria, founder of a company called Masienda, bought and exported eighty tons of landrace corn from small farmers in Mexico in 2015, and when I spoke to him in 2016, he expected to export four hundred tons that year. In 2017, his company struck a deal to distribute tortillas made of landrace Mexican corn in Whole Foods stores throughout the United States. Some farmers told him that previously the prices and demand were so low they were better off feeding their corn to their animals than trying to sell it. Today, however, "top chefs" in Europe and North America are searching for and willing to pay a premium for ancestral corn, and Gaviria buys it from them. "There seems to be no more coveted addition to a restaurant kitchen these days than a hulking metal mill for grinding corn softened with ash or slaked lime," writes Victoria Burnett in the *New York Times*.[34] Enrique Olvera of New York's Cosme and Rosío Sánchez of Hija de Sánchez (formerly of Noma) in Copenhagen buy Gaviria's corn and grind it themselves. Daniela Soto-Innes, chef de cuisine at Cosme, marvels that she has routine conversations with other US chefs about which variety of landrace corn they prefer—Cónico, Bolita, or Chalqueño.[35] Similarly, a New York City–based Mexican philanthropist told me he was shocked when dining at "high-end" Mexican restaurants in the city like Cosme, Empellón Cocina, or the more casual Tacos Número Uno in Chelsea Market to hear "gringos" confidently debating the relative merits of huitlacoche, insect larvae, mezcal, and other previously esoteric and down-market delicacies. That Mexico's ancestral peasant food is surging in popularity and status at a moment when two decades of globalization, trade, and industrialization of agriculture have endangered the viability of small-scale farming and displaced millions is not a coincidence.

TELLING STORIES

Who gets to tell stories? In today's distracted and content-saturated landscape, we are exposed to a lot of information, but not always a story. Content becomes relevant and memorable only when it takes form and weight through the weaving of narrative. Stories are one of the oldest ways human beings have to make sense of the world, and the ability to tell a good story has always been a talent we reward with status and admiration. But narrative capital, like all kinds of capital, is not evenly distributed, and just as with other kinds of capital, those who already command more than their share of other kinds of resources and status are at a clear advantage in getting "their" stories heard, even when they have appropriated the stories of others. When Chef Redzepi notes that tortillas have yet to have their story properly told, he can only be referring to the food story bank of the elites, in which a small, highly mobile, and privileged global foodie set ranks elite chefs, their restaurants, and their cooking styles, philosophies, and ingredients in an ever-changing hierarchy. They collectively, and usually not in any sort of coordinated way, set trends, raising the popularity of foraging or fermenting, for example, or by elevating certain ingredients in newly fashionable ways. Stories have always been told about corn, and the food systems that have grown up around it—indeed the foundational myths of the Mesoamerican peoples revolve around exactly that story. But whose stories are they?

Redzepi knows that the price a product commands goes beyond the material and taps the symbolic. The utilitarian value of things has never been enough to account for their price in the market. Wealth is generated precisely by layering additional markers of value and distinction on top of the basic product; if the consumer can be told a story about a particular organic peach grown on someone's family farm, just a few miles away, watered by crystalline mineral springs, it can be priced higher than other peaches.

"Mexican food," though wildly popular in the United States, may have needed extra fuel for its fire of redemption. Associated in the popular imagination with grease, melted cheese, and ground beef, it is seen as filling, easy, and unsophisticated.[36] The food many people in the United States think of as "Mexican" is unrecognizable to many Mexican people, and far from the rarefied world of high-end restaurants. That is where stories come in. The groundwork for the story being told today began, perhaps, in the 1980s and early 1990s. That is when rumors spread in the United States that perhaps flour tortillas were not "authentic," and we began to see the beginning of restaurants promising "traditional" food. Some of the variations on this were short-lived—for example, the explosion of "Southwestern" cuisine restaurants outside of the Southwest, with images of kokopelli, and lots of blue and red corn tortillas. This interest in "authenticity" did not rupture completely the stranglehold that melted cheese seemed to have on the American imagination, and still does.[37] But, we also begin to see greater awareness of what food in Mexico is actually like, and a simultaneous move in food trends more broadly toward freshness and away from processing. The possibility for a growing public to enjoy these trends is aided by the rise in year-round availability in the United States of avocados, chiles, mangoes, and limes since NAFTA. The growing popularity of fresh Mexican food led to simultaneous explosions of available food at both ends of the price range—taco trucks serving Mexican street food gained new credibility and visibility among non-Mexicans in urban spaces, while red snapper *a la veracruzana,* and other, fancier, dishes were served at restaurants marked in guidebooks with $$$ and $$$$ signs for their high prices.

But for the true alchemist's victory, Mexican cuisine would have to be reduced to its most basic elements. If twentieth-century diners rewarded restaurants for sophistication, in the twenty-first century, restaurant patrons are as likely to seek out lowbrow as they are highbrow foods. After years of ever more arcane "molecular," "fastidious," "hermetic" gastronomy, we see now that overly fussy restaurants are being brought down a few notches, as with the recent gleefully scathing review of one of the most elite restaurants in recent memory, Per Se, by the same *New York Times* reviewer who crowned Cosme: Pete Wells.[38]

The norms of a farm-to-table ethos reward "simplicity"; a $98 tasting menu called the "Farmer's Feast" at Dan Barber's iconic Blue Hill in

Greenwich Village, New York, features such simple courses as an impeccable single radish lying next to a single carrot, greens still on, sprinkled with salt. For $98, most diners have to be told a hell of a story to enjoy a raw, naked radish. Barber has been working on that story for longer than most, generating an entire philosophy around growing, preparing, and eating food that has been enormously influential. He primed the elite restaurant world for Cosme, a paean to corn, by instructing us to reward food that can be traced back to a particular place, even a particular farmer working a particular plot of land. In his book *The Third Plate: Field Notes on the Future of Food,* Barber focuses the better part of a chapter and frames his whole worldview on a plate of polenta.[39] He made it from corn that he had midwifed into existence by giving a farmer a cob of New England Eight Row Flint, an heirloom variety that dates to the 1700s and was nearly extinct. A rare seeds collector gave a desiccated cob to Barber, who in turn gave it to a farmer, who planted and grew it. Barber writes of the result: "It wasn't just the best polenta of my life. It was polenta I hadn't imagined possible, so corny that breathing out after swallowing the first bite brought another rich shot of corn flavor . . . How had I assumed all those years that polenta smelled of nothing more than dried meal? It's really not too much to ask of polenta to actually taste like the corn."[40]

A clue that there is some social alchemy happening in all of this is the frequent use in food writing of a French term to describe one of the most central attributes of food distinction today—*terroir*. It is the word for one of the characteristics traced and qualified by France's protectionist wine appellation and regulation system and refers to the idea that the particular environmental characteristics of a place give things produced in that place—wine and champagne, especially, but also cheese, cured meats, and more—a unique taste that cannot be approximated even when an otherwise identical product comes from a different place. If place matters, in theory so do the particular political histories of control over that place, and oftentimes, struggles for rights, legitimacy, resources, and domain—even though these are often omitted. Terroir is just one more in a large toolkit of words for distinctions that are value added to products, enabling some products to stand out from a sea of others that are, in other senses—such as nutritional or use value—identical and interchangeable.[41] When a food is elevated to *cuisine,* it is not about its power to fuel the human body, or even its capacity to bring people together around a table, but its function as a vehicle of value that enables some to profit wildly by it. For an outsider to acknowledge certain foods as special is a necessary step because it is rarely, if ever, the original producers and consumers of a food that can give it distinction in the supranational, elite sphere of haute cuisine.[42] Thus, Dan Barber, René Redzepi, and Enrique Olvera together, in different locations and moments, succeed in telling different chapters of a story that brings corn to its apex of value. It is not enough for something to be "a perfect mouthful," but it must evoke a particular set of ideas and represent the perfect iteration of corn.

We humans do not always trust our own instincts about value and instead assign it in a cumulative and highly social fashion. Something simple can accrue value simply by its journey through elite cultural realms; things are rarely recognized in situ for having value on their own. On the contrary, the fact that something is highly valued by people native to a place has been inversely correlated historically to its market value until it is extracted from that place and inserted into larger global circuits, usually by brokers who pass little, if any, of the profit back to the original producers. Jorge Gaviria of Masienda notes that even the maize farmers themselves who continue to grow black, red, and other unusual varieties of landrace corn in rural Mexican communities disparage their crops. While they value the corn for their own household consumption, they see little to no market value for it.[43] Masienda solves their logistical problems—the meager economic or physical infrastructure available to subsistence farmers in Mexico to transport their products out of their communities—but more compellingly solves a symbolic problem, creating value for a product undervalued in its place of origin. We will explore the paradox of landrace corn rising in value at the same time that commercially grown corn has become fully commoditized, transforming markets, industries, and even bodies as it fuels the production of cheap food and the prosperity of multinational corporations.

A PARENTHESIS: QUINOA

A few years ago, socially conscious foodies were mortified to learn that quinoa, the "superfood" that had come to be known and appreciated outside of its place of origin in the Andean highlands among those who pursue organic, vegan, and other plant-based diets, could have some ethical baggage. Although it cooks and is eaten like a grain, quinoa is a seed with a very high proportion of protein. Quinoa became ubiquitous on menus, at salad bars, and on some people's shopping lists. But the same moment that the UN named 2013 the Year of Quinoa, an article in the *Guardian* raised questions about the ethics of eating it.[44]

Quinoa has long constituted a staple in the diet of Andean highland farmers in Bolivia and Peru, who were suddenly able to sell their harvests at unheard of prices due to the crop's global popularity. Economically, it made sense for them to sell their entire crop and purchase white rice imported from China for their own consumption with the cash. Further, the profitability of quinoa meant that many farmers chose to no longer grow other crops, making them entirely dependent on a continued rise in the global demand for quinoa.[45] The irony that economically privileged health food enthusiasts in the Global North would literally take a nutritious and local food product out of the mouths of Andean peasants generated a great deal of hand wringing for some and schadenfreude by others who enjoy mocking the fickle preferences of elite foodies.

Since then, when I've discussed this book and the state of corn in Mexico with friends and colleagues, some have interrupted me early on by saying, "Don't tell me, corn is like quinoa!?" It is increasingly clear that there are some parallels, but there are also unique aspects to corn—it is a massive commodity compared to quinoa—with 865 million metric tons grown worldwide in 2011, and has major industrial uses such as ethanol, animal feed, sweeteners, starches, and fillers, in addition to more direct kinds of human consumption. The sheer scale of production and multinational economic impact of corn cannot be compared to quinoa. Nonetheless, landrace corn's appeal may exceed supply. Jorge Gaviria, founder of Masienda, is keen to avoid a "quinoa moment" for heritage corn and argues that he has built ethical controls into his business model. He ensures that each farmer he purchases from has set aside enough corn for household consumption. He does not tell farmers what to grow; instead he tells them that if they have extra of certain varietals after harvest, he'll buy it. He is careful never to share the names or specific locations of the farmers he purchases from. Nevertheless, he acknowledges that other, less ethical, speculators could come in behind him and buy out the entire supply of subsistence farmers in the region. The preventive mechanism for that, he explains, is love for the crop; *amor al arte* is the phrase used in Spanish.[46] The farmers he works with were already growing landrace corn for their consumption alone, even if it lost money, because that is what they like to eat. The fact they can sell the surplus instead of leaving it to rot in the fields or feeding it to their animals ensures they will have enough to eat and more cash in their pockets. But the scalability of such a model is tricky. The more popular and pricy landrace corn becomes in global markets, the less incentive exists for farmers to keep their focus on small scale and subsistence, and the greater the profit motive for speculative brokers willing to cut ethical corners.

Tortilla consumption in Mexico is declining. Long Mexico's most archetypal food, its consumption dropped 15 percent in the first four years of this century alone.[47] In cities, the decline has been even faster. In 2010 in rural areas, per capita consumption was 217.9 grams per day, but in urban areas, only 155.4,[48] a difference Salvador Villalpando, a researcher for the National Institute of Health in Mexico, attributed to "a status issue."[49] The Ministry of the Economy, in a 2012 report on the "corn-tortilla value chain," attributed the decline in consumption to multiple factors: the cost of tortillas (from an average of 9 pesos to 12 per kilo in five years, and a rise in price of 279 percent since 1994), but also the increase in availability of "new fast food products" and "life style changes," leading to greater consumption of packaged and ultraprocessed foods from breads and muffins to pizzas and chicken nuggets.[50]

With NAFTA, Mexico sought to move its economy away from agriculture, a process we'll explore in detail in the next chapter. NAFTA provided a compelling rationale and push toward de-peasantization and the removal of federal supports of the agricultural sector. The architects of economic policy probably underestimated how brutal that would turn out to be as well as the ripple effects for public health, migration, and more. Even though Mexico pushed for a phased extinction of tariffs and limits on US corn imports in the early phases of NAFTA implementation, these were less part of a plan to protect farmers in the long term than an effort to soften the initial blow to rural livelihoods, even while policies were pursued that together accelerated the decline of the farm sector. The low cost of US-grown corn compared to Mexico's at the start of NAFTA was perceived as a threat to Mexican farmers while also understood as a benefit for the economic policymakers' plan to purchase corn Mexico would no longer grow to sustain the population's food needs. Within fifteen years after the implementation of NAFTA, 40 percent of corn in Mexico would be imported from the United States. By the same period, ethanol production came to claim a large share of US corn, driving up the cost of US corn, and corn prices globally, and in theory creating an incentive for Mexican farmers to get back in the game. But it was too late. Mexico had already undone the distribution channels and market supports that had previously made Mexican corn more viable. Changes in eating habits (more meat and processed foods, less milpa-based cuisine), the rise in the cost of tortillas, and the increasing alienation of Mexico's poor from the land have contributed to the decline in consumption of Mexico's ancestral staple.

Here, I explore the initial effects of NAFTA on corn. Corn is the most contentious commodity in trade between Mexico and the United States. Fearing a glut of cheap US corn, Mexico conditioned its signing of NAFTA on certain protections to its corn growers, but these quickly expired. Mexico also agreed to give up most of its subsidies for corn cultivation.[51] While Mexico today exports more farm products to the United States than vice versa ($23 billion in agricultural imports from Mexico to the United States, $18 billion from the United States to Mexico),[52] the comparisons are, to use a fruit metaphor, apples to oranges: Mexico's exports are a small slice of the overall US economy, while US exports to Mexico constitute a large slice of its economy.[53]

NAFTA altered the viability of corn farming in Mexico, initially by creating a marketplace in which small-scale farmers could not compete. In the United States, corn subsidies continued to dominate the annual farm bill after NAFTA, protecting industrial agriculture from the vagaries of market fluctuations. The result? Cheap US corn flooded the Mexican market and made it difficult for small-scale producers in Mexico to grow corn for the market, or even for subsistence.[54] "Product dumping" further weakened the market. US exports of corn to Mexico climbed more than 400 percent between 1997 and 2005, a fifth of it "dumped," or expelled from the market to protect US producers, costing Mexico $6.57 billion.[55] By the time ethanol came to claim 40 percent of US corn in 2010, driving up global corn prices and stimulating a speculative frenzy that also drove up land costs, the damage was done.[56] The costs in rural economic decline and national GDP as a push factor for migration, in biodiversity, and in health are almost incalculable.

For Mexico, NAFTA initiated the march toward what food and trade analyst Timothy Wise has identified as Mexico's import dependency: for nearly all major agricultural products, Mexico has doubled, tripled, even quadrupled imports between 1990–1992 and 2006–2008.[57] This marked a shift away from agriculture and toward food security, and depended on Mexico being diagnosed at the onset of NAFTA with a "corn deficit." Because of the "corn deficit," the NAFTA signatories repeatedly agreed to suspend the tariffs that had been planned to slowly expire to protect the Mexican corn industry. A staged extinction of tariffs on US corn was one of the few protections Mexico insisted upon, so that the costs of exporting to Mexico would stay high and protect Mexican growers until at least 2008. These were coupled with quotas, also to expire in 2008, to limit the total quantity of US corn allowed to enter the Mexican market.

Of course, characterization of US corn as cheap and efficient in the early 1990s was not entirely what it seemed, as it is the most heavily subsidized crop in the United States, receiving between 1995 and 2014 a staggering $84,427,099,356 in a variety of subsidies: deficiency payments, direct payments, crop insurance premium subsidies, price support payments, countercyclical programs, market loss assistance, and other programs.[58] Ostensibly a means to aid farmers' ability to weather periodic ups and downs in the market price of corn, climate vagaries, and other unknowns, the subsidies were not pegged to the market. Even as global prices have risen in the last decade with corn's rising use as an ingredient in ethanol, subsidies also rose—not simply protecting farmers from the whims of the market but insulating them from any exposure to it at all. Subsidies allowed them to profit whether their crop succeeded or failed entirely. At the same time, crop supports encouraged agribusiness to further consolidate, increasing the acreage of land cultivated while decreasing the number of farmers cultivating it.[59] Far from being a boon to the small farmer, also endangered in the United States, subsidies act as an incentive toward corporatization, conglomeration, and mechanization.

These subsidies for US producers, while now more heavily concentrated in crop insurance premium subsidies, persisted, even while as a condition of NAFTA, Mexico agreed to eliminate both its crop supports and the agency that promoted and protected growers of corn and other basic food stuffs, CONASUPO, the National Company of Popular Subsistences. Since its founding in 1965, CONASUPO had supported the cultivation of particular foodstuffs as a means of combating extreme poverty and marginalization.[60] When subsidies are factored into calculations, US corn was not so "cheap" after all.

Nonetheless, let's return to the question of Mexico's "corn deficit." Mexico's demand for corn was reportedly so high with NAFTA that the signatories agreed to suspend tariffs and exceed quotas long before 2008 to meet it. This was seen as important for jump-starting the meat industry, dependent on corn as feed. Dramatically lower feed costs contributed to dramatically higher quantities of meat produced. So, the tariffs and quotas built into NAFTA as protection were actually effectively ignored from the start: instead of phasing out corn tariffs in fifteen years, as planned, the tariffs were phased out in thirty months. The planned fifteen-year transition period was compressed between January 1994 and August 1996, when prices fell 48 percent.[61] Direct payments to corn farmers to soften the transition were introduced when these were phased out, but they have not been evenly distributed or reliable.[62] The fall of corn prices in Mexico to international levels (set by the United States, the world's largest producer) was one immediate consequence of NAFTA, resulting in the bottom falling out of the already razor-thin profit margin of Mexican corn growers. But the issue is more complex. In theory, Mexican corn was still protected, but corn *products* were not subject to tariffs or quotas. So, while "free" trade in corn as a commodity was to begin in 2008, it began in 1994 for corn products (starch, filler, feed, syrup, flour, chips, etc.).

What did that mean in practical terms? While building a dam to prevent a flood of US corn, Mexico left the floodgates open for "corn products." And when even the open floodgates were not enough, quotas and tariff policies were adjusted to allow for even more corn products to enter. Even more insidious, virtually the entire "corn deficit" was met with US yellow corn (Central Illinois Yellow Corn and American Gulf Yellow Corn, mainly).[63] These varieties of corn in Mexico are used primarily for animal feed, chips and other snacks, syrups, and cereal. It is very different from almost all of the corn (91 percent) grown in Mexico, largely white corn, favored for human consumption, including commercial sales (corn flour, masa, and tortillas) and direct household consumption. Very little of imported US yellow corn is eaten *as corn* (in tortillas, corn flour, etc.). So what we see as a result of increased US corn in the Mexican market is increased consumption of the processed foods that use corn byproducts (mostly syrups and starches), accompanying a decline in consumption of tortillas. This corresponds to prices: while corn prices have come to mirror international prices (for US-grown yellow corn) and fell in the decade after NAFTA began, along with prices for products made with corn syrups and starches, tortilla prices (made from Mexican white corn) rose, drastically. This was arguably more damaging for consumers than beneficial for corn growers. Availability also rose, with corn syrup exports from the United States to Mexico up 863 percent since NAFTA.[64] When Mexican sugar producers tried to prevent a flood of corn syrup–sweetened products from edging out their business, Cargill sued them for violating the conditions of NAFTA.[65] Thus, the suspension of tariffs and approval of "over quotas" had little to do with responding to a "corn deficit," which in most people's eyes would imply a food shortage.[66] But yellow corn is not food, at least not as it has been defined for most of human history. [67] As a corn grower in the documentary *King Corn* (Woolf 2007) phrased it, referring to the Iowa cornfields spread out to the horizon before him, "We aren't growing quality. [It's the] poorest quality crap the world's ever seen."

It seems absurd that yellow industrial corn and white landrace corn when destined for such different applications would even be considered in the same category of analysis. A 2012 Mexican Ministry of the Economy report noted that tortillas were ranked second in importance in the typical Mexican family's shopping cart (after beef), but on average represented only 3.1 percent of the average household food budget. For Mexicans in the poorest tenth of the population, however, tortillas represented 10 percent of their average food budget. The rising costs of tortillas, 33 percent in five years, should alert us to food insufficiency among those with the least resources. Indeed, malnutrition has risen in recent years as Mexico's small-scale cultivation of corn has declined and imports of corn have climbed.

In *The Omnivore's Dilemma,* Michael Pollan writes that while we think of early Mesoamericans as "people of the corn," it is really the United States in the early twenty-first century that deserves the moniker. Indeed, US corn consumption exceeds that of all other nations, at 280 million tons per year. Per capita average annual corn consumption in the United States is about .87 metric tons, nearly four times Mexico's at .24 tons. That consumption includes all kinds of corn: high-fructose corn syrup, starches, cereals, corn-fed livestock, and so on.[68] In fact, most of the corn Americans eat is delivered via the meat and poultry that have consumed it first.

TIME TO MAKE THE TORTILLAS

It is 7 a.m. in Santo Tomás Tlalpa, Puebla. The roosters have been crowing for a while now, and the donkeys have chimed in with their tone-deaf but enthusiastic refrain. The local teenagers, piled onto the intraregional bus, are getting ready to go to the closest public high school, in Tehuacán, the midsized city about twenty minutes away. Here, in the Tehuacán valley, southeast of Mexico City, it is said that corn was first cultivated by a female midwife.[69] There is a line at each of the four *molinos,* corn mills, in this small town. A few decades ago, there was only one molino, and women lined up at four in the morning with their buckets of soaked, nixtamalized corn. But migration has changed things in more than one way: some migrants have invested in mills—the machine, though decidedly low tech, is pricy, and the calculus was that corn grinding would always be needed. So, now each of the four neighborhoods in this town has its own molino. Migration has taken away a lot of the working-age population, however, so while there are more molinos, there are fewer people to eat the fresh tortillas that are the end-product of the laborious process of turning hard, starchy corn kernels into warm, soft, chewy tortillas. Also, migration has resulted in an influx of migradollars, not only the remittances that migrants send, but also the income generated by migrant investments in small businesses. So, with this influx of money, some buy their tortillas already made from the tortilla factory for 12 pesos a kilo (about 67 cents US). The teenagers who live in town now are more likely than a generation ago to continue their education; they can be seen standing at the bus stop with wet hair neatly combed and maroon sweaters over their school uniforms, perhaps with a box of milk or a granola bar in hand—but without having had a hot breakfast including fresh homemade tortillas.

It is estimated that in the colonial period, the many different, laborious steps required to make fresh tortillas for an average household required forty hours per week, almost all of it accomplished by women.[70] This included hand-grinding the corn on a stone metate. Class status could be measured by the presence or absence of hired help to do this labor. It is also possible to imagine that for families of lesser means, this labor alone would be reason enough for having a large family; the labor requirements were steep. The practice of sons bringing their wives to reside in their parents' home, patrivirilocality, which is still common today in this region of Mexico, was also in part favored by the labor intensiveness of the basic diet. No wonder that technological innovations like the corn grinder, and later the tortilla factory, represented massive transformations in the labor burden of women. Now, we will look at the strategies deployed by families in one part of Puebla state, who use corn as one element in a complex subsistence strategy.

ASUNCIÓN MIAHUATLÁN, PUEBLA

Fernando Escamilla and Hortensia Cordero explained to me the circle of life in which corn cultivation is the center. They are corn farmers I interviewed in Asunción Miahuatlán (*miahuatlán* is a Nahuatl word for an ear of corn), and like many people in this region, they speak Nahuatl as their home language. Both are lean and fit, although the gray in their hair and the ages of their children indicated they were in their sixties. They gestured with hands worn from hard work, but soft and strong. I spoke to them in their neighbor's living room. The smell of roasting chiles wafting from the kitchen made the air heavy and piquant. They grow *criollo* corn—by which they mean native landrace corn as opposed to hybrid corn—on small plots of land a walking distance from their home in Asunción Miahuatlán.[71] It is largely rain fed, although sometimes they pay for irrigation when rain is scarce. Their corn takes six months to grow, but each harvest provides them with enough corn for their household's consumption for half the year. Every day, Hortensia soaks a bucket of dried corn in mineral lime and water, nixtamalizing it to prepare it for grinding, using techniques developed by ancient Mesoamericans that maximize the bioavailability of corn's nutrients and enhance its digestibility. Every morning, she takes the corn she soaked the day before to be ground at one of her town's mills, for 2 pesos (13 cents US). From the ground corn masa, she makes tortillas. In addition, depending on the occasion and her mood, she will make atole, tlacoyos, tamales, or memelas for her family. The couple also sell corn husks out of her husband's furniture workshop. The corn husks are in high demand at Christmas and Candelaria, festive occasions when people tend to make huge vats of tamales, which are wrapped and steamed in the husks. She and her husband sell sacks of three hundred husks for 18 to 25 pesos ($1.20 to $1.50 US). The price is determined largely by how much her neighbors charge for their sacks, with each trying to remain competitive with the other. They also charge the goatherds who live near their land a few pesos for the privilege of grazing their goats on the zacates, or fallen stalks, after harvest.

Their corn, they told me, "does not like to be crowded, it's bothered by other plants," but traditionally corn milpas in many parts of the region were intercropped with squash, tomato, and bean plants, a lively and intertwined ecosystem containing the main crops of everyday consumption. While Fernando and Hortensia plant their vegetables on separate plots, they speak of the circular and self-sufficient production cycle that marks their seasons and their lives. They say it is helpful for weathering the ups and downs of other economic activities. While Fernando also makes furniture, he does not depend entirely on it, and many people I spoke with described having multiple survival strategies involving producing as well as selling various items. Like others I spoke with, he described himself as a *poquitero,* a jack of all trades who earns a little, *un poquito,* from each of a variety of endeavors.

This is by no means a strategy for the generation of wealth. On the contrary, Fernando and Hortensia are vulnerable to market forces, as well as climate, and operate on a razor-thin margin of economic viability, going into debt some years, breaking even others, and only rarely generating anything like a profit. Nonetheless, the fact that their own subsistence needs are covered insulates and protects them. We will see how people like this family are being drawn away from this kind of livelihood by changes in farming and the status of farming in the overall economy.

HYBRID VERSUS CRIOLLO

Not far away from Fernando and Hortensia, Don Miguel is representative of a quickly diminishing club. He, too, insists on growing his own corn. His father never put his name on the ejido paperwork that would have allowed him to access communal land, so he had to buy land instead.[72] The ejido program was a proud legacy of the Mexican Revolution, administering rights to collectively held land, but it has been rolled back in recent years. Don Miguel has several small and awkwardly shaped plots sprinkled around his hometown, San Diego Miahuatlán. All together, they add up to somewhere between one and two hectares. He plants corn on one, and on the others, he might grow tomatoes, chiles, quelites, or sorghum, varying a bit each year.[73] At the moment I visited him, he was growing a bumper crop of sorghum, which he was hustling to sell for animal feed. He wanted to get it sold and harvested before it dried too much on the stalk.

While my farm skills and knowledge are embarrassingly thin, it does not take a genius to notice that the sorghum stalks and corn stalks look remarkably alike, two kissing cousins that only at the end stage of development develop into very different looking crops. The sorghum is a royal burgundy color and has small and organized rows of seeds, like corn that forgot its husk and grew outward, almost like a flower, instead of inward into a kernel. It's a beautiful plant.

Next to the sorghum, his cornfield had been harvested already and the zacates, or corn stalks, were lying along the ground like a giant had been called away from playing pickup sticks. Nothing in the process is wasted; even the discarded zacates are sold as animal feed. The corn Miguel harvested would last his family of five most of the year, providing enough for their daily consumption of tortillas and the occasional atole or tamales. I asked him if his children, now adults, help him. His sons, he said, make more money working in the *granjas,* the egg farms that dot the countryside all over Tehuacán. The self-contained, compact, white-roofed

Figure 1. Don Miguel and his sorghum, Puebla, 2015. Photo by the author.

buildings make it clear that "free-range" is not a moniker added to the advertising for these eggs, but "white" is; all of the industrially produced eggs are uniform in color. Eggs, formerly a very local and low-yield business, have been industrialized in this region, and the two largest producers here now distribute eggs all over Mexico.[74]

The egg farms pay more than other kinds of farmwork, as much as 300 pesos per day (about $20 US). Miguel told me he is happy with his current situation: he has enough land to grow corn for his family and to supplement his income as a driver, and he is largely able to work it himself, while his sons spend most working days at the egg farms. When necessary, he hires *peones,* or day laborers, at around 100 pesos a day (less than $10 US) to help. His sons occasionally take a day off to join him at harvest time, and he invests 1,200 pesos in the services of a tractor to prepare the land for planting and to harvest. To buy more land would require more capital input and more risk, and would not necessarily pay off in yield.

Miguel insists on growing criollo corn. It is the ragtag cousin of *híbrido,* hybrid corn, which has made inroads here in the birthplace of corn. He is lucky compared to a lot of small-scale corn growers because he gets free water. The availability of water can make or break small corn farmers today. While most farmers I spoke with told me that it used to be feasible to rely only on rainfall, *temporal,* to nurture the milpa, now it is a risky proposition that results, always, in a smaller crop than corn grown on irrigated fields. Criollo is known to produce smaller, lighter, and fewer *mazorcas,* ears, per stalk than híbrido. A few farmers, due to necessity or because it is not their main economic activity, depend entirely on rainfall for their milpa to grow. But most have to buy water, irrigating by the hour a few strategic times during the development of the crop, sometimes more if the skies are especially stingy.

An urban legend about the regional egg magnate has to do with the locally held opinion that rain is unfavorable for the egg business, causing muck and runoff problems that are expensive to mitigate. I was told matter-of-factly by corn farmers in Malacatepec, a town to the east of the city of Puebla, that when heavy gray clouds form in the sky, the egg man sends small planes into the clouds to bust them up—ruining the chances for small farmers to irrigate their crops for free. The lucky few have access to a still functional aquifer or some other source of free water. Miguel's fields lie downhill from the road where the city of Tehuacán dumps storm runoff. Other farmers told me they used black or gray water to irrigate their fields. The safety of using wastewater to irrigate food crops is questionable, but it is a wide practice.

Criollo corn is widely acknowledged to be *más sabroso,* tastier, than yellow or hybrid. It is also less labor intensive: it grows tall and flourishes with the little rainwater that falls on it. Fernando Escamilla spoke about corn plants as if they were children. Hybrid corn, he told me, is like a fussy baby; it is very delicate, finicky. It requires a lot of water and pesticides, and only grows short, uniform stalks. The stalks are laden with heavy mazorcas, but it requires a lot of attention. Criollo corn, on the other hand, is more resilient and less demanding. It can survive with rainwater and a little irrigation here and there. He told me his milpa had been sown a few weeks before and now it was knee high. It's cute, he told me: "Está chula mi milpa."[75] Even though the hybrid corn is considered to be a foreign transplant, it is not tall like people here describe the *gringos* and *ingieneros,* the agronomists who promote it. While corn farmers here refer to themselves as *chaparritos,* short, their criollo corn stalks reach for the sky. They grow so tall that they are known to topple over in the wind, but farmers use millennial strategies to support their height and prevent them from being knocked over. Hybrid corn is unimpressive height-wise, quite short and squat, but able to withstand gusts of wind.[76]

Peel back the husk and the two kinds of corn are remarkably different from each other. Criollo corn is a riotous and unruly cluster of kernels wedged in against each other, more like a colorful mosaic than subway tile. Hybrid corn grows kernels that sit in neat little rows, uniform, even boring, and taste is not its strong suit. It's also expensive. A twenty-five-kilo sack of hybrid corn seed—sufficient for sowing a hectare—in the Miahuatlán region runs about 1,800 to 2,000 pesos ($120–$130), more than twenty times the cost of criollo, which is only 60 to 80 pesos a sack. Moreover, the hybrid corn must be purchased anew every year. I asked the family of Javier Cruz in San Diego Miahuatlán why and was told, "Se acaba rápido" (it's finished quickly). If replanted, it attracts *plaga,* which can refer both to insects and blight, and it doesn't grow as plentifully. They told me that the seeds have chemicals that make it grow faster—four months from planting to harvest, versus six for criollo corn—but also deplete it more quickly.

This is part of its genetic engineering. It is designed to be sterile, not fertile. Seed companies argue that genetically ensuring planned obsolescence enables them to justify their investments in research and development. Large multinational biotechnology firms hold patents on the varietals and will sue seed savers for copyright infringement. NAFTA makes such lawsuits easier and more profitable. The patenting of seeds and aggressive pursuit of violations of copyright for practices such as seed

Figure 2. A resident of the Tehuacán region demonstrates the difference between criollo corn (left) and hybrid corn (right), Puebla, January 2015. Photo by the author.

saving ensure that farmers have to purchase seeds from the corporation each year.[77] For farmers like the Escamilla family, it is not easy to see saving seeds from the corn they grow themselves as theft of someone else's property.

Criollo corn, on the other hand, has been selected and replanted from one harvest to the next for millennia. When corn is picked, its husk is removed, the ears are dried in the sun, and the kernels are stored in twenty-five-kilo sacks for sale or consumption until the next harvest. In fact, the selection of the best mazorcas for drying and planting the next season has been the key human intervention in corn's evolution in this region, accelerating and fine-tuning the selection of favorable traits over time. In this way, corn in each region—not just Miahuatlán broadly, but specifically in the hills, and the valley, on the wet side of the slope or the dry side—is perfectly suited to its own microclimate and conditions. Farmers might buy, sell, trade, and share seeds because of friendship and need, but also because a neighbor's varietal might be more suitable in an especially dry or wet year.

Corn species in this region, I was told by the farmers, have been adjusting to the climatic shift toward aridity over the last two decades, but not quickly enough. The region never returned to predrought conditions after a severe drought in the mid-1990s, and now local aquifers are drying up. Miguel Olivares told me he remembers there being more rain in the past—criollo corn could almost always thrive *de temporal*, with rainfall alone. Now, he said, almost everyone irrigates their milpa. Water scarcity has gone from a recurrent risk to a constant crisis.

Why, then, if hybrid corn requires more water and pesticides, costs more, and behaves like a spoiled baby, would anyone grow it? That is a question the farmers in Asunción Miahuatlán ask themselves. Asunción Miahuatlán is a Nahuatl-speaking town where the indigenous language has not declined but has resurged in recent years; the people there described themselves to me as a self-sufficient and proud unit. Most people in town, they told me, still grow enough of their own corn for household consumption, and they report receiving no help from the government. While government agencies are actively aiding farmers in many parts of Mexico to adopt hybrid corn, increase productivity, and combat pests, diseases, and drought, farmers here tell me the help is not worth the costs, both financial and symbolic. First, they said the help is distributed according to political affiliations. Towns that promise to fall in behind a particular candidate and party can expect to receive help, whereas those who remain unaffiliated or ally themselves with the opposition, they say, are left in the cold. Further, the ejido program is not seen as having benefited many here. "No estamos dentro de los programas" (We're not in any programs), Fernando Escamilla and his wife told me. In this way, this town has become one of a few that without calling a lot of attention to it, are resisting the larger push toward genetically modified corn and industrial agriculture.

Josefina and Javier Cruz, on the other hand, in San Diego Miahuatlán, proudly grow hybrid corn. San Diego Miahuatlán is closer to the semi-urban sprawl of Tehuacán and its regional market, and customers there prefer hybrid, Josefina told me. In addition to keeping a good portion of the corn they grow on three hectares for household consumption, they sell *elotes* and *esquites,* and hybrid ears of corn command 10 pesos a piece, while criollo corn only sells for 6 pesos each. The difference between corn for elote and corn for grinding is not always one of species but of time on the stalk. Elotes are harvested earlier and must be consumed faster, while grain corn is left on the stalk another month. Fresh corn on the cob is eaten as elotes, served on the street from carts. The corncob is speared with a stick and grilled, and then slathered in mayonnaise, chile powder, and cotija cheese. Esquites is another variety of snack, also grilled fresh corn, but the kernels are removed from the cob and layered with sour cream, herbs, chiles, lime, and salt, and it is eaten from a cup with a spoon. These are popular snacks, and apparently lucrative enough to shape the Cruz family's overall production scheme. They explained that 10 pesos per ear make it worth the family's investment in the seed, six separate irrigations, and pesticides.

We see this same pattern repeating in multiple contexts. In the next chapter, we follow goat farmers navigating between older and newer ways of working. Powerful trends in government funding, corporate practices, purported consumer preferences, among other drivers, push small-scale producers toward larger scale and more industrial farming practices that require more expensive and complicated inputs, consume more water and other resources, and entail greater risk. Some, like the stubborn farmers of Asunción Miahuatlán, articulate their resistance to these trends matter-of-factly: we're already marginalized from larger national trends, whether government support or corporate pressures, so we'll keep doing what we've done since our ancestors' time, thank you very much. Does such resistance make these farmers and their families more likely to survive the threat of climate change, increased industrialization of agriculture, and the dismantling of the ejido system and small-scale agriculture, or does it doom them to obsolescence? Time will tell.

These are variations on one of the main questions of this book: what is gained and what is lost by the shifts in ways of producing, distributing, and eating food in Mexico and the United States over the last twenty years? Social scientist Judy Hellman described the "gentlemen farmers" she encountered while conducting research in Mexico in the last twenty years, who insisted on growing their own corn, even at a loss, because they enjoyed eating fresh, white corn tortillas.[78] This is an example of nonrational behaviors and nonmarket forces in the language of economic theory—all of the realms of human action in the universe (such as "culture") that are outside of or defy economic rationality.[79] But are these quixotic characters who can absorb the costs and hurt no one in their pursuit of eating and sharing their favorite varietals of corn simply remnants of an outdated and obsolete mode of production that can be expected to become extinct along with its last practitioners, or be "rescued" by elite chefs? We will continue to explore in the coming chapters whether there might be ways to ensure farmers' long-term sustainability, value the biodiversity of Mexico's corn, and ensure that its traditional foods remain available, and not only to the rich. Will we need to "remember" the ancient art of grinding corn and making tortillas from space age internet videos?

3 Laying the Groundwork for NAFTA

GOATS

Bertoldo Juan Palacios Castillo has been herding goats for fifty years, like his father and grandfather before him. He lives on the outer perimeter of Santo Tomás Tlalpa, in the state of Puebla, with his wife and six children. He raises native goats, *chivos criollos*. His goats, he is quick to point out, are scrawny. They have little meat on their bones and the females produce hardly enough milk for their own kids, let alone his. He shrugs his shoulders and laughs amiably, as though even he is not sure why he bothers with them—it is not because they're good business! In spite of his deprecation of his business smarts, Mr. Palacios is an expert in his domain.

Even though he can only sell his goats for 80 to 100 pesos, he does not invest much in them. Criollo goats, he explains to me, thrive on what this land has to offer. When I first visited the area in 2002, I was struck by how dry it was. I knew a lot of people had migrated to the New York area from this region because they could no longer make their living there, and my secret question was how they had ever made a living off this arid landscape. What I did not realize then, or until years later, was that this land, dotted by a multitude of cactus species, is home to a teeming assortment

Figure 3. Goatherds outside Asunción Miahuatlán, Puebla. Photo by the author.

of plant, animal, insect, and human life that have coexisted, and thrived off of each other, for millennia.

Every day, after a quick breakfast with his wife, Mr. Palacios or one of his sons takes his herd of goats to *el monte,* the hills that rise behind their home. There, for two or three hours, the goats graze on zacate, *acahuale* (native sunflowers), and compost. He takes them to visit the stream that is fed by a local aquifer (it is rapidly diminishing, but for now, still available). He is home by lunchtime. His dogs deter coyotes, but they are not very good at herding, so he directs the herd using whistles. For the most part, though, everyone knows what they are supposed to do. And the meat, he tells me, when his goats are slaughtered, while minimal, "*es bien sabroso*"—it is very tasty.

Recently, however, he was approached by a government agronomist who suggested that he take advantage of credits available to him to invest in *cabros finos,* fancy goats. The new, improved goats yield much more meat than the *chivos criollos* he has always raised. While his goats sell for 80–100 pesos at a month of age, the fancy goats sell at fifteen days for 500 pesos, a huge price difference. He is worried, though, about the inputs required. I ask him to explain. Well, he tells me, first there is the insemination, then the expert advice. While there are loan and assistance programs available to help, he would have to learn a lot, and because these goats are *delicados,* they need to be monitored more closely by veterinarians. I ask if he incurs a lot of veterinary costs for the goats he currently raises. He laughs, "No, pues, estos chivos se cuidan solos" (No, these goats take care of themselves). His goats are sturdy and resilient. The government's goats need more water than he currently has available, so he would have to build new troughs and corrals, and pay for water delivery. They also require a special food enriched with antibiotics because they cannot digest the rough vegetation his current breed of goats eat. They are taller, and less fleet of foot, so they can't be allowed to roam on rocky or steep hillsides because they fall. Worst of all, their meat is tasteless.

I tell him he is not convincing me that the new goats are worth the trouble. Even though his goats yield less meat, I remind him, he also invests little in them. True, he replies, and everyone in this town favors the taste of chivo criollo. He would have to go into debt to invest in the government goats. Nonetheless, he tells me, that is the direction things are going, and he may as well make the change now.

Bertoldo's dilemma is one faced by countless small-scale farmers in Mexico. People like Bertoldo have managed to make a living from limited resources, operating at a thin profit and with little support, growing crops and raising livestock uniquely suited to the local conditions. Nonetheless, he is under pressure to "modernize," to invest his own resources in innovations brought from somewhere else, to fulfill others' ideas of progress, by raising what he calls "fancy goats." As Josefina, in the last chapter, noted, her customers wanted hybrid instead of landrace corn (*maíz criollo*); similarly, the fancy goats do not taste as good, but they somehow seem modern and command higher prices than the more rustic but by all accounts tastier and more hardy chivos criollos.

This chapter locates NAFTA within the longer arc of Mexico's economic and development policy. Starting with the late nineteenth century, I examine trends and shifts in Mexico's economic history and orientation, particularly the ways in which the state viewed the countryside's role in its development project. I follow the pendulum swings of successive governments between protectionism and openness to foreign investment. Influenced by macroeconomic theories developed in the United States, Europe, and Latin America, as well as homegrown ideas about sovereignty, Mexico has, over time, chosen successively to open or close its doors to foreign investment in the interest of development and prosperity. While each government has promised growth, ideological differences have shaped the path political leaders imagine lead to that goal.

Beyond ideology, even longer standing ideas about modernity and efficiency have endured. I will demonstrate how the stated goals of NAFTA fit neatly within this history. Mexico's federal elected officials, since the long rule of Porfirio Díaz (president for seven terms, 1876–1911, a period commonly referred to as the Porfiriato), have viewed the countryside as a place of backwardness, and the nation's cities as sites of modernity.[1] This is not unique to Mexico, of course, but there we see a particular array of ideas about rural communities, especially indigenous ones, in terms of their capacity for development and their relationship to the nation's idea of progress. As we will see, the predominantly negative views of the countryside are ironic because it has in fact always provided the resources for Mexico's development. Industrialization relied heavily on growth in agricultural production to meet the sustenance needs of workers who migrated to cities, but those who have consistently subsidized modernization have not been given credit. Tracing this arc allows us to see that these understandings of development preceded NAFTA and set the stage for it. Today, even as NAFTA has only delivered economic growth and prosperity to a few, these old ideas about rural people are revived in new, perverse ways, allowing those most vulnerable to the effects of globalization to be blamed for their own health and economic problems.

In this chapter, we first examine the formation of the Mexican state after independence, particularly the crisis that brought an end to Porfirio Díaz's three-decade rule and launched the Mexican Revolution. After exploring the ways that the leaders of the Mexican Revolution framed the countryside and its relationship to the country's modernization, we will turn to the postrevolutionary government's efforts to achieve industrialization and prosperity. Throughout the twentieth century, the government sequentially closed and opened the nation to outside investment. Throughout, the Mexican state played a robust role in economic policy, trade, and development. This role did not diminish until austerity measures, externally imposed as part of debt restructuring, obliged Mexico to unequivocally open its doors to outside investment and designate a smaller role for the federal government—an approach that endures today. Even while these episodes have marked radical shifts in orientation and conceptualization of the conditions for development and prosperity, one constant has remained: the idea that the countryside is a drag on the nation's progress. This idea persists today and is deployed anew as justification for the government's destabilization and abandonment of small-scale farming.

We can see that in each major period in Mexico since the Porfiriato, the state has sought to "modernize" the economy and make agricultural production more "efficient." This is so even though definitions of the terms "modern," "efficient," and even "agriculture" have changed frequently, as have the arrangements for production and distribution of labor and resources. The Porfiriato favored large landholders and industrialists, and its authoritarian approach as well as the way it allowed for the concentration of wealth and power in the hands of few allowed it to continue for so long. While the Mexican Revolution was fought to undo that inequality and redistribute land and resources, its leaders nevertheless still favored an industrial vision of modernity. If the revolution succeeded, it promised to liberate *campesinos* from the feudalism of archaic land distribution that favored wealthy *hacendados* and their massive landholdings, but rather than a more just rural economy, "the Mexican revolutionary gaze had already framed peasants and decided their fate."[2]

EFFICIENCY

A key notion in conceptualizations of modernity is the idea of efficiency, a means to marry science and technology with on-the-ground "know-how" to increase productivity as quickly as possible. The idea that Mexican corn is inherently inefficient is a recurring theme, traceable back to the conquest era—but in the last few decades, it is US corn production that provides the counterpoint to Mexico's, shaping ideas about progress and modernity. The United States is the most prolific producer of corn in the world, by a country mile. To what is that productivity owed? Is the United States simply better at growing corn? Large-scale industrial corn, the paradigm of "efficient" corn production, has short-, medium-, and long-term costs to the environment, health, and biodiversity of corn-growing regions and beyond. Efficiency can be fetishized above other values, ignoring "hidden" or "external" costs and leading to crop yields being held up as a metric all should employ. Setting aside the obvious emphasis on efficiency as a metric of worth and viability, is US corn actually efficient? The case of corn in Mexico demonstrates how theories of free trade are often at odds with economic realities and how measures like "efficiency" are not straightforward.[3] The United States produces a whopping 9.6 metric tons of corn per hectare, while the next most productive country, China, produces 5.3 metric tons per hectare. Mexico, in contrast, produces between 1.5 and 3 tons per hectare.[4] Because so much of corn growing is still done by hand, to produce one ton of corn requires 17.8 labor *days* in Mexico, versus 1.2 *hours* in the United States.[5]

Further, the corn itself has been altered. "Ancient Mexican corn," Pollan explains in an interview in the documentary *King Corn,* had a higher protein content than contemporary corn species, especially the few varieties of yellow corn grown most widely in the United States. Pollan describes today's dominant breed of corn as an urban crop—grown in "corn cities," stalks that thrive in cramped conditions, and are "Roundup Ready," genetically modified so they can be sprayed with Monsanto's trademarked glyphosate herbicide without dying. Corn that requires no weeding favors further mechanization. Its protein, sugar, and starch content have also been altered. Most of the corn grown in the United States is not for direct consumption; in fact, it cannot be consumed directly, the way heirloom

Mexican corn can be eaten fresh (*elotes* and *esquites*) and for grain (in the form of *masa* for tortillas or tamales).[6] Most corn grown in the United States is used for biofuels (40 percent) and animal feed (36 percent). Of the remainder, only a small amount is used for food for human beings—that is, if by food we mean high-fructose corn syrup.[7] The high sugar content of such corn favors its use as animal feed in industrial feedlots and processing into food additives. Corn-fed cattle grow quickly, even though they also require antibiotics and other medications for the acidosis and ulcers that result from their consumption of grain, which they as grass eaters have not evolved the capacity to digest.

As dysfunctional as critics paint the corn industry in the United States today, if we put it into the context of United States–Mexico relations, it is the holy grail. The almost absurdly prolific cornfields of the midwestern United States have been idealized as the key to the puzzle of Mexico's prosperity and development and part and parcel of a vision for development centered on NAFTA. In the narratives constructed in advance of and since the signing of NAFTA, US agro-industry's unprecedented productivity would liberate the Mexican campesino and propel Mexico's economy into the twenty-first century. In this model, efficiency is the measure by which an agricultural endeavor's merit must be measured. "Comparative advantage," the idea that each place should specialize in what it does most efficiently and purchase the rest of its products on the global market, is a categorically different idea from self-sufficiency. Within this framing, if US productivity per hectare at 9.6 metric tons obliterates Mexico's 1.5 to 3 tons, Mexico should not grow corn. This conclusion has been supported by what I argue is faulty logic in conceptualizations of food security and Mexico's development model.

These models promote a fetishization of efficiency, which is imbued with the magical power to overcome inequalities between and within nations, accelerate economic development, and produce wealth.[8] However, its believers are blind to its costs. The inefficiency of Mexico's small-scale farms has been taken as gospel in most of the country's discussions of economic and trade policy since long before NAFTA—even before the Mexican Revolution. However, before we debunk the logic of efficiency, I wish to ask first whether—even if true and factual—it is a valid measure of worthiness. If we follow the logic of efficiency and concede that Mexico should no longer produce but simply import all the corn it needs, what is lost? There might be reasons that Mexican farmers wish to continue to grow corn even if it is not efficient. In fact, we widely recognize that practices known to operate at a loss are sometimes still worth it. Corn cultivation deemed "inefficient" may still have social, political, cultural, health, and other benefits. It may even have economic value by measures that go beyond yield.

Moreover, Mexico's small farms actually are and have been efficient. Efficiency is, essentially, a ratio of investment and effort to yield. Unfortunately, it seems that in macroeconomic policy discussions yield is too often used as an indicator of efficiency—but this is only half of the equation. Higher levels of investment are assumed to command higher yields—but lower yields can be highly efficient if they result from smaller investments. As with Don Bertoldo's goats, small-scale corn farming yields little compared to other methods, but it does so with minimal input—the biggest inputs being labor and, in some cases, periodic irrigation. Smaller inputs can be more economically and environmentally sustainable. Even while laborious compared to industrial corn farming, which is highly mechanized, milpa-based corn farming is very compatible with other subsistence and economic activities, whether complementary crops, animal husbandry, craft production, or wage labor, among others. Milpas use the nooks and crannies of Mexico's diverse terrain, maximizing land use in ways that industrial farming never could.

This kind of reciprocal balance between land, labor, and life is referred to by Zapotec farmers as *mantenimiento*.[9] This relates to long-standing ideas in Mesoamerica about the moral value of conservation and resourcefulness.[10] Rather than being an adaptation to scarcity, this notion holds that "making do with what you have" can turn out to be more than enough.[11] With their reliance on heirloom seeds saved from one year to a next, and the minimal use of chemical inputs, small-scale farmers usually not only meet their food needs—with some left over for market—but also ensure biodiversity and environmental sustainability. Small-scale farmers engage in a complex economy of investment, effort, and market price, as well as intangibles like the comfort of eating food one knows to be wholesome, clean, nourishing, and plentiful.

The idea that small-scale agriculture is inefficient, and therefore a drag on Mexico's development and prosperity, is a myth that emerged in the colonial period and gained steam over the course of the twentieth century. Porfirio Díaz's motto was "order and progress," and he combined a firm, autocratic hand with an openness to foreign investment. However, most of the population, at the time made up of landless peasants and migrants to cities, were hungry, living in crushing poverty and continual scarcity, and exploited by ruthless elites. The revolution was principally fueled by demands for land reform. Unfortunately, these demands did not translate into actual redistribution of land when the leaders of the revolution seized power until the presidency of Lázaro Cárdenas in 1934.

Both the pre- and early postrevolutionary governments saw larger landholdings as more modern and efficient than small ones. Even though ideologically these successive governments were polar opposites, they shared views that favored consolidation and expansion of large-scale agriculture to modernize the economy toward industrialization. They invested in large-scale commercial agriculture and industry and saw this model as the key to feeding a growing population. After the revolution, enhanced productivity on large farms was expected to free the Mexican peasant from debt peonage. Nevertheless, in every period, it was rural dwellers that subsidized Mexico's industrialization—not bad for a woefully "inefficient" sector.

In fact, the subsidy provided by Mexico's rural peasants has been both national and transnational—with displaced Mexican farmers and workers and their extended kin also providing labor in periods of high demand and growth of the US economy during World War II and again in the last decades of the twentieth century. "Unskilled" and mobile laborers, at the bottom of the wage hierarchy, fostered the prosperity of Mexico's industrial elite at their own expense and through their own labor. This is because so many families have historically moved in and out of the wage sector and sustained themselves through small-scale agriculture, in time with the expansions and contractions of regional, national, and binational market conditions. The burden of economic growth was disproportionately shouldered by those paradoxically blamed for their country's backwardness.

This paradox, and yawning inequalities between the landed and landless, led to Mexico's revolution and its promise of more equity, but the revolution did not resolve these issues. As we explore how ideas about development changed during and after the revolution, we will see that views about rural people did not change much at all. We will trace these ideas to the period leading up to the implementation of NAFTA, and its aftermath.

LAND AND THE ROLE OF THE STATE

In the face of widespread hunger and a lack of access to land for meeting basic subsistence needs, millions were willing to take up arms in the Mexican Revolution.[12] Emiliano Zapata was the most iconic advocate for land redistribution to the peasantry, but it was José Venustiano Carranza, the son of a wealthy landholding family in Northern Mexico, who became the first president after the revolution (1917–1920), with a vision of development through private enterprise that dominated the period.[13] It was not until after the 1934 election of Lázaro Cárdenas that land reform was undertaken in earnest, with the creation of the *ejido*, a system for distributing land to be communally held and cultivated. Unlike every other man who has held the presidency in Mexico, Cárdenas thought development depended on the fostering of a prosperous rural sector, to be achieved through equitable access to land, credit, technical assistance, and social services.[14] During the Cárdenas administration, the countryside was transformed. The amount of land dedicated to privately owned farms was halved, while that of ejidos increased fourfold.[15] For a very brief period, between 1934 and 1940, the countryside, and the ejido as a form of land distribution, was seen as central to Mexico's prosperity and targeted with massive investment. Efforts were made to distribute land and productive resources more equitably. In turn, small landholders' productive capacity surpassed the yield per hectare of larger, privately owned farms.

Cárdenas's successor, Manuel Avila Camacho (1940–1946), very quickly shifted back to an emphasis on industry, not agriculture, as the key to development. His administration abandoned the ejido and ceased land reform efforts. Avila Camacho's administration placed its bets on "the vital energy of private initiative" and sought to "increase protection of private agricultural properties."[16] Nevertheless, in spite of total disinvestment on the part of the federal government, the yield of small-scale farms continued to outpace that of large-scale farms.[17]

When people began to move in massive numbers to the cities in 1940, sprawling urban settlements emerged that depended on produce from the countryside to meet their nutritional needs. If farmers were to become urban workers, they still needed to eat, and industrial farms were seen as the answer. A great part of the peasant population shifted to the industrial and service sectors, often moving to squalid conditions in the capital and other cities. Anthropologist Cynthia Hewitt de Alcántara notes these moves were out of necessity, with former peasants "supplying cheap labor or eking out a subsistence livelihood without making demands on the public treasury."[18] Interestingly, agricultural production increased in that period for both small and large farms, but for small holdings this increase occurred in spite of disinvestment from the state, and for large holdings, it followed a massive infusion of new investment.

But the rise in productivity still could not keep pace with the needs of the growing urbanized population. In the 1960s, rising hunger and inequality led to greater state involvement and coordination of food regulations. CONASUPO, the National Company of Popular Subsistences, was created to organize all of the state's regulatory activities involving food, including its efforts to regulate the markets of staples (corn, among others), create a more efficient and rational relationship between producer and consumer, eliminate inefficient and dishonest intermediaries, and protect low-income consumers and producers, allowing access to basic foods and a livelihood from productive activities.[19]

These efforts had succeeded by the 1970s: Mexico had gone from a period of importing food for subsistence to being a net exporter of food. Increased government intervention, protections, and tariffs, along with a focus on food sovereignty and the application of technology and chemical inputs, increased productivity.[20] But these government interventions to promote and increase large-scale food production in the 1960s further hastened the decline of small-scale corn farming.[21]

There was an understanding that corn was the most important element of the Mexican diet and that if people had tortillas, they would be OK. As a stopgap to combat urban hunger, the state intervened in maize production, providing price supports and subsidies intended to keep the price of tortillas affordable for all. The value of the tortilla went beyond its role as a staple starch—filling, cheap, and plentiful. Its symbolic weight as an emblem of culture, comfort, and identity meant that it was not treated like a neutral food product even as the economy shifted toward greater commoditization. In spite of government intervention to "rationalize" production and consumption, maize was accorded privileged status, not quite converted into an ordinary commodity. According to Lind and Barham, "Maize and tortillas circulated in protected markets, reinforcing the cultural criteria that viewed the tortilla as somehow incommensurable and incapable of being subjected to an unregulated free market economy."[22] Elected officials focused on how to make the cultivation, harvest, preparation, and consumption of corn more efficient and modern in an urbanizing society. They thought hunger and market bottlenecks could be mitigated through technological advances enabling stockpiling and siloing of corn, and production of dried, nixtamalized corn flour. They sought technologies to mechanize the time-consuming process of making daily tortillas, with such labor viewed as antiquated and unproductive for a nation trying to develop. Mass production of tortillas was achieved by advances in machinery and by the development of dry corn *masa*. Now often referred to by the name of the most commonly available brand, Maseca, dried corn masa enables home cooks to reconstitute the nixtamalized ground corn flour with water to make tortillas. It is also commonly used today by many neighborhood tortilla factories, where a machine churns out hot tortillas from the sacks of dried masa that can often be seen stacked on a pallet in a corner. People in cities rarely find a tortilla maker soaking and grinding corn for tortillas.

For some, the mass production of corn masa meant a fall from grace for the iconic food: rural sociologists Lind and Barham note: "The shift to dry flour [is] the desiccation or drying out of the maize dough and perhaps, symbolically, we might speak of the desecration of the tortilla culture."[23] This may, paradoxically, also have enabled corn's elevation as a kind of cultural emblem, divorced both from its use as a daily food staple and from its centrality to the country's economy.[24]

If the shift in the 1960s toward mechanization of every step corn took from the field to the table desacralized the tortilla, the government's turn toward structural adjustment and globalization has hastened its downfall. Previously a basic food product endowed with tremendous symbolic import and a direct relationship to Mexico's idea of itself and its origins, the tortilla became a special product requiring special intervention, and then, finally just a product, as interchangeable as any other. Lind and Barham write that insertion into the market meant that first the tortilla had to be established as fulfilling a nutritional requirement, fungible with other foodstuffs, like bread. Then, for full equivalence in the marketplace, a kilo of tortillas had to be comparable not only to bread but also to items as disparate as a spoon or a cup or an hour of labor, and all had to be assigned value using currency, on a single scale.[25] That conversion of a singular emblem, corn, into a good in the marketplace exemplifies the conversion to market logics of all kinds of value, as we will see in later chapters. It also, arguably, is what enables corn's redemption by chefs Enrique Olvera, René Redzepi, and others who have reclaimed corn as a sacred material in their artful cooking, ripe for redemption and elevation.

After the Mexican Revolution and through to the present, we see drives for development at any cost alternating with efforts to achieve and maintain political legitimacy with a populace largely excluded from or disadvantaged by national policy intended to promote economic growth. Anthropologist Jonathan Fox notes that the postrevolutionary state's origin in an agrarian revolution that promoted notions of an inclusive national heritage obligates it to respond to popular mobilizations with at least the appearance of representation of their concerns in the political system.[26] However, those ideals have not translated into substantive investment in small-scale farming or rural communities on their own terms. Rural, as well as marginalized urban populations, are seen as continually in need of intervention—education, technical support, modernization—in order to become part of the government's idea of development, with their role in sustaining such projects overlooked at every stage.

1980–1982 PARENTHESIS

Mexico's pursuit in the twentieth and twenty-first centuries of modernization and urbanization has taken two main forms. For some presidents, progress and prosperity were imagined to rest with foreign investment and trade, while others have taken a protectionist stance, seeing foreign investment, from the United States especially, as a threat to Mexico's autonomy and self-sufficiency. Throughout, the postrevolutionary state has been an activist state—intervening aggressively in the nation's economy and productive sectors.[27] Because of the robust federal government and single-party rule for most of the twentieth century, we can see in those periods of orientation outward that Mexico has been a lab for social, economic, and technical experiments. These include the Rockefeller Foundation project from 1941 to 1956 that developed the "Green Revolution."[28]

With the administration of Enrique Peña Nieto (2012–18), we see an unprecedented effort by the Mexican government to not only make the country open to private and foreign investment, but to actively court it, with an energy reform privatizing Mexico's oil sector, as well as education and health reforms undoing some of the oldest tenets of the government's relationship to its citizens. If we return to the metaphor of the pendulum to understand the ways that Mexico's food and trade policies have oscillated between openness to the outside and protectionism against external forces, the swing toward openness represented by NAFTA was first preceded by a swing in the other direction—with a concerted effort to maintain a closed, self-sufficient economy.

Jonathan Fox calls 1978–1982 one of Mexico's "most autonomous moments." As the 1970s came to a close, riding the tide of an oil boom, the Mexican government envisioned its purpose as one of administering abundance rather than addressing poverty.[29] But everything changed in 1979, when a poor harvest brought a reality check. Grain imports had to double to prevent mass hunger, while the transportation infrastructure was strained to its limits, carrying more food than ever from producers to consumers. Mexico had become increasingly dependent on imported food, and the "technocratic modernizers" of the federal government feared that Mexico would spend 50 percent of its oil income on food imports by 1985 and 75 percent by 1990.[30] Mexico had begun experimenting with the idea of comparative advantage, in which it would leave the growing of corn and other agricultural products to the United States and other more "efficient" countries and use revenues from its own industries (especially oil) to meet its other needs.[31] But the experiment was getting ugly as hunger spread.[32]

To respond to a growing food crisis, Mexico invigorated its coordinated food system, Sistema Alimentario Mexicano (SAM), through which it increased grain price supports and funded subsidized credit, crop insurance, agro-chemicals for non-irrigated land, staple food marketing and processing, and food subsidies.[33] SAM's stated objective was for Mexico to meet all of its basic food needs, and with a systems approach analyzed the entire food chain with the intent of increasing the area under cultivation, integrating agro-industries, and improving processing and distribution. Mexico City's explosive growth in the period was partly possible because massive food markets, especially the Central de Abastos, created a space for those who cultivated the land and those who purchased their products to come together.[34] The experiment, though short-lived and truncated by the 1982 debt crisis, succeeded for a time in empowering rural communities, heightening the accountability of elected officials and government bureaucracies, and systematizing a vast and disorganized food system.

It is striking that less than a decade later, self-sufficiency in grains and other foods would cease to be a primary goal of the state, with the mantra of comparative advantage defeating it once again. At the end of the 1980s, this experiment in autonomy and self-sufficiency would be replaced by a desperate pivot outward.

BANK NATIONALIZATION

The pendulum representing Mexico's openness to foreign investment did not swing away from the protectionism of the oil boom era by itself. There were people working very energetically to push it that way. I was told this while sipping tequila atop the Empire State Building.

I was standing in a gorgeous beam of late afternoon sunlight on the top floor, invited as a guest of the consul general of Mexico to the annual celebration of Mexican Independence Day in New York in September 2015. As darkness fell, the lights of the building that night would be tinted red, white, and green in honor of Mexico. While it was an annual event, this, to my knowledge, was an unprecedentedly high-altitude affair, and not only because the tequila was served from a $200 bottle on the eighty-sixth floor.[35] The people gathered in this rarefied space possessed distinguished professional and diplomatic profiles. While accepting a bite-sized portion of shrimp ceviche from a waiter in black tie attire, I began chatting with a man standing near me. After a few moments of small talk in which I mentioned that I was working on this book, my interlocutor told me that I should read the definitive account of how NAFTA came to be, a story in which he, as it happens, had played a starring role. Within a couple of days, the monograph he mentioned arrived on my desk with his compliments.[36]

The book asserts that a precipitating factor in priming Mexico's willingness to open itself to trade with its more powerful neighbors to the north, opening the possibility for NAFTA, was, ironically, its last and most spectacularly protectionist move. In 1982, faced with low oil prices, a falling peso, and impending default on international loans, then president López Portillo (1976–1982) announced the nationalization of Mexican banks with a speech aimed at arousing nationalistic sentiments. He declared, "In recent years a group of Mexicans led, counseled, and supported by private banks, have taken more money out of the country than all the empires that have exploited us since the beginning of our history."[37] The speech was a hit with the general public but was perceived as a direct affront to Mexico's investors, both foreign and domestic.

López Portillo's promise to keep Mexican wealth in Mexico drove business interests mad, and the economy faltered. The peso was devalued and Mexicans saw their buying power plummet. Mexico defaulted on its international loans and explored programs to nationalize the banks. Meanwhile, the International Monetary Fund prepared a new $3.8 billion loan package premised on Mexico radically reforming its economic policies through structural adjustment and an end to import substitution.[38]

In the meantime, the binational business community got busy characterizing Mexico's president as "failed," spreading rumors that he was chain smoking, unshaven, and padding around the presidential palace in a bathrobe, completely incapable of leadership. They formed a consortium of ultrawealthy US and Mexican businessmen to conspire to plant the seed for NAFTA long before it would grow into reality. The initial germ of the idea was not heavily laden with notions about development or the transition of Mexico's economy into twenty-first-century industries, which would later be articulated as the primary rationale for the trade agreement. It was not imagined as a way to ensure equal footing between two (and later, three) radically unequal trading partners. Instead, it was about protecting the interests of an elite few who had been excluded from the

Mexican government's idea for itself, and saw themselves as victims of protectionism (tariffs, duties, and subsidies), piracy (toothless and out-of-date copyright and intellectual property protections), dumping (the off-loading of surplus products on another country, causing market value to plummet), and import substitution (the effort to replace imports with domestically manufactured equivalents). They wanted the doors of Mexico's economy open to their chemicals, pharmaceuticals, banks, industries, and farm products. They pushed, hard, for "liberalization," by which they meant that they wanted Mexico to stop its hindrance of US imports and investment in its efforts to protect its own interests, retain national control over energy, and avoid the settlement of disagreements through a common dispute procedure. The fostering and brokering of US investment in Mexico was in itself a strategy to get—and stay—rich by an elite subsector of Mexican business people.

Important groundwork was laid by the US-Mexico Business Committee (MEXUS), a standing committee created by the Council of the Americas and chaired for most of the period by Rodman Rockefeller, son of the New York state governor, and scion of the uber-wealthy oil and banking family. MEXUS was joined in its work by the American Chamber of Commerce of Mexico (comprised of 2,800 corporations that accounted for 85 percent of foreign investment in Mexico) and the US Chamber of Commerce. Rockefeller articulated a particular model of trade integration: "The fundamental idea is that there is really only one motor powerful enough to drive the economies of our two countries toward sustained growth. That motor is our joint private sector."[39]

The role that the MEXUS played in laying the groundwork for NAFTA was intended to take place behind the scenes. Players at the time shared an informal credo: "Let's try to avoid publicity," and they accomplished much of their "quiet, not flashy" work by issuing semi-anonymous "non-papers" lacking any letterhead or institutional provenance, which they would leave lying in rooms in which bilateral trade was to be discussed; the papers would then be distributed anonymously to high-level decision makers.[40] The incredibly central role that this groundwork played in getting NAFTA on the table a few years hence, and determining the specific shape the agreement would take, could have been lost to history. But some of the key players eventually sought to clarify their participation. Rockefeller himself, who was granted an Aztec Eagle Award, Mexico's highest honor for a non-Mexican, as well as Guy Erb and other architects, made sure they left a belated but thorough paper trail, including the celebratory monograph by George Grayson sent to me after the cocktail party at the Empire State Building.

What happened with this shift from a protectionist, inward-looking focus on self-sufficiency and autonomy to an outward-focused economic and political model in which prosperity was seen to lie in openness to the outside, private investment, and a diminished role for the state? Avocados provide one answer.

AVOCADOS

From a 2016 interview in *Bloomberg Markets* magazine with former Mexican finance minister Pedro Aspe Armella (1988–1994):

> Question: Mexican cuisine is a great example of the benefits of globalization, so in Mexico what food or drink would you point out to your kids as an example of the way they also benefit from globalization?
>
> Answer: A good example would be a guacamole taco. Why? Because it is a mix of two very Mexican food items (corn and avocado). While avocados grown in Mexico are the best in the world and are exported to many countries, the demand for corn in Mexico exceeds the domestic supply. A relevant portion of corn consumed in Mexico has to be imported. Thus, it can be said that Mexico takes advantage of its competitive advantage to grow avocados, a high-margin crop, to export them and get the necessary resources to import the corn, a low-margin crop, to fulfill the domestic demand. Without free trade, we could not have enough tortillas for our avocado.[41]

When NAFTA was initially passed, Mexican avocado growers did not see an expansion of their markets. On the contrary, Florida avocado growers, fearful of the influx of cheaper and more plentiful Mexican avocados, ensured that the trade agreement included new limitations on imports so that they could continue to dominate the US market. An indication that NAFTA catered to corporate interests, in spite of its ostensible purpose promoting free trade, these protections almost single-handedly decimated the avocado export industry in many states in Mexico. In Puebla, historically a migrant-receiving state, this decline precipitated the mass migration of *poblanos* to New York City.[42] Prior to NAFTA, Puebla's avocado farmers were not limited in the exports they could ship to the United States, so the trade agreement presented a new and major threat to their livelihood. Today, the deals cut by Florida farmers more than two decades ago have been rolled back and Mexican avocados dominate the significantly expanded consumer market in the United States. But this was too late for most Puebla avocado growers, most of whom did not return to Mexico after migrating. In 2015, the avocado was declared the "favorite fruit" of the US, and consumption has risen to four times its 2000 levels.[43] Now a staple on restaurant menus in typical applications like guacamole, but also often as an add-on to sandwiches and burgers, avocados are even having a moment with "avocado toast," consisting basically of smashed avocado on bread, causing a sensation.[44] But the corn tortillas on which the former finance minister's children spread their guacamole may now be made of US corn, as the protections that Mexico implemented against a flood of US corn have also expired.

FOOD SECURITY VERSUS FOOD SOVEREIGNTY

Within the logic of comparative advantage, each country should produce what it does most efficiently and purchase the rest. The ability to purchase is viewed as a kind of security. But security goes beyond buying power on the global market. It encompasses trade regulations and relationships, economic capacity, and ideas about relative efficiency. It also evokes notions of safety, as in a nation's ability to protect itself from unanticipated events and the reliability of global finance structures to facilitate the transfer of capital across markets. Food security is very different from self-sufficiency, an idea that was at the root of many Latin American countries' nationalistic and anti-imperialist economic policies from the 1950s to 1980s. The main strand of these policies, import substitution industrialization, envisioned economic development to originate in a country's ability to provide for itself alone by producing all of its own goods, replacing imported goods with locally made equivalents. But by the mid-1980s, most Latin American countries had been forced to give up their import substitution programs as part of structural adjustment programs imposed by international lenders.

What does structural adjustment mean for food systems? Structural adjustment promotes a particular model of food security. Defined in 1974 by the Food and Agriculture Organization of the United Nations, food security is "the availability at all times of adequate world food supplies of basic foodstuffs to sustain a steady expansion of food consumption and to offset fluctuations in production and prices."[45] At the national level, it is the ability of a nation to meet its population's nutritional needs, not necessarily by producing its own food, but by purchasing it.

To the nonspecialist, food security may not sound controversial until it is contrasted with the term *food sovereignty,* defined by the international peasant movement la Via Campesina as "the people's right to healthy and culturally appropriate food produced through ecologically sound and sustainable methods, and their right to define their own food and agriculture systems."[46] Food sovereignty requires democratic control by the people over food systems, including production and provision.[47] If self-sufficiency in food, food sovereignty, is a commonsense notion involving a nation's ability to provide for its population's basic needs, food security is a purely market-based concept. For food security to be achieved, it does not matter how, where, and by whom food is produced. A nation can be maximally food secure even when it produces no food whatsoever, if it has the resources to purchase all of the food its people need. Thus, within logics of comparative advantage, Mexico, the ancestral birthplace of corn, need not continue to produce corn, but might be better served producing Volkswagens and Audis, and purchasing corn and other foods from foreign nations.

DEPENDENCY

The underlying logic of free trade and globalization is that all of the world's economies are on the same path of progress toward economic development. This unilinear path necessarily places the more "advanced" economies further along on a road that the "developing" economies must also travel. Interventionist policies and programs within the logic of the Washington Consensus promoted by international lending agencies and trading partners imply that the inevitable sequence of development can be sped up. Such acceleration is framed as a charitable service the developed world can provide to the developing world while simultaneously making alternative visions of development inconceivable. This logic, modernization theory, was all the rage in wealthy nations throughout the twentieth century, and has only recently been publicly questioned by the institutions that promoted it.[48] But others counter that the development and prosperity of industrialized nations have rested entirely on the sacking and pillaging of poorer countries and regions. "Development" for them is, instead, exploitation.

Scholars of the Global South have critiqued modernization theory for overlooking the centrality of cheap raw goods and materials from the "third world" to the growth of "first world" prosperity. World systems theory, developed by Immanuel Wallerstein and elaborated in its specific Latin American expression as dependency theory by Raúl Prebisch, Henrique Cardoso, and the economists of UN Economic Commission on Latin America (ECLAC/CEPAL), among others, posits that wealthy countries, the center, have always exploited unfair terms of trade to increase their own wealth, while the hopes for development of poorer countries, the periphery, have been continually postponed and undermined.[49] Colonialism's extraction of raw materials and resources provided the fodder for the machines of industrialization. In the post- or neocolonial world, parasitic relationships between former colonial powers and territories continue to organize global trade and economic relationships. Only because of the relationship of economic and political dependence between center and periphery could the center become wealthy enough to dominate the global economy.

Dependency theory recommends that countries in the periphery reclaim the terms of their own development, along with their own resources and systems of production. Policies of import substitution promoted local production of all the goods the market demanded, rather than receiving them at a markup as imports. Governments reclaimed the terms of trade with protectionist policies designed to shield them from the coercive imposition of goods from imperialist nations. Dependency theory defies the premise posited by modernization theory that "poor" and "underdeveloped" nations are inherently "backward" and behind on the path of progress, in need of intervention to speed up.

For Mexico, both modernization and dependency-oriented views of development have been cited in efforts to promote the turn of Mexico's economy away from the countryside and toward the cities. While industrialization and urbanization have been viewed by Mexican political leaders as a pathway on which the rural countryside and its inhabitants needed to embark, if we instead acknowledge that the rural countryside is the resource on which Mexico's prosperity has always rested, the view is different. Rural communities, blamed for being culturally exotic, backward, ignorant, and reluctant to change, have always had to nimbly adapt to changing economic conditions, often with little to no structural support.

We can see that family sizes, decisions about migration, economic and productive activities, and subsistence strategies have all been malleable, constantly changing with market conditions. Often the accommodations and arrangements that people make to adapt to changing market conditions favor those who own land and control production in rural and urban areas. Solutions that poor families in Mexico have implemented in response to economic crises include diversification of productive activities (making handcrafts, selling prepared food, working as day laborers on others' land, growing food for household consumption and for market, growing a variety of crops to hedge risk), dispatching family members to other activities, and migration to cities and to the United States. In all of these domains, many people become "*poquiteros,*" engaging in *un poquito de todo,* combining lots of different activities, selling all kinds of different items, and moving between regions and areas within regions, in order to make a living. This adaptability and flexibility in the face of changing market conditions takes the pressure off the state to improve economic conditions for all. The state's responsibility for poverty and limited job and educational opportunities is deflected, while families engage in a whole series of strategies to meet their basic needs. In this way, the "growing pains" of development, as some economists call the painful process in which Mexico has turned away from agriculture and toward an industrialized economy, have been borne by people from the countryside. Even so, these families subsidize the economic progress of their nation.

Similarly, on a multinational scale, in the last two decades, we can see that Mexico, the weakest partner in NAFTA, contributed to the prosperity of the strongest partner, the United States. Whether through increased consumption in Mexico of US products, or migration to jobs in the United States, Mexico's people have subsidized the US economy. And as marginalized populations have been blamed for the Mexican countryside's "inefficiency" or its economy's "lack of productivity," Mexican migrants and Mexico itself serve as a scapegoat in the United States in moments of economic stagnation, a target to be accused of "stealing" jobs that the economy has failed to create or stealing entire industries through outsourcing.

NEOCOLONIALISM

> We cannot stop global change. We cannot repeal the international economic competition that is everywhere. We can only harness the energy to our benefit. Now we must recognize that the only way for a wealthy nation to grow richer is to export, to simply find new customers for the products and services it makes.
>
> —Bill Clinton, Dec. 8, 1993

In this quotation, US president Bill Clinton, hailing the imminent launch of NAFTA, frames globalization as an unstoppable tide while also reinforcing the logic of it as something that can increase the prosperity of industrialized nations via market expansion. While he and his counterpart, Mexican president Carlos Salinas, discussed NAFTA in other moments as a plan for mutual prosperity, here, the veil slipped a bit, revealing that for the already wealthy United States, NAFTA would be a way to get wealthier. Implicit within economic ideas about food security and free trade are our understandings of the place of nations in global hierarchies of power and resources. While "free" trade is marketed to smaller economies as a means to "level the playing field" and "eliminate barriers" in the global economy, the price to play is a willingness to undo subsidies, protections, tariffs, and price supports.[50] The United States, like many larger economies, actually does not practice what its dominant financial institutions preach in that it heavily subsidizes its own agricultural commodities and engages in other state-led manipulations of national and international markets (often at the behest of big business as much as for the ostensible purpose of protecting consumers or small-scale producers). The market reforms imposed on countries like Mexico in order to receive loans from multinational lenders and to enter the global market as a favored trading partner of more powerful economies benefit US corporations that then are able to enter those markets with little restriction. In this way, trade agreements are framed as a favor larger economic powers do for smaller ones while they are also a boon to multinational corporations, which rush into the space created by the suspension of tariffs and protections.

To understand NAFTA's impact on Mexico, it must be framed as the latest example of a neocolonial relationship between the United States and Mexico. Late capitalism and neoliberalism are the most recent iteration of the relations of dominance that have subjected the countries of Latin America to the influence of a more economically powerful nation since the conquest by Spain and Portugal. Whether because they pass under the radar of many due to their eye-glazing minutiae, their exclusion from democratic debate and decision making, or because they are framed as belonging only to the sphere of international commerce, trade agreements are not always subject to widespread public scrutiny or skepticism, or seen as an example of overreach by powerful nations.[51]

Mexico has been a laboratory for policies that frame foreign direct investment as the path to prosperity and development. Mexican economists, educated in elite US institutions, pushed their nation to adopt structural adjustment programs and measures to attract foreign direct investment. In spite of Mexico's tradition of protectionism, outwardly oriented policy makers have succeeded in undoing its nationally controlled assets and protections.

The effects are deep and numerous. As a result, we see an acceleration of the industrialization of Mexican agriculture and of its food system as a whole, hastened by an influx of patented chemical inputs into agriculture and livestock production. A shocking 42 percent of Mexico's food supply is now imported from the United States.[52] The way that foods are grown and processed in Mexico has come to bear a striking resemblance to US production methods. NAFTA has massively expanded the Mexican market for imported grain commodities (corn, soybeans, wheat), chemicals, processed foods, and sugars. Exports to the United States of Mexican berries, tomatoes, cucumbers, and other fruits and vegetables have exploded, even while there are widespread reports that eagerness to profit from this trade have led to horrendous labor and human rights abuses in slavery-like conditions on Mexico's export-oriented industrial farms.[53]

What are the consequences of Mexico's reorientation toward foreign investment and free trade? What are the health consequences of the decision of Mexico's political leaders to value food security over food sovereignty? In this chapter, I located the North American Free Trade agreement implemented in 1994 within the longer arc of Mexico's economic and development policy. Ideas about agricultural production in Mexico's countryside in the lead-up to and aftermath of NAFTA are propped up by very specific and traceable myths about efficiency, productivity, and the capacity of rural dwellers to progress. Almost all governing regimes since the Porfiriato have located the cause of Mexico's "underdevelopment" in the countryside. This is inaccurate, given the consistent productivity, resourcefulness, and industriousness of the country's rural people. It is the countryside and its inhabitants that have subsidized every wave of the country's development. We can connect this to the ideas of the technocrats in the late twentieth century who implemented NAFTA: Mexico's future was seen to lie in increasing its manufacturing base and the transitioning of people off the land, with their imagined future prosperity enabling them (former campesinos, and also the nation as a whole) to purchase their food rather than grow it.

The ways NAFTA was envisioned working did not spring up sui generis in trade negotiations with the United States and Canada, but are premised on very specific, historical ideas about the countryside and its inhabitants, and their eligibility and capacity for democracy, productivity, innovation, and change. Today, while Mexico has achieved many of the objectives it sought when it signed NAFTA in terms of industrial development and integration with the global economy, the same discourses of underdevelopment have not disappeared, and are revived again and again to provide cover for the gaps and exclusions inherent in Mexico's economic development model. Persistent poverty and chronic disease are not embarrassing exceptions to a happy story about how Mexico has prospered, but are in fact the outcome of development policy. In one generation, the leading causes of death in the Mexican countryside went from malnutrition and infectious diseases to diet-related chronic diseases. As we will see in the next chapter, this cannot be easily blamed on a suddenly voracious Mexican sweet tooth—although that does not stop many from trying.

We will explore in the next chapter how Mexico's bargain in NAFTA to promote its place as a low-cost manufacturing site at the expense of its agricultural sector has had perturbing public health consequences.

4 NAFTA

FREE TRADE IN THE BODY

UNA TIENDA, REPOSITORY OF DREAMS

Doña Yolanda has owned her *tienda,* a small store, in Santo Tomás Tlalpa for twenty-seven years, but in the last decade, her sales have plummeted almost to nil with the installation of four other tiendas within two blocks of hers in this sleepy town and the arrival of Walmart a few miles away. Migradollars, remittances from those who have migrated, mostly to New York City, have funded the competition. A widow with grown children, Yolanda says that she keeps her store open because she would be bored to death at home. At least with the store, she can say hello to her neighbors and catch up on gossip. However, she tells me these days rather than patronize her store, her neighbors prefer to hop on the bus that takes them, for 7 pesos (about 40 cents US) to Tehuacán, where they can shop at Walmart or its cheaper knock off, 'tá Barato (a play on the words "It's cheap!").

Tiendas in general have lost the air of idiosyncrasy they used to have when the shop owner would make up her own mind about what to stock. On the way home from school, or on quick runs from home, children and their parents could buy bottled water, soda, and cartons of milk, but they

Figure 4. Doña Yolanda in her tienda, Santo Tomás Tlalpa. Photo by the author.

could also typically find some house specialty: homemade gelatin, tortas, or fresh cut fruit served with generous sprinklings of lime juice and chile powder. She mentions that she thinks this shift has had a negative effect on nutrition in town. Before, she tells me, people did not eat all these Sabritas and Gansitos all the time.[1] I ask if she has considered stocking fresh fruits and vegetables and she says it's hopeless. If she sells fresh foods, people say her prices are too expensive (with fruit lacking the soda companies' extensive distribution structure, she would have to take the bus or a taxi to the market to stock up, paying retail prices), and if she looks for a value-added option, like fruit salad, she says that her neighbors buy it once and then complain that it's too expensive. She experimented once with selling a common street snack—spears of sliced mango, watermelon, and cucumber in a cup—but her customers did not buy them fast enough and they went bad. Her best customers are the children who live in the homes surrounding her store; they have a few pesos of spending money and are eager to spend it on a treat of soda or chips. Her best days, now, are the days that people get their cash installments from Prospera, the federal conditional cash transfer program. Packaged foods, with far-off expiration dates, sit on the shelf, losing no value as Yolanda waits for her neighbors to come into a little cash.

Tienda proprietors enter contracted agreements with a distributor—Coca-Cola (Femsa) or PepsiCo—which brings them free of charge the refrigerators, racks, and signage that are the most significant startup costs for a new tienda. These exclusive agreements determine not only the brands of soda, water, and sports drinks they stock, but also the full spectrum of other sweet, salty, and spicy snacks and candies they sell. These distribution networks and the equipment the corporations provide to franchisees favor the display and sale of a great variety of packaged foods and beverages.

Talk to recent Mexican migrants in the United States, and as often as not, you'll find they share the same goal: to open a small store in their hometown. While occasionally I have encountered someone who wants to build a small factory for grinding onyx stone, or a tortilla mill, the most common entrepreneurial pursuit is a tienda. Many migrants have told me in interviews over the years that with $5,000 they can outfit a tienda, with $10,000 "un super," a slightly larger tienda, still often housed in the street-facing front room of a multigenerational dwelling. With a tienda, migrants calculate, they can live and earn in their home communities, and thus avoid future migratory journeys. They acknowledge the slightly gouged prices that tienda owners charge for the convenience of leaving one's house in slippers to pick up a bottle of cooking oil, a package of sugar, or a soda. They calculate that this margin of profit could be exactly what they need to ensure a long and comfortable retirement in their home communities. But the age of the tienda may be ending. Instead, we see Walmart and Oxxo expanding across the country.

In the last chapter, we examined how ideas about the countryside and the desirability of foreign investment as a path to development have changed over the course of Mexico's history, contributing to its willingness to conform to US expectations at the time that NAFTA was negotiated. In this chapter, I focus on the aftermath of NAFTA. I examine how the Mexican landscape has changed since NAFTA, with the transformation entailing a rise in the availability of processed foods and beverages, and also less visible shifts. NAFTA resulted in changes to Mexico's food system that in turn led to consequences for the health of the Mexican population. We trace the ways that US food and beverage corporations have entered the Mexican market and the effect of these on the health of Mexican people. We see how free trade gets into the body and why the effects are more complex than a mere increase in the quantity of processed foods and beverages available.

OXXO

"I love Oxxo!" This startling exclamation was from a colleague at a university in the city of Puebla. Oxxo, like the comparable 7–11, itself just behind Oxxo in its conquest of Mexican market share, is a convenience store that caters primarily to those who drive.[2] In the last decade, Puebla has begun to bear a striking resemblance to Los Angeles, California. Previously most well known for its quaint and well-preserved colonial center, historic churches, and conservative social climate, it is now a sprawling suburban city and thought to be a haven—from drug violence, urban congestion, and the inconveniences associated with living in many other Mexican cities.[3]

Here, as in LA, the car is king, and most of the city's growth in the last decade can be seen in the rampant spread of new, shiny shopping centers. The state government was historically based in the city center in a colonial building on the main plaza, but that is now a ceremonial relic. Instead, the state government is housed in a set of mirrored skyscrapers, surrounded by moats, sitting in the center of a vast, paved esplanade that conveniently obscures the view of the multilevel parking garage that lies underneath. Across the "street"—a multi-lane loop of a highway without stoplights or cross walks—is the biggest and newest shopping center in the area, anchored by Liverpool and Palacio de Hierro, the Macy's and Nordstrom of Mexico, but also featuring Nike, Sephora, H&M, Starbucks, and other international brands. My colleague who loves Oxxo works at an institution tucked amidst all of this—a small and young satellite of a larger private university system—housed, like the government, in a new building that is oriented toward its parking lot and designed in a way that maximizes its exclusivity and security. Surrounding this recently developed area are gated residential communities and a ring of new condominiums for the city's newly rich—all steel and glass contemporary architecture.

Radiating out from this new hub, far from Puebla's colonial heart, are countless strip malls, most dominated by US franchises: Subway, Home Depot, Starbucks, KFC, and McDonald's. To get from one part of the city to another, one traverses stark new bridges, rising above ground level like white-painted steel sailfish, constructed by the state governor in as ambitious a plan to physically leave his mark on a city as any government official since Haussmann in nineteenth-century Paris. The bridges, supposedly "people friendly" with some new bike lanes and pedestrian paths, are really about sustaining the viability of a car-centric elite in a city designed as utterly without concern for urban functionality as Los Angeles was. Without dramatic and rapid investments in improving the urban architecture—including adding a second deck to the city's main north-south artery, set to open soon—the city and its commerce might grind to a halt. Historically, Mexico has been a country that was always physically shaped by the needs of carless walkers. Most Mexican cities, at their heart, are in fact utterly hostile to cars—Mexico City being an example of a megalopolis whose traffic reaches almost total paralysis on a daily basis. In contrast, in the city of Puebla today, government officials and functionaries, shoppers, and university faculty and students can conduct all of their day-to-day business of governing, shopping, eating, working, teaching, and learning without setting foot on a street or a sidewalk, moving from one sanitized environment to another in a private car. Compared to most of the rest of Mexico today and in the past, this is a vastly different lifestyle.

Often, Oxxo stores are attached to a Pemex gas station, and more than anything they offer the products convenient for those who move by car: bottled water, soda, chips, ice, and beer. Now, Oxxo has also branched into bill payment. This is what appealed so much to my colleague: instead of standing in line at the utility company, phone company, and so on, she can pay all her bills at Oxxo when she stops for gas on her way to work in the morning. Lest waiting in lines for such tasks should become the last and most democratic obligation of Mexicans, they can now pay their bills in the convenience of the Oxxo.

DEVELOPMENT AND DOMINANCE

What did the three countries that signed NAFTA expect to get out of the deal? What were their expectations and ambitions? Who were the anticipated beneficiaries? Who was expected to be disadvantaged? The answers to these questions have to do with the definition of economic prosperity and development held by the political leaders of each country as well as the relationship between the government and the interest groups that stood to benefit or be harmed by the deal. Part of what makes trade deals appealing is not just the economic benefits imagined to await signatories, but social benefits as well, especially access to patterns of production and consumption associated with ideas of progress and modernity. With NAFTA, consumption has come to be as economically important as production. While production—and its demand for ever lower costs—was a central concern of capitalist formations in previous eras, with globalization, the sustainability of the capitalist model and its profits depends on continuous expansion of markets. Perceived "market saturation" in one location can be addressed by turning to other locations.[4] Growth in market reach carries with it a need for expanded distribution, expanded production, and, to fuel all of this, expansion of desire. Ways of consuming are promoted through marketing that taps into ideas about who people are and who they wish to be. People are encouraged by advertising to imagine themselves to be modern and cosmopolitan through the consumption of certain kinds of products.

While earlier phases of economic development around the world were focused on infrastructure (water, roads, electricity) and growth of productive activities and industries, today we see development defined increasingly by the expansion of consumption. Consumer goods reach even areas where basic infrastructural issues are not resolved, and in some cases, it is private distribution networks that advance the infrastructural aims of nations. Distributors of processed foods and beverages literally pave the way to communities previously ignored by vendors and historically left out of development plans by the state. A coordinator of the Puebla state government's food distribution service for malnourished children and the disabled told me that many of the communities she serves in the marginalized Sierra Negra region did not have roads until recently. Her job required her to spend hours each day navigating bumpy, unpaved rural routes in a four-wheel drive vehicle. When paved roads were built, she told me, the first to use them were the Coca-Cola trucks.

The vision of development that Mexico adopted with its outward turn in the 1980s echoed the one promoted for Mexico and other recipients of multinational development aid in its package of structural adjustment reforms. It is one that coincides neatly with the continual drive of corporations to expand markets and seek cheaper raw materials and labor for production. While the idea of free trade is premised on governments "getting out of the way" of private entrepreneurship, in reality, trade deals depend on collaboration between the private sector and the government. Corporations are expected to undertake and profit from enhanced opportunities for investment, human and material resources for production, and exports and imports. But the private sector depends on governments to maintain conditions that are favorable to their investments by ensuring security and providing the legal and regulatory framework in which trade operates. Security is an expansive concept that can mean everything from addressing issues related to crime, to mechanisms for minimizing corruption, to ensuring spaces for resolution of disputes and copyright infringement.

It can be difficult to untangle private and public interests in trade deals because intersectoral collaboration is so embedded. While trade is typically an arrangement between allies, US investments in its military are not irrelevant to trade. Military might can be an ultimate guarantor of US interests (we can look back to "gunboat diplomacy" at the dawn of the twentieth century for examples of the military reinforcing US objectives in trade and other arenas). But heavy US investment in its military has other implications for trade: technologies developed in wartime can be turned to highly profitable consumer and industrial goods. A lot of the technological innovations and chemicals in food production and processing came from wartime, and the research and development funded by military investments.

The most iconic transnational food or beverage corporation is Coca-Cola. Its ubiquitous red-and-white swish logo are known the world over. What is less known is the historical link between Coca-Cola and US military power.[5] Before World War II, Coca-Cola was largely associated with the Southern United States, a regional drink. Although it was already available in other parts of the United States and even sold abroad, it did not yet have the market dominance it would come to have after the war. But during the war, fully 95 percent of soft drinks sold on US military bases were Coca-Cola products.[6] Soldiers, stripped of the comforts of home, were encouraged to assuage their homesickness with Coca-Cola. Arrangements were made by generals to move the company's bottling operations closer to the fronts at which soldiers were stationed, resulting in the establishment of a Coca-Cola bottling company as a gesture indicating a place's friendliness to US interests.

US corporate influence and military force have always gone together. Even today, while we are not at war—cold or otherwise—with our hemispheric neighbors, our economic clout is unequivocally tied to our military might. Although Mexico is an ally, the United States has significant military investments in Mexico, ranging from the Mérida Initiative to border security.[7] And the wars we have discursively declared (on drugs, on terrorism) provide the conceptual underwriting that enables a massive arms buildup on our borders and also in the territories of our allies. It is possible that the countries the United States has interfered in the most, with the highest level of migration to the United States and the highest levels of foreign direct investment, will demonstrate the highest rates of diet-related illness.[8] While the partnerships the United States has with its southern neighbors are largely framed around "mutual peace and prosperity," it is clear that the military strength of the United States is a powerful tool for ensuring that trading partners like Mexico do their part to keep conditions right for investment. Security, prosperity, and expansion of markets are bundled in a single package. Sidney Mintz described this as follows:

> Power over labor and resources employed in the production of food undergirded the unhampered operation of the corporate system, closely coordinated in this instance with the will of the state. Even in times of politico-military crisis—some might say particularly in such times—corporate power neatly integrated with the state bureaucracy firmly underwrites the successful execution of what are defined as broadly societal tasks. At such moments, the power of the state seems far less irksome to corporate America.[9]

We can see this throughout Latin America. For a vivid example, we can look to the role of the United Fruit Company in Guatemala. The company's contributions to Guatemala's development included its built-to-order railway system, which was ideal if you were a banana trying to get to a shipping port, but rather irrelevant if you were a person trying to get from one place to another in your own country. In 1954, Guatemala's democratically elected president, Jacobo Arbenz, promised his people to nationalize industries and restrict trade, but the United Fruit Company perceived these promises as threats and sought to ensure an uninterrupted supply chain between tropical plantations and northern urban markets. That year, Arbenz was overthrown in a US-backed coup that reinforced the collaborative relationship between US corporate interests and military force.[10]

Corporate interests have perhaps reached their highest level of influence in the neoliberal era. The neoliberal political and economic policies dominant since Ronald Reagan in the United States and Margaret Thatcher in the United Kingdom promote a disinvestment in the public sector and propose market solutions to society's problems.[11] It is not possible to argue for broad-based structural management of food systems when a privatization of many of the functions of the state has been built into the economy. Ideas about how illnesses are caused and how they can be treated cannot be separated from the same habits of mind that have produced a faith in market solutions to intractable problems like economic development and income inequality. Whether it is the state's responsibility to guarantee access to sufficient and healthful food, health care, and education is a question answered by the choices nations make about the structure of their economic and political system. By opting into a liberalization of its economy premised on foreign direct investment, Mexico took a big step away from the protectionist and activist role the state envisioned for itself during the revolution. Buzz words like "empowerment," "inclusion," and "responsibility" have replaced words like "rights," "sovereignty," and "solidarity." In other words, the state's role has become one of enhancing the access people have to a selection of products, behaviors, and habits—"healthful" and not—while remaining deafeningly silent on the transformation of the Mexican food landscape with the invasion of ultraprocessed foods and disinvestment in locally grown, unprocessed staple foods.

With each move toward foreign investment and each expansion of access to the products of industrialized globalization, Mexicans were promised prosperous "modern" lifestyles. While there has always been a strong vein of Mexican nationalism opposing what is framed as cultural imperialism on the part of the United States, that has not stopped Mexico from being a major market for US products and technological innovations. Even while ideas about what constituted Mexican modernity were different from the US version, neither the dominant nor the oppositional ideological camps gave much importance to traditional ways of sourcing, preparing, or eating food.

One of the key bargains implied by the deal was for Mexico to shift from a model of food sovereignty based on small-scale subsistence agriculture to one of food security, as discussed in the previous chapter. With the latter model, Mexico would compensate for loss in the productive sector with gains in buying power, ensured not only by its favorable trading status with its North American neighbors but also by its anticipated industrialization and economic growth. In other words, Mexico's newfound prosperity would enable its people to eat like those in the United States, without having to rely on an agricultural sector long deemed inefficient and underproductive.

In Mexico, as in many places around the world, many innovations in food processing were welcomed with open arms. Technologies that were developed in the United States were also useful in other places. Arguments that were made in favor of the industrialization of food in the United States, especially in the post–World War II period, were adapted to local contexts. Early industrial processing of food went far to reduce food-borne illness in the still nascent days of refrigeration and transcontinental shipping of food. Processed food was marketed as a boon for busy and working mothers, who were told they could be liberated from the drudgery of food preparation by the science and technology of time-saving appliances, mechanization, and processing. These technological developments became symbols of prosperous modernity—a modern kitchen, modern food, and a modern life. These were bundled together with ideas about child rearing and lifestyles premised on atomization—to break into particles—drawn from atomic research but a metaphor for the fragmentation, individuation, and "nuclear" families of modern life in the postwar suburb. The liberatory appeal of these images cannot be forgotten, as they promised a life of prosperity, health, greater mobility, and more time for women, in which they could have greater "freedom" and take on jobs without "neglecting" domestic duties. When some older women in the United States today raise an eyebrow at the choice of some millennials to make their own bread, pickles, or soap, we are reminded that a life of unrelenting housework is not so far in the past for middle-class women, and not in the past at all for many working-class women.

Earlier innovations in food production and systems of distribution made food and other agricultural products produced at a small scale more widely available, expanding consumption but not always transforming it. In contrast, the changes brought by globalization have dramatically changed diets. Today, processed foods amount to 80 percent of food sales globally. The industry itself plays a role in producing changes in diet, rather than simply responding to latent demand.[12] The rise in numbers of supermarkets, possession of cars and refrigerators, female labor participation, emulation of "Western culture," and advertising are factors in transformations in Latin America since the early 1990s.[13] In Mexico, we see a dramatic influx of US supermarkets, emblematic of a shift toward industrialized food, including Walmart, which possesses a lion's share of the market.[14]

Together, chain retail stores have now overshadowed the previously dominant tienda. Ninety percent of food purchases in small towns were from tiendas in 2003, in contrast with only 30 percent in cities with populations above 250,000.[15] Today, that urban/rural distinction has been lost. And, because of corporate distribution arrangements that supply tiendas with racks, signage, refrigerators, and a continuous supply of products in exchange for exclusive vending deals, the distinction between tiendas and retail convenience stores is also being lost. Across the republic, retail stores account for 35 percent of food sales, tiendas for 30 percent, and open air markets only 25 percent.[16] Mexico's Chamber of Commerce estimates that for every convenience store that opens, five tiendas close.[17] What could be wrong with convenience? Oxxo was on target to open its *fourteen thousandth* store in Mexico in 2015, for an average of three stores per day.[18] Its parent company, Femsa (Coca-Cola's Mexican division), fills the 24-hour convenience stores with Coca-Cola products: soda, and also bottled water, vitamin water, chips, snacks, and other processed food items. Oxxo recently surpassed Soriana to become the second largest chain in Mexico, after Walmart, which has captured 20 percent of the food retail sphere in Mexico.[19] Big box stores (Walmart chief among them) are now often found at the point at which major roads meet the edge of nearly every city. For example, Tehuacán, a midsized city with 250,000 inhabitants, has four Walmarts, one on each corner of the city's footprint. Tehuacán remains a major market center for its region—with rural farmers traveling from low- and high-altitude municipalities to gather there and sell their goods—but now every market vendor and shopper must pass a Walmart to get to the city's colorful and bustling central market.

This growth in retail chain stores changes what and how people eat. Drawing on Hawkes, Popkin, and other scholars of nutrition transition and the globalization/diet nexus, we can see that the rise in diet-related illness and obesity in Mexico following the free trade agreement makes perfect sense. It is not a coincidence, but rather a logical outcome of NAFTA. We can see this looking through the lens of foreign direct investment in food industries alone: US companies invested twenty-five times more in Mexico's food industry in 1999 than 1987, with three-quarters of that investment in the arena of processed food production. And from 1995 to 2003, sales of processed foods expanded 5 to 10 percent each year in Mexico.[20]

The rise in prevalence of noncommunicable chronic diseases in Mexico is correlated with the nation's restructuring of its economy.[21] Economic transformation has not only entailed development in the broad sense but has also specifically promoted the market penetration and affordability of processed foods while simultaneously stunting the market reach and affordability of basic subsistence, minimally processed, and locally produced foods.

NUTRITION TRANSITION

The expansion of global markets for and by industrialized food and beverages has impacted the ways that people eat around the world. Globally, economic development has been linked to changes in food consumption and a rise in noncommunicable diseases.[22] One way of understanding this is through the process known as "nutrition transition." Barry Popkin is the leading scholar on nutrition transition, a concept he developed to capture the "dynamic nature of diet." Popkin periodized five phases in human history: the age of collecting food, the age of famine, the age of receding famine, the age of degenerative diseases, and the age of behavioral change.[23] Popkin characterized lower- and middle-income countries in the last quarter of the twentieth century as transitioning from the period of receding famine to the age of degenerative diseases. Obesity and diet-related diseases caused by a surfeit of food, as opposed to the old constant of hunger, were already plaguing the upper-income countries. In the last phase, health is improved as populations come to terms with the surfeit of calories available to them and pursue health-promoting lifestyles that allow them to emerge from the era of degenerative diseases. The key actionable question for Popkin and his colleagues is whether sound public policy, education, and strategic incentives/disincentives can shorten the age of degenerative diseases for lower- and middle-income countries.

Ironically, in spite of massive increases in agro-industrial productivity, statistics of world hunger have remained stagnant, and like many middle-income countries, Mexico has achieved some key goals of globalization and development without having vanquished malnutrition, poverty, and other problems associated with underdevelopment.[24] Mexico has come to bear the "double burden" of malnutrition alongside diseases marked by caloric excess.[25] UK-based food policy expert Corinna Hawkes notes that globalization exacerbates uneven dietary development between rich and poor: "As high-income groups in developing countries enjoy the benefits of a more dynamic marketplace, lower-income groups may well experience convergence toward poor quality obesogenic diets, as observed in Western countries."[26] The "globalization/diet nexus," as Hawkes calls it, is characterized by "food trade and global sourcing, foreign direct investment, global food advertising and promotions, retail restructuring (supermarkets), emergence of global agribusiness and transnational food companies, development of global rules and institutions that govern . . . food, urbanization, cultural change and influence."[27]

The concepts of dietary convergence and dietary adaptation help us understand the ways that globalization fuels nutrition transition. Dietary convergence refers to the "increased reliance on a narrow base of staple grains, increased consumption of meat and meat products, dairy products, edible oil, salt and sugar, and a lower intake of dietary fibre" that characterizes the "Standard American Diet" (SAD), or "Western diet."[28]

Dietary adaptation is characterized by "increased consumption of brand-name processed and store-bought food, an increased number of meals eaten outside the home and consumer behaviors driven by the appeal of new foods available."[29]

Globalization enables multinational corporations to situate themselves effectively for producing desire and demand where previously it was minimal.[30] To be able to eat the foods associated with cosmopolitan modernity is appealing when they previously were not available, but before long, as they become ubiquitous and more affordable, they are no longer associated with higher social status. Now that people around the world have access to the same varieties of soda, chips, and fast foods, consumption of them—especially when it can be characterized as "excessive"—has become associated with lower social status. Status and prestige—always implicated in dietary differences—are now associated with minimally processed, locally produced foods, which are coveted by wealthy elites while food that has traveled the farthest and undergone the most radical transformations from its raw ingredients is associated with lower class status.[31] This is a change from the days when European royalty in the conquest and colonial eras demonstrated their class distinction by consuming Mexican chocolate sweetened with Caribbean sugar—imported at great expense.

Nutrition transition did not begin with the latest phase of globalized trade. Moving to cities is associated with greater consumption of what some call "superior" grains (rice or wheat as opposed to corn or millet); ground and polished grains, food higher in fat, more animal products, more sugar, more packaged and processed food, and more food prepared away from home.[32] Economic factors, such as greater purchasing power from working in a wage economy instead of subsistence agriculture, better transportation and more food markets in urban areas, intersect with social factors. These include the ways that people use food to express community, identity, and belonging; changing norms about what constitutes foods that are good to eat (in terms of taste, health, etc.); and changing social dynamics in households and communities. For example, the shift toward women's wage labor participation powerfully influences household food production. Modernization and industrialization contribute to reduced use of human labor. Mechanization and processing of food can imply significant changes in the distribution of labor for preparing food and also in the characteristics of the food consumed. Popkin writes, "Food preparation technologies, along with home electrification, washing machines, dryers, vacuum cleaners, piped water, and so forth, have transformed home production from a time-consuming, often back-breaking, full time occupation of peasant or working-class women."[33]

But technological changes did not always alter the kinds of food that people ate, even as it might dramatically alter who was producing and preparing food, and in what contexts. In Mexico City for much of the twentieth century, elaborate state-funded food distribution networks ensured that the agricultural products of the countryside reached the cities and were within reach of city dwellers.[34] But networks for food production and distribution had already served an urban concentration of population in the central valley of Mexico for centuries, preceding the arrival of the Spanish. Famously, Moctezuma II dined daily on fresh fish from the Atlantic and Pacific oceans as well as on foods from all over the Mexica empire in the capital of Tenochtitlán, today Mexico City. His subjects were able to consume an infinite variety of foods produced in diverse ecosystems near and far.[35] But in contrast to earlier innovations in the production and distribution of food in Mexico, NAFTA presented more of a threat to milpa-based diets.

TRADE POLICY IN THE BODY

But how, exactly, does trade policy get into the body? Mexico consumes more soda than any other country; is that fact alone sufficient explanation for the rise in obesity? Some would say it is. The logical solution, according to Popkin's model, is "education," so that Mexico can push through the age of degenerative disease into the age of behavior change. We can see that trade agreements and globalization generally contribute to dietary transition. But the transformation NAFTA implied for Mexico went well beyond increased availability and marketing for processed foods and beverages.

One key place to see NAFTA's impact is in the regulations governing commerce, trade, food systems, and food safety. While decisions about what food to purchase and consume are made at the household and individual level, how those products are regulated and the additives and chemicals used in their production are governed by regulation. Free trade agreements could not gain political legitimacy or support without their promise of a shared regulatory environment.[36] The main fear in liberal democracies about trade agreements is that they will result in a loss of jobs in wealthier countries as corporations establish operations in nations with the cheapest labor and materials costs. Trade unions and environmental advocacy groups warn that trade agreements constitute a "race to the bottom": a cycle of chipped away jobs, labor protections, and environmental standards. This has been amply demonstrated in public health scholar Nicholas Freudenberg's book *Lethal but Legal: Corporations, Consumption and Protecting Public Health,* which chronicles the ways that globalization has allowed corporations themselves to set the standards for regulation, supplanting the historical role of the state. Proponents of free trade say competition drives investment and leads to prosperity. In this way, they argue, trade partners are obliged to adopt regulations that protect workers and the environment while furthering corporate agility, mobility, and productivity.

Central to an increasingly globalized food system in which food processing occurs on a large scale, often in separate phases and distant locations from food production and consumption, is the regulation of food quality as well as standards for wages and worker safety. Within this framing, when we consider NAFTA and other agreements involving the United States, there is an implicit assumption that the United States enjoys the highest level of standards and the developing nations have to rise to meet them. This process, it is promised, will raise the living standards of citizens in all of the signatory nations while protecting US workers from job loss to cheaper labor markets. The fact that the trade agreements adopted by the United States are so appealing and profitable for US corporations might be our first clue that they are not an effective means for the promotion or protection of labor and environmental standards. In fact, trade agreements accelerate the abandonment of a country's existing standards and protections, within the same logic of unfettered trade that is used to justify them economically. Rather than raising their standards, many countries are obliged instead to drop regulatory and industrial protections. To the extent that there is a leveled regulatory environment, it cannot be understood as a good thing.

When the federal governments of Mexico, Canada, and the United States together laid the regulatory framework for NAFTA, they sought to make capital in North America mobile across borders, to lower constraints on investment and expansion of markets, and to facilitate the expansion of corporate products. But the regulatory framework was modeled on that of the United States (with tremendous input from the business sector). Canada, not as dependent on the potential economic gains, was able to retain a greater degree of regulatory autonomy.

Self-regulation of food production is a norm that was imposed on Mexico by the United States as part of NAFTA. "Self-regulation" and a minimization of regulation generally are among the central tenets of a pact US corporations made in the early 1970s and that has been a key component of trade agreements.[37] Safety measures and inspections of one industry are seen as attacks on all industries, evoking howls from corporations as they seek to protect their own unfettered ability to do business and downplay risks to workers and consumers.[38] Mexico's pro-business agency, ConMéxico, is one of the most powerful Mexican institutions promoting the transnational corporations' mantra of self-regulation. We see with the Trump administration in the United States an even greater emphasis today on elimination of regulations, and pressures for the same are commonly heard in Mexico and promoted by the current pro-business president, Enrique Peña Nieto. Corporations have fostered ideas about the inefficiency of government and the need for government to "get out of the way" of private enterprise and innovation. In Mexico, opinions about government's inadequacy to regulate have less to do with opposition to regulations as a concept than with allegations of corruption, the idea that the government cannot be trusted to inspect or regulate. An enduring skepticism of government transparency and the assumption that graft undercuts any potential regulation have led to many people expressing a general lack of trust in government. This, too, has served the profit interests of corporations.

While mechanization of food production implies standardization of processes, professionalism, and a presumption of inspections and standards that protect food safety, the factors that have led to food in Mexico and in the United States being more highly processed are the same factors that have minimized government regulations. Nestle, Schlosser, Pollan, and others have shown how the US food industry is oriented around maximization of efficiency and minimization of costs, not safety for consumers.[39] A small number of inspectors are charged with food safety. Rather than anything approaching a systematic mechanism for inspecting the foods we eat, a combination of random and spot checks, "self-regulation," and reactive responses to problems in the supply chain (recalls of foods tainted with listeria, for example) have meant that much of the food consumed has never been inspected. Some argue that security of the food and water system is a ticking time bomb, given the trends toward consolidation of food systems, with more and more food retailers using an ever smaller number of distributors and suppliers. A problem in one area can easily spread to affect the whole food system when a small number of companies control larger and larger segments of the food chain. Food industry lobbyists and the agencies charged with food safety seem to have revolving door policies in which policy makers, regulators, and inspectors often come from the corporate food sector and return to it after public service. An expansion of the US food system to include Mexico and Canada only exacerbates the issues associated with consolidation and massive chains of food production and distribution.

When livestock and plants destined for our plates have been subjected to countless interventions and inputs, chemical and otherwise, how do we know we can eat them? While some attempt to consume only unadulterated foods, subscribing to classification regimes like organic, non-GMO, and so on, for most people, deciding what to eat is a constant navigation of availability and affordability, and continual assessment of what is considered edible. Ideas about what is edible and how "clean" food is, or needs to be, are culturally specific. While food that is safe and clean is presumably a universal desire, anthropologists have demonstrated amply how definitions of these concepts vary across times and places and also serve to highlight distinctions groups draw between themselves and others.[40] Urbanization and class stratification provide a myriad of ways in which social groups can set themselves apart from others. The Zapotec farmers González writes about in the state of Oaxaca use the adjective "clean" to refer to the beans and corn they produce themselves, on their own land. But wealthy urban dwellers in Mexico, as in other places, sometimes use the adjective "dirty" to refer to countryside-residing people and their foods. In supermarkets, prepared and packaged foods traffic in illusions of cleanliness and reliability, even while the food supply in an era of industrialized agro-industry is highly susceptible to mass contamination events (such as salmonella, listeria, E. coli, etc.).[41]

When Mexico signed NAFTA, it agreed to adapt to the United States' regulatory environment, opening the way for the heavy use of chemical inputs in farming and food processing. Even before the trade agreement, Mexico fostered the dominance of industrial agriculture over subsistence agriculture, but NAFTA's promise to erase the border for commerce resulted in an erasure, too, of most barriers on the use of chemical inputs. Changes in food production not only alter the circumstances in which food is grown or processed, but also its chemical content. Consumers have been exposed to a cocktail of chemicals in our environments, homes, and in the foods we eat with effects on the internal chemistry of the body that are only beginning to be known. Some of these chemicals change the way the body metabolizes food, some alter signals of satiety and hunger, and some produce cravings (even addictions) for more sugar, fat, and salt.[42] Others alter the gut flora, wiping out some of the "good" bacteria that play a role in all other bodily processes, from digestion and nutrient absorption to mood.

In NAFTA's first decade alone, chemical exports from the United States to Mexico rose 97 percent.[43] Given the incredible growth in chemical sales since NAFTA, the bonanza Mexico's market offers to US chemical companies might by itself justify the massive number of dollars they annually spend lobbying Congress for favorable policies—$55 million was spent by 108 companies in 2015 alone.[44] In spite of NAFTA being a three-way trade deal, Canada subscribes to regulations of chemicals that are more like those of the European Union than the United States. For example, Canada banned bisphenol A (BPA), while Mexico and the US allow it. It is a chemical used in plastics, such as baby bottles, plastic food containers, canned goods, and more, and is a proven endocrine disruptor. Despite Mexican scientists' warnings and many calls for its prohibition, it continues to be permitted in Mexico, along with a spectrum of other chemicals used in consumer and industrial applications.[45]

As discussed above, US corn produces dramatically higher yields because of the intensive nature of its production with a vast quantity of inputs—fertilizers, herbicides, insecticides, genetic modification of hybrid seeds, and so on. The heavy use of antibiotics in livestock production not only enables animals to proceed at a faster pace to slaughter, but is also used to prevent infections. While pigs and chickens in Mexico have long been fed corncobs, among many other things, the industrial corn they are fed on factory feedlots is more starchy, has less protein, is harder to digest, and makes up a larger portion of their total diet than the landrace corn they were fed in the past. Cattle, evolved as grass-eating ruminants, are simply not equipped to digest corn, and their ability to do so depends on prophylactically treating the constant infections in the digestive tract they suffer from when they are fed corn instead of grass. The tight conditions and inappropriate feed of industrial farming mean cattle are often perpetually sick and continually fed antibiotics.[46] It is logical that the antibiotics and other chemicals used in the production of the animals themselves and their feed pass through to human beings, who are eating larger quantities than ever of the resulting "cheap" meat, milk, and eggs. It is also logical that eating larger quantities of those animal products could result in accelerated growth (resulting in childhood and adult obesity, as well as early puberty), decreased biodiversity in the gut, antibiotic resistance, and other endocrinologic and metabolic effects.[47]

Besides the increase in availability of processed foods and beverages, mechanisms for their distribution throughout Mexico, and a rise in the use of chemicals in food production, there are other factors that may play a role in the rise in obesity rates. Antibiotics are considered one of the greatest achievements of human ingenuity and have saved the lives of countless millions. Paradoxically, they also have systematically reduced the biodiversity in the gut of people in industrialized nations, leaving it less able to digest, regulate bodily processes, and metabolize nutrients. Where only recently any colony of bacteria were viewed largely as infectious menaces to be eliminated with good science and innovation, today we see many referring to gut flora in decidedly more flattering terms, as a mutualistic ecosystem that is necessary and beneficial to the survival of the host.[48] There is growing awareness of possible connections between diseases, auto-immune disorders, digestive ailments, and allergies with overly sterile environments, lack of exposure to pathogens and bacteria, and overuse of antibiotics. While countless generations faced high rates of mortality from easily transmitted infections that are generally routine and minor today, we see rising evidence that antibiotic use can be taken too far, with those living in highly controlled and overly sanitized urban environments developing a reduced capacity to manage even low levels of exposure to bacteria, allergens, and toxins.

Parenting advice in the early twenty-first century tells those worried about asthma and allergies to be sure to get a dog or a cat, expose their infants to peanuts, and not overuse antibacterial soap and hand sanitizers. Children who are routinely licked on the mouth by a pet, exposed early on to allergens, and challenged often by low levels of noxious bacteria may have improved immune system responses later in life, with fewer allergies, auto-immune disorders, and asthma.[49]

Use of antibiotics in animal feed was considered a revelation in the early twentieth century, "a superfood to produce cheap meat."[50] The prevention and treatment of the infections resulting from industrial livestock's overcrowding, poor living conditions, and inappropriate feed have been given as reasons for routine antibiotic use; their role in boosting and speeding growth was seen as an exciting bonus.[51] Creepy experiments to see if the same results could be achieved in human beings were considered encouraging. In one experiment, the antibiotic chlortetracycline was given to "mentally defective" children in a Florida orphanage in the 1950s; they grew an average of 6.5 pounds each year, while untreated children grew only 1.9 pounds.[52]

In a 2002 article in the *Journal of Alternative and Complementary Medicine,* environmental researcher and medical doctor Paula Baillie-Hamilton suggested that environmental causes might be responsible for the abrupt rise in obesity in the United States in the latter half of the twentieth century. Genetics, she notes, change at a glacially slow pace. Shifts in lifestyle and qualitative and quantitative alterations in the average person's diet play a role but do not go far enough to explain the recent abrupt and meteoric rise of obesity and chronic disease. Rather than the quantity of food consumed, she posits that it is the quality—specifically the chemicals used in and to produce processed food—that is a likely culprit. The well-chronicled rise in obesity and diet-related illnesses in middle-income countries with globalization may not be fully explained by an increase in availability and consumption of high-calorie foods and sugar-sweetened beverages that trade policies have placed within easier reach of people living in newly expanded markets, but have to do also with the qualitative shift in chemical composition of foods consumed.

The assumed rise in calories consumed and decline in calories burned is not consistently supported by data or the simple but unsubstantiated energy balance theory, promoted by some dietitians and medical professionals. This is the idea that weight is an outcome of a simple equation of calories in and calories out. This formula is praised as being simple, unequivocal, impossible to misunderstand, and an effective teaching tool for health and nutrition educators. It also, conveniently, means that there is no such thing as "bad" food. Individuals bear the responsibility, in this model, for ensuring they burn the same number of calories as they ingest to maintain a stable weight. This view holds that anything can be consumed if one's energy expenditure is sufficient to burn it off.

But, the body reacts very differently to some kinds of calories than it does to others. Recent studies show that the amount of calories absorbed from food, and the way that food is metabolized, varies from person to person and can be affected by multiple internal and external factors.[53] Our bodies may even work against us by plateauing the use of calories at a certain level of physical exertion.[54] A polemical infographic in the *Atlantic* magazine entitled "Exercise in Futility" summarizes these studies, showing that in spite of dramatic increases in exercise among adults in the United States in the past few decades, obesity prevalence has risen, too.[55]

It is possible that risk and causality for obesity and diseases like diabetes are attributable to a complex mix of social determinants, personal behavior like diet and exercise, chemical exposures and environment, and genetic or epigenetic factors. Nonetheless, as will be explored in the next chapter, much of what we hear about "solutions" to diet-related illness focus only on individual behavior and diet, even while public health scholars argue that intervention is most effective at the population level.

Our understandings of how obesity and diet-related illness develop and how they can be treated influence the scope of our imagined solutions. Energy balance theory in its elegant simplicity of calories in and calories out deflects attention from the content of food and the ways that chemicals impact our ability to digest and metabolize foods and the processes of all of our cells. The prevalence of energy balance theory, in its many itera-

tions, has led to an emphasis on physical activity and calories consumed that overlooks the chemical composition of processed foods and beverages and the effects of consuming those chemicals.

Heavy use of antibiotics and chemicals in industrialized food production are viewed by some as a necessary aspect of a modern food system. Science and imaginative intervention into "natural" processes of plant and animal growth speed them up, enhance them, and otherwise interfere in response to market demands and other considerations. For some, this is progress and improvement, while for others, meddling with organisms and the environment in which they grow represents a dangerous practice with unpredictable consequences.[56]

Synthetic chemicals began to be broadly used in the United States in the post–World War II period.[57] Some chemicals were found to induce growth. This was seen as useful to speeding up the time it takes for livestock to be ready for slaughter. Many chemicals have multiple applications. The same chemical might be used in a drug to treat anorexia to boost weight gain and then used on livestock to speed growth. These chemicals, even when used in very small quantities, can be detected in people, as well as being transmitted in utero and in breast milk. Further, they can alter genes, an epigenetic phenomena, that can be carried over from one generation to the next, in ways more abrupt than can be attributed to conventional genetic mutations. Some pesticides, herbicides, and other chemicals used in farming boost growth in less predictable ways. For example, Villeneuve and colleagues published research in 1977 that demonstrated that rats exposed to the pesticide hexachlorobenzene gained significantly more weight than those who were not exposed, even when their food rations were reduced by 50 percent.[58] In a time when antibiotics are routinely fed to livestock to prevent infection and to speed growth, increasing numbers of researchers are asking whether antibiotics are the "X factor" contributing to dramatic gains in only a few decades in human BMI.[59] Research by Martin J. Blaser and his colleagues at his lab in the Schools of Medicine and of Microbiology at New York University is exploring the relationship between the changing human microbiome and contemporary ailments like asthma, allergies, and obesity.[60]

In sum, mounting evidence indicates that obesity is not simply a result of an imbalance in the equation of calories in and calories out. In fact, many of the most basic precepts about prevention or reversal of obesity lack evidence and may be the product of specious, circular thinking and assumptions that are not in fact proven. Even the premise that obesity is in itself harmful is not settled.[61] Is a calorie a calorie, no matter the quality? What are the causes of obesity? What are the solutions for obesity? How does one lose weight? Are any of the major recommendations for weight maintenance or loss proven to work? None of these are settled questions.

The controversial idea that it is not only quantity of food but additives and residues of chemicals used in production that may explain the abrupt rise in obesity in the last decades is gaining strength due to evidence from scientific studies. Summing some of them up, anthropologist Julie Guthman, in her book *Weighing In: Obesity, Food Justice, and the Limits of Capitalism,* questions whether we really understand how people gain weight.[62] She critiques the prominent explanations for and solutions to obesity as an example of "coproduction," in which "science helps produce the social worlds it is intended to explain." The circular and specious reasoning she signals goes like this: obesity is caused by cheap, fast, nutritionally inferior food and a built environment that discourages physical activity, and so, the solution is better food and health-promoting renovations of the built environment, such as the addition of bike paths and sidewalks.[63] The assumption is that eating too much food causes obesity and that behaviors—eating less and better food, and exercising more—are the solution. However, there is evidence that people do not necessarily consume greater quantities of calories than in the past. And the rise in infant obesity contradicts the idea of a causal relation between calories, exertion, and obesity, with infants being "a segment that doesn't go to the movies, can't chew, and was never that much into exercise."[64]

SOLUTIONS?

What are the effects of a lack of consensus on the causes and treatment, and even harmfulness, of obesity? If researchers are not in agreement about the causes of obesity, or even whether it is necessarily a problem, they will not agree on what must be done. Etiologies, the understanding of how a disease is caused, are rarely reducible to a single vector or agent.

Instead, most diseases and syndromes are understood to be multifactorial, with differing understandings among experts, those who experience the diseases, and others, depending on causes, contributing factors, treatment, and the possibility of prevention. Even though etiologies of obesity are remarkably discordant, a rather facile equation drawn between excess calories, insufficient exercise, obesity, diabetes, illness, and mortality has contributed to the framing of diet-related illness as an urgent public health crisis for Mexico. Indeed, with an average of eighty-six thousand deaths attributed to diabetes in each of the last ten years, Mexico has reason to be concerned.[65] But, who benefits from the "confusion" surrounding the purported causes and solutions to this "epidemic"?

Marion Nestle demonstrates that efforts to make proper nutrition and the effects of diet on health seem hopelessly complex have been a strategy of food corporations that counts on consumers throwing up their hands in confusion.[66] Cultural anthropologist Emilia Sanabria traces the way "ignorance" about the causes of obesity is actively driven by the profit interests of the food and beverage industry.[67] We can be forgiven for finding the latest in nutritional advice at any given moment baffling: is it sugar that is bad, or fat? How bad are carbs? Are carbs fine, but gluten the issue? What does it mean to follow a "paleo" diet or to eat "clean"? Nutritional fads and data are rarely differentiated in a reliable way in consumer-oriented media. It is common in mainstream magazines directed to women and families, for example, to see advertisements by corporations on facing pages with recipes that promise better health through nutrition—for example, a recipe for low-fat macaroni and cheese opposite an ad for a new low-fat Kraft cheese product. Nutrition literature distributed in both the United States and Mexico in clinics and hospitals is often produced by transnational food corporations and focused on use of the products they manufacture.[68] The influence of corporations on advertising, media, and even scientific research means that consumers are right to be wary of reports demonizing or donning a halo on certain kinds of foods. But in reality, as Pollan has argued, the only nutritional advice that has been consistently corroborated by scientific research can be summed up in ridiculously simple terms: eat food, not too much, mostly plants.[69]

Industrial food and beverage producers, as publicly traded corporations, have a mandate to their shareholders to increase profits, even if the market for their products appears to have reached saturation and even when there is evidence that the products are harmful. How do corporations continue to grow the market for their products? First, companies seek to increase consumption of the things they sell. This is the role of advertising: to encourage consumers to pick particular products, increase their consumption of them, and remain loyal to brands. So, for example, we see the growth of Coca-Cola from a medicinal elixir to a special occasion treat, to a beverage framed as suitable for consumption in everyday contexts. But to expand consumption beyond that requires greater creativity—different varieties and flavors of soda, responding to perceived trends in preferences for taste, color, packaging, and product features. It also requires suppression or dilution of evidence that the products can be harmful.

Transnational food corporations, and especially sugar-sweetened beverage corporations, have heavily subsidized research into the energy balance theory, and melded these investments into their marketing plans.[70] Much of this research has been conducted in major academic institutions. Some of it has been conducted in industry-funded "think tanks" where researchers produce reports with scientific-sounding data. Energy balance theory is important to them because it implies that a calorie is a calorie, no matter what it is comprised of. If there is no such thing as "bad" foods or beverages, then one must simply manage total caloric consumption in relation to exercise to increase, reduce, or maintain weight. One manifestation of energy balance theory that we see if we look at the soda corporations' own discussion of obesity prevention is their emphasis on "hydration" as a crucial element in health, particularly for "active lifestyles." This is the idea that dehydration is a significant enough risk that intake of fluids of any kind is advisable, and it allows for "energy drinks" and even soda to be considered part of an active, healthy lifestyle.

This argument was aided by the invention of diet soda, Tab, in 1963, in response to the emergence of concern with weight gain. In earlier epochs, a bulging waistline was associated with wealth and privilege, but in the twentieth century we see the inversion of this, with thinness coming to be a desired attribute among elites and its pursuit driving the development of "diet" products. With the development of synthetic and low-calorie sweeteners in the latter half of the twentieth century, we see the definitive conversion of soda's image from an indulgence or treat into an anytime drink with, presumably, no deleterious consequences. The association of saccharin with cancer notwithstanding, the march toward what PepsiCo now calls "good for you" and "fun for you" products, was underway, with the underlying logic being that each food and beverage corporation would try to corner the market on a range of products with options for everyone.

When even the seemingly infinite game of product diversification proves insufficient for ensuring an annual rise in profits, market expansion is key. To expand markets, food and beverage corporations have had to simultaneously pursue various strategies. One is to try to replicate the broadly shared warm and fuzzy (cold and fizzy?) feelings about their products that they enjoyed in the United States in the past. Coca-Cola has long been marketing its product as one that brings people together with songs in ads like "I'd like to buy the world a Coke," or the recent campaign of names on the outside of cans, with ads encouraging us to buy a friend a can featuring their name.

This requires active suppression of the rising tide of data on the harmful effects of consumption of their products. There is growing evidence that consumer advocacy organizations in Mexico have been subject to spying by the government, while activists and scholars working to address Mexico's obesity and diabetes epidemic have faced death threats.[71] While it is unclear whether these threats are part of a coordinated, official effort by the government, it is clear that there are multi-billion-dollar interests at stake in continued growth of the Mexican market for processed food and beverages. To suppress data about the health effects of consumption of processed foods and beverages when marketing is increasingly global and consumption of media is not constrained by borders isn't easy. But this process is aided by the concurrent shift toward what can be summed up as a "consumption for all" model of economic development.

Raising the questions that one needs to answer to test the relationship between increased use of chemicals and a rise in obesity and chronic disease in the US and our trading partners requires a dramatically different political economy of research and in fact, different ideologies. An emphasis on the individual, an irrefutably central aspect of the US creed, orients us to downplay social and structural aspects of health.[72] This orientation is part of the economic policies and role of the state promoted by the United States via international lending and trade deals.

How we think about personal choice and behavior influences the ways we conceive of etiologies and solutions for diet-related illness. Discourses of healthism, consonant with notions of neoliberal governmentality, are deployed as prevention *and* solution in ways that obscure collective and political responsibility for the population's health. Within models of self-care, in which each individual is responsible for his or her health, collective concern and responsibility are hampered. Energy balance theory reinforces our idea that weight is under an individual's control and an outcome of choice and discipline. Theories about obesity hypothesizing that it might be linked to a rise in exposures to an untested and unquantified soup of chemicals in our air, water, and food require a much bigger frame of analysis than the individual. In the next chapter, we will analyze how the Mexican government has framed and is addressing the "obesity epidemic" and the rise in diet-related illnesses, especially diabetes.

5 Deflecting the Blame

POVERTY AND PERSONAL RESPONSIBILITY

TLACOYOS

"Tlacoyos need a marketing campaign." This was the assertion of Alejandro Calvillo when I interviewed him in Mexico City at the nonprofit he directs, El Poder del Consumidor (Consumer Power). Like many traditional Mesoamerican foods, the tlacoyo begins with ground corn, or sometimes a combination of corn and garbanzo or lentil flour, that is then stuffed with beans, cheese, and sometimes herbs, huitlacoche (corn fungus), or other fillings before being cooked on a *comal*. After toasting on both sides, it is layered with green or red salsa and a sprinkling of fresh cheese. The organization El Poder del Consumidor is well known for cheeky and sometimes aggressive campaigns critiquing corporations and conflicts of interest in government. At Christmas, they received a lot of press when they placed an actor dressed as Santa Claus and a four-meter tall inflatable Coca-Cola can labeled "diabetes" in the iconic font in Mexico City's Zócalo, the nation's largest and most visible public square. They call out misleading advertising, for example, accusing Sidral Mundet, an apple-flavored soda that is bottled by the Coca-Cola company, of misrepresenting the amount of juice in the drink (it's only 1 percent).[1] They are one of the

Figure 5. El Poder del Consumidor staged an action in Mexico City's Zócalo just before Christmas, with this inflatable Coca-Cola can labeled "Diabetes." Mexico City, December 2014. Photo courtesy of El Poder del Consumidor. Photo by Aaron Borrás.

organizations that has joined the Alianza por la Salud Alimentaria (Alliance for Nutritional Health) to advocate for a stronger public health response to the health effects of the rising dominance of processed foods and sugar-sweetened beverages in Mexico.

Tlacoyos can generally be purchased for 60 cents to a dollar in Mexico City, from street vendors or modest food stands. Calvillo insisted that there are no processed food items that can rival the nutritional value or affordability of the tlacoyo. However, as with tortillas, consumption of foods like the tlacoyo is declining in Mexico. The conversion of food preparation from a small-scale activity in the household to a globalized, transnational corporate activity has wrought changes not only in content and quality of food but also in its valorization. The most significant cost to the production of industrial food is its marketing. Processed foods employ the cheapest possible ingredients and save on production costs through automation and massification. Reducing costs to a fraction of what it might cost an individual to make a food product enables corporations to spend handsomely on marketing to generate a desire for products of dubious nutritional value.

The slang term "vitamina T" refers to the list of snack foods that happen to begin with the letter *t* that many Mexicans will tick off with chagrin—tacos, tamales, tortas, tostadas, tlacoyos, tlayudas, and so on—the tempting, delicious, and ubiquitous *antojitos* that one can find anywhere in the republic.[2] These are often listed as an embarrassing indication of Mexicans' weakness for junk food. We'll come back to the idea of Mexicans' weakness for junk food, but first, street foods are often not "junky" at all. In fact, I know of few places that offer as many options to eat a fresh, hot, handmade meal on the street as Mexico's cities, and it is possible to observe and consume many kinds of food without ever setting foot inside a permanent eating establishment. The recent food truck craze in the United States has nothing on the time-honored Mexican tradition of *puestos* (food stalls that line sidewalks in just about any urban area).[3] Besides puestos, I've eaten food served from tricycles, taco trucks, pickup trucks, baskets carried on someone's elbow, back, or head, and even delicious bean *tacos de canasta* out of a bicycle basket.

The association of convenience and street-level commerce with low social status taps into age-old Iberian social and gender mores about the

propriety of being on the street. In the colonial period, elites, especially well-bred women, were expected to stay indoors, hidden from the eyes of unrelated males. Working-class and slave women had no choice but to work on and travel through the streets, whether as market women, domestic servants, or small-business owners. The link between public visibility and sexual availability continues to be reproduced today. Similarly, food that is made or sold in the street, and those who prepare and consume it, is disrespected, and now with public campaigns about obesity and diabetes at a fever pitch, street food is attacked as being easy, dirty, fattening, and bad. Periodic campaigns in the interest of public hygiene since the nineteenth century have sought to regulate and control outdoor food sales, and street food continues to be criticized by many wealthier people and in tourist guidebooks for being "dangerous" and "unsanitary." In fact, street snacks are just as likely to involve a slab of jicama (*jicaleta*) or spears of cucumber and mango with lime, an ear of corn, or a cornmeal pocket stuffed with beans as they are to involve the infamous "Dorilocos" (Doritos dressed with a mountain of toppings), deep-fried quesadillas, or torta de tamal, so it is not correct to assume that street food is inherently unhealthy; it can be as artery clogging or as full of fresh fruits and vegetables as any other kind of food.

This chapter examines Mexico's multisectoral strategy to combat obesity and diabetes, a public health response that has won it accolades internationally and been praised for its progressiveness. I critique the response for not being as progressive as its reputation or as civil society advocates had hoped and for resting on some rather unprogressive, indeed retrograde, ideas about gendered roles and responsibilities, as well as about rural and low-income populations. We can see that the aftermath of NAFTA is not just a changed food system, but in fact a revision of the relationship between the state and its people. NAFTA is not simply a contract between nations to govern commerce, but about the signatories agreeing to subscribe to specific market-based ideas about how to solve society's problems. The main assertion: poverty, inequality, and chronic disease are issues to be addressed with market solutions. Rather than take responsibility for the structural changes to the nation's economy and food system since NAFTA, the government of Mexico has framed citizens as consumers, free and capable of purchasing the goods of health and well-being in the marketplace. If diet-related illness has risen in the aftermath of NAFTA, it is, the logic holds, because Mexicans need to be educated to be better consumers, not because their political leaders have transformed the context in which they make their lives.

MEXICO'S STRATEGY FOR DIABETES AND OBESITY

I walked down the sidewalk toward the Ministry of Health in Mexico's capital on a chilly morning in December 2014. As I proceeded down the street, two middle-aged men behind me were speaking animatedly about their cholesterol levels. Arriving at my destination, I boarded the elevator. As we rode upward, two workers were talking about weight. "I'm afraid to step on the scale," the man said, "I don't want to know." The woman, wearing the smock of the custodial staff, smiled and leaning slightly toward him. "I already lost ten kilos," she said. I arrived at my floor as the man exclaimed and praised her accomplishment. That talk about health, weight, and weight loss should spill out even onto the sidewalks surrounding the health ministry is an indication of the prevalence of preoccupation with Mexico's diabetes and obesity "epidemic."

Even though this was the central office of a government ministry, it also had the feel of a clinic. The elevator doors were plastered with posters recommending that foods be steamed or broiled, not fried, and that soda consumption be minimal. The plate glass windows of the lobby had massive posters promoting the ministry's current campaign: "Mídete, Chécate, Muévete." Weigh and measure yourself, have a checkup, and move your body. With the country facing a massive increase in noncommunicable chronic diseases, including a deadly epidemic of diabetes, this building is the headquarters of Mexico's largest coordinated public health campaign yet.

There, I interviewed a high-ranking official in the federal government's Ministry of Health, la Secretaría de Salud. She eagerly spoke to me about the health ministry's recent adoption of a national strategy for the prevention of overweight, obesity, and diabetes.[4] Her first insistence, like that of everyone in the government I spoke with, was as follows: diabetes and obesity are multifactorial problems that require multisectoral solutions.

Figure 6. Poster at the health ministry, December 2014. Photo by the author.

One of the first projects of the strategy was the collaboration between the health and education ministries to remove sugar-sweetened beverages and energy-dense foods from within schools and to ensure that when children are served food at school, it is healthy. It should be noted that Mexico does not have a federal school lunch program, in part because the public primary school day is only four hours long. Instead, children eat a *refrigerio,* or snack, at 11:00 a.m., and then are assumed to eat lunch, typically the family's main meal, after they go home at 1 p.m.[5] In many communities, it is still common to see mothers arriving at school at 11:00 a.m. with a hot meal for their children. But if that does not happen, children often purchase a snack. Some schools offer an extended school day that includes lunch, while others serve hot or cold breakfasts to low-income students, but these tend to be an exception.

When I asked the health ministry official about the results of a pilot project in which mothers of students were asked to cook food for the children's morning meal, she exclaimed, "¡Era peor!" It was worse! "The moms

Figure 7. At 11:00 a.m. on weekdays in many small cities and towns in Mexico, it is possible to see a parade of women carrying small woven plastic bags with a hot meal to children at school. January 2015. Photo by the author.

would serve them a fried *sope* topped with *frijoles, queso, y crema*."[6] That the anecdote she shared centered on a sope—a fried sope, no less—as the mothers' contribution to a "healthy" lunch program was surely intended to enlighten me as to the complexities of the Ministry of Health's efforts to address the rising problem of diabetes and obesity in Mexico. Perhaps inadvertently, this high-ranking member of the ministry's staff also revealed some of the assumptions behind the health ministry's strategy against obesity.

Assessing the Mexican government's current multisectoral strategy against obesity, overweight, and diabetes requires contextualizing it within the government's overall approach to its citizens' well-being. It also requires looking at changes in the last decades in the state's role in providing goods like health care, poverty remediation, education, and food security. Over recent decades, the government has withdrawn or reduced some features of that care and other services for its citizens. The shift in Mexico's approach to serving its citizens can be generalized as a move toward "self-care." This shift places the responsibility and the solution to major issues, such as health and poverty, in the hands of individuals. The focus on "shared responsibility" and "co-management of risk" occludes the larger systemic changes that have altered the choices available to the public. In fact, while the shift in responsibility from the state to the individual has been happening, we have also seen a privatization of previously nationalized and collective goods, such as petroleum and the ejido system of collective landholding. So, at the same time that there has been a "decentering of expectations of welfare from the state," citizens have been encouraged to be flexible, resourceful, and most of all, accountable for their own health and well-being.[7]

The very idea of public health and welfare is premised on expectations and understandings about the public sphere, the common good, and the responsibility of state and non-state institutions to ensure and protect them. Even while consumer choice and empowerment are promoted as means for overcoming some of the bureaucratic intransigencies of welfare systems, a shift to self-directed care and advocacy undermines the central promise of "public health," which assumes a state role in protecting the well-being of all. It draws into question the state's concern for the common good when it can be observed eliminating and privatizing systems oriented toward collective well-being. As I argue throughout this book, in examining the rise of chronic disease in Mexico, we must be attentive not only to the changes in the ways Mexicans eat over the last two decades, but also to the larger food system and the ways that food is distributed and marketed, within national projects of economic development and political transition.

Of course, individual behaviors and choices play a role in chronic disease—what we consume and how much we exercise are not trivial—but to imply that people have succumbed to junk food and sedentary lifestyles and brought on an epidemic of chronic disease just in the last twenty years defies logic. A predilection for sweet foods has been well established as a constant in human history, one that has only expanded as trade, technology, and marketing have heightened the availability, affordability, and desirability of sugar, other sweeteners, spices, and other flavorings.[8] The global expansion of production, marketing, and distribution of what Nicholas Freudenberg calls "hyperpalatable" foods manufactured using "supernormal stimuli" cooked up in laboratories by food scientists is a response to and capitalization upon that predilection.[9] The desire for such foods did not emerge sui generis in the last three decades. As Linda Fried, dean of the Mailman School of Public Health at Columbia University, notes, "Evidently, genetics haven't changed. Willpower hasn't changed. Conditions have changed."[10]

Nonetheless, the larger economic and political forces that have enabled global market expansion and increased buying power are not always blamed for the expansion of chronic disease. In fact, when we look closely, we see that corporate interests have promoted a dispersal of causality and culpability for the public health consequences of the consumption of their products at the same time that their industries have expanded globally.[11] Further, political leaders in many nations around the world have opted to promote economic development in the short term, even when it is accompanied by elevated health costs in the long term. They have eased the market penetration of products whose consumption can be harmful to health within campaigns for the promotion of foreign investment, job creation, market leveling, and so on, and have systematically dismantled formerly robust systems designed to prevent just such an invasion of foreign products (price supports, tariffs, quotas, import substitution, subsidies, and so on). The shifting of culpability and responsibility for chronic disease to individuals, within a frame of self-care and individual responsibility, serves corporate interests and profit motives, especially when that framing is consonant with how the nation has long conceived of economic expansion and comparative advantage. As such, the particular ways that Mexico's public health policies center upon individual knowledge, actions, and responsibilities, and evade addressing structural forces, are worthy of scrutiny. Here, we continue such a project of scrutiny.

IS DIET-RELATED ILLNESS THE GOVERNMENT'S PROBLEM?

The World Health Organization (WHO), the Food and Agricultural Organization of the United Nations (FAO), and the Organisation for Economic Co-operation and Development (OECD), among other

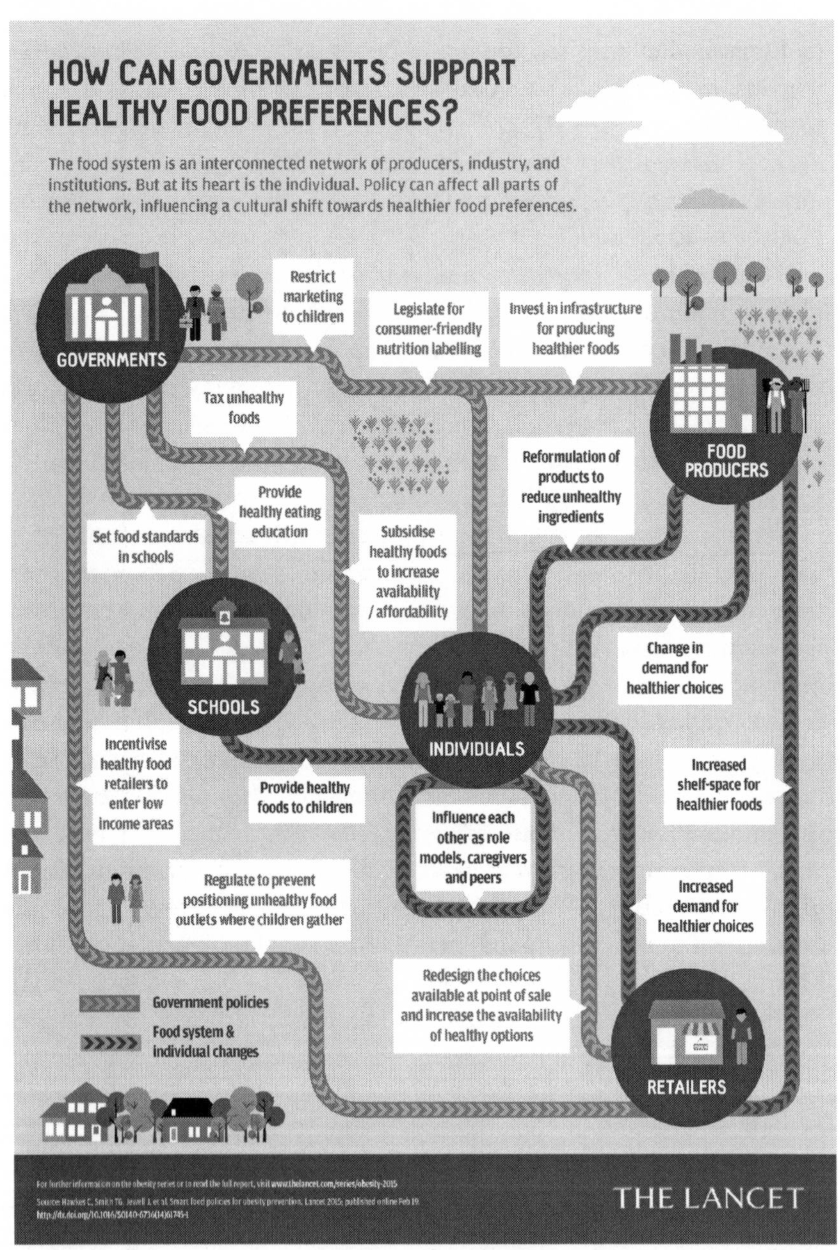

Figure 8. Infographic: "How Can Governments Support Healthy Food Preferences," *Lancet,* Special Series, Obesity, 2015, www.thelancet.com/infographics/obesity-food-policy.

multinational entities, call obesity a threat to health, productivity, economic development, and child development in countries around the world. The threat is often noted to be particularly high in middle-income nations experiencing nutrition transition as a feature of economic development, globalization, and urbanization. Contributing factors include alterations in lifestyles, buying power, food availability, and habits, and the prevalence of fast and processed foods.[12] Scholars have implicated multinational enterprises in the rise in chronic disease globally, and have also spurred efforts by the WHO and the OECD, a market-oriented coalition, to oblige multinational enterprises to address the growing health and productivity costs of diet-related illness. While no campaign, agency, or program has successfully reversed the rise in obesity and diet-related illness in a population, interest in doing so is widespread.[13] Although the UN did not convene its first high-level meeting of the general assembly on obesity until 2011, scholarly and civil society efforts to measure the effectiveness of campaigns and locate responsibility have been building.

A 2011 special issue on obesity of the *Lancet,* one of the oldest and most respected peer-reviewed medical research journals, was clear and incriminating: "The simultaneous increases in obesity in almost all countries seem to be driven mainly by changes in the global food system, which is producing more processed, affordable, and effectively marketed food than ever before. This passive overconsumption of energy leading to obesity is a predictable outcome of market economies predicated on consumption-based growth."[14] Indeed, the *Lancet*'s 2011 summation is consonant with the approach of some of the most aggressive, and to date effective, anti-obesity policies. It closely corresponds to what Thomas Frieden, former commissioner of the New York City Department of Health and Mental Hygiene and later director of the US Centers for Disease Control, identified as the "healthy impact pyramid," in which efforts to address socioeconomic determinants of health at the systemic or structural level are deemed to have the greatest impact and return on investment in the long term, while individual education and behavioral change, at the top of the pyramid, have the least: "Interventions focusing on lower levels of the pyramid tend to be more effective because they reach broader segments of society and require less individual effort. Implementing interventions at each of the levels can achieve the maximum possible sustained public health benefit."[15]

However, by 2015, the *Lancet* had shifted toward a greater emphasis on the individual. That shift was not supported by data. How the *Lancet* describes obesity, as well as its causes and solutions, has global influence. The journal influences etiologies of obesity, and we see that in 2015 it moved away from laying the blame for the rise in diet-related illness on the expansion of markets for processed foods, market-based economic policies, and changing food systems, and instead hedged with language about multifactorial causes and multipronged solutions. While they rightly acknowledge that no phenomenon as widespread and complex as obesity can be reduced to single causes or solutions, the shift away from pointing fingers at processed food and beverage corporations is exactly what corporations have lobbied for with lawmakers, and advocated for with proprietary and sponsored research programs. Marion Nestle has written convincingly about how food and beverage corporations strategically foster the notion that the causes and solutions to obesity are confusing or complex, and we can see the *Lancet*'s shift as a possible result of corporate efforts to influence thinking on the issue.[16]

In its 2015 special issue on obesity, the *Lancet* published a flowchart summarizing approaches to combat obesity. In it, the individual is at the heart of the food system. Government is given an important role in heading up efforts through a few major strategies that research indicates can be effective: taxing unhealthy foods and subsidizing healthy ones, restricting marketing directed to children, mandating better nutrition labeling, and in schools, setting standards for meals, providing nutrition education, and regulating availability of unhealthy food options. However, the illustration visually reinforces the centrality of individuals and families. In this same issue, in its editorial statement, the *Lancet*'s editors argue for a "balanced" approach to obesity, implicating both structural and behavioral factors as contributions to obesity. It is impossible to ignore echoes between the phrasing here advocating a "balanced" approach and energy balance theory, the idea heavily promoted by food and beverage corporations through sponsored research and lobbying. An emphasis on balance implies that responsibility is shared and causality is diffuse or unknown. "Balance" implies that there are no bad foods or beverages, simply that good and bad must be balanced, so one does not outweigh the other. Where structural factors are named, they are not given the weight they are in Frieden's pyramid, but are just one among many competing factors. Transnational food corporations endorse such characterizations, or at least howl less about them, because they are not singled out for blame for diet-related illness.

Like the *Lancet*'s 2015 approach, Mexico's anti-obesity strategy emphasizes "top of the pyramid," small-bore efforts. Even while the strategy was designed as a multipronged approach, structural or systemic interventions have been minimized while the messaging to individuals and the focus on education and behavior has been expanded. To briefly summarize the strategy:[17] in 2012, presidential candidate Enrique Peña Nieto announced his commitment to address Mexico's growing epidemic of diabetes, as well as correlated factors of obesity and overweight. It was estimated that a concerted public health strategy could save fifty-five thousand lives per year.[18] After he was elected, in 2013, he announced the multisectoral National Strategy for the Prevention and Control of Overweight, Obesity, and Diabetes. Here, I will focus on three main parts of the Mexican government's multisectoral response to diabetes and obesity: the soda tax and regulations on food marketing; the anti-poverty program currently called Prospera, and La Cruzada en contra del Hambre, or the Crusade against Hunger.

SODA TAX

In 2013, Mexico achieved something remarkable: its legislature passed a tax of 1 peso per liter on sugar-sweetened beverages. The tax was part of a package of reforms promoted by the recently inaugurated president Enrique Peña Nieto, and passed by the Mexican legislature. Interestingly, the tax was approved against the wishes of the minister of health and was advanced instead by the economic ministry, interested in addressing rising public health care costs through an expansion of the tax base.[19] The tax resulted from a concerted effort by some civil society organizations and consumer advocates to push hard for a policy response to the growing "obesity epidemic." The Bloomberg Foundation, following on Michael Bloomberg's unsuccessful attempt to pass a portion size cap when he was mayor of New York City, pumped millions of dollars into Mexican nonprofits and think tanks to push for strong policies like the tax.

In her 2015 book entitled *Soda Politics: Taking on Big Soda (and Winning!),* Marion Nestle praises the policy.[20] In fact, the *and winning* of the title refers precisely to Mexico and a similar tax passed in Berkeley, California. In the book, and at a December 2015 talk at the CUNY School of Public Health, Nestle lauded Mexico's efforts, which are praised as one of the few successfully implemented national taxes on sugar-sweetened beverages in the world.[21] Preliminary data published by independent researchers indicates that the tax has resulted in a decline in the consumption of soda, 5.7 percent in the first year and 9.7 percent in the second, to approximately 13.7 liters per person per year, down from a projected 15.6 liters without the tax.[22] However, conversations with some of the advocates for the tax indicate that it falls short of what they wanted and what they thought would work.

The main pillars of the strategy were publicly opposed by large multinational food and beverage corporations. In spite of their continued vocal opposition, it later became clear that behind closed doors, the government handed corporations a victory in the significant narrowing of the scope of the policies. While the policies were supported by a broad coalition of government, civil sector, and business entities, the main academic public health institutes and civil society organizations were excluded from final negotiations. For example, policies regarding package labeling were left to "self-regulation" by multinational corporations. Scholars and advocates unsuccessfully lobbied for a stoplight labeling system, something more like the Ecuadoran system. Many had also pressured for food guidelines that take into consideration food systems and food justice, like the Brazilian system, which states, in part: "Access to reliable information on characteristics and determinants of healthy diets contributes toward people, families, and communities increasing their autonomy in making good food choices; it also contributes to leading them to demand the compliance to the human right to adequate food."[23] Mexico's current labeling results in what many have critiqued as confusing and misleading recommended daily allowances and portion sizes that contradict WHO recommendations for daily sugar and fat consumption. Critics point to conflicts of interest that have marked the design and implementation of the Estrategia.[24]

Efforts to strengthen and target the campaign after the initial passage of the soda tax have been unsuccessful. In March 2015, the congress

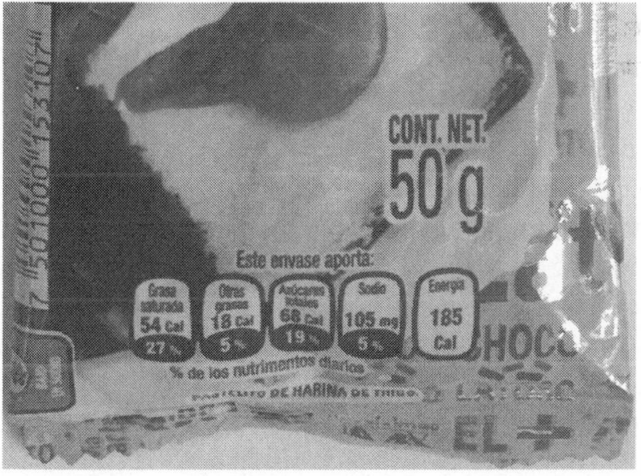

Figure 9. Stoplight nutrition labeling (top). Photo by Marcelo Aizaga. Current Mexican nutrition labeling (bottom). Photo by Marisa Macari.

rejected legislation seeking to refine three major principles of the strategy against obesity: front-of-package stoplight labeling, clarification of regulation of marketing to children that acknowledges that children are exposed to marketing at times and in venues not regulated by prior legislation (advertising during programming families watch together like *telenovelas,* on the internet, etc.), and the concretization of some of the principles of the strategy in the form of a general law for the prevention and treatment of overweight and obesity.[25]

In addition, Mexico no longer has subsidies for healthier food cultivation and production intended to increase consumption of healthful foods by making them affordable, and has reduced direct provisioning of fresh foods through most of its social service programs. Perhaps most significantly: the strategy is undercut by the economic policies that have significantly and possibly irrevocably reconfigured Mexico's food system. If we look at the strategies that have been implemented to date, while they are structural in that they are government mandates that regulate certain aspects of availability and marketing of sodas and calorie-dense foods, they do so in ways that seek to foster and depend upon behavioral change rather than structural change.

A soda tax generates resources that can be used for prevention and treatment at the same time that higher costs are shown to discourage consumption slightly. In this case, a large portion of proceeds from the tax are ostensibly dedicated to the installation of potable drinking water fountains in public schools across the republic.[26] A tax on foods and beverages alone does not incentivize the purchase of more healthful options or bring them within easier reach of low-income communities. Product labeling is dependent on the consumer analyzing and making choices about purchases and consumption. Regulation of publicity and marketing also is intended to shape decision making and preferences, or more specifically, to mitigate the negative influence of marketing of hyperpalatable processed foods. But on their own, such regulations do not offer information leading to other choices or make those choices more affordable. None of these addresses or improves the food landscape, food provision, or availability of healthy foods, or promotes sustainable or traditional foodways. Further, trends in both federal poverty prevention and mitigation and nutritional support programs have contributed to greater exposure of low-income Mexicans to a commoditized food economy, made small-scale subsistence practices more precarious, and monetized social assistance and food aid.

I would argue that this strategy has closed the front door while leaving the back door wide open. The tax is precisely the kind of measure vociferously opposed by industrial food and beverage corporations around the world. Since the early 1970s, many transnational corporations have followed the playbook outlined by corporate lawyer and later Supreme Court justice Lewis Powell in a confidential memo to the United States Chamber of Commerce entitled "Attack on American Free Enterprise System," encouraging corporations to team up to respond to any affront to their ability to grow and engage in commerce across state, federal, and international lines, even when peddling products with poor track records for health and safety.[27] We can see that trade agreements like NAFTA empower corporations to globalize markets and production while also marshaling resources to defend from regulations and other perceived attacks by civil society and governments.

The soda tax in Mexico was opposed by then health minister Mercedes Juan, who has a checkered history of conflicts of interest with corporations, having been on the board of directors of FUNSALUD, a private health foundation primarily funded by Nestlé.[28] One of her predecessors in the post, Salomón Chertorivski Woldenberg, is the son of Isaac Chertorivski Shkoorman, founder of ConMéxico, a trade group with the exclusive purpose of expanding the Mexican market for consumer goods.[29] With this level of collusion between those whose purpose is to please stockholders by selling more goods and those who set health and economic policy, it is not surprising that policies sometimes seem made to order to the specifications of corporations. Noisy complaints by corporations and their allies that taxes and other large-scale efforts to address the public health consequences of products like soda are regressive, a threat to personal liberty, examples of a "nanny state" and so on, serve to veil the major concessions made to corporations throughout the legislative process. It is part of the corporate playbook to complain loudly at *any* regulation while simultaneously working behind the scenes to co-opt or pressure away the most far-reaching attempts at regulation. Independent public health scholars and institutions in Mexico, and globally, argued that the tax should be at least 2 pesos per liter to have the desired effect. In negotiations, it was reduced to 1 peso per liter. A year after the tax went into effect, proponents of the tax had to fight against proposals to eliminate or dilute the tax, reducing it for low-calorie or low-sugar beverages while maintaining it for fully sweetened beverages. In the aftermath of the tax, corporations have continued to imply that the tax has failed and to generate confusion and debate as to its efficacy.

Current president Enrique Peña Nieto came into office in 2012 with an elaborate slate of drastic reforms of Mexico's energy sector and educational system. Privatization of the state-owned petroleum enterprise, Pemex, even partial, was long considered the "third rail" of Mexican politics: untouchable and deadly to political aspirations. He intended to implement a vast sell-off of state infrastructure and productive capacity to multinational investors. Further, he had in his sights the national teachers' union, one of the nation's largest and most powerful constituencies, and a bastion of working-class solidarity and mobilization, in spite of constant allegations of corruption. His proposed education reform would diminish the teachers' power of collective bargaining. These reforms generated anxiety and significant opposition, as did his party affiliation with the Partido Revolucionario Institucional, or PRI, which came back to power with his election. He also raised eyebrows with his mediagenic campaign and ties through marriage to Televisa, Mexico's biggest media conglomerate. He needed a great deal of political capital to pull off what some consider a peaceful coup—what his main opponent in the 2012 election called "the biggest plunder in human history."[30] His national and international image have only been further tarnished since he took office by astounding violations of human rights and rampant corruption and impunity.[31]

When I learned about how he aligned forces early in his term with more progressive voices on the soda tax, promising to sign the legislation even as the congress pushed it well past where the Health Minister herself wanted to go, I had to wonder whether the soda tax was a chit sacrificed by Peña Nieto in the interest of gaining favor from legislators for his larger reform project, or at least to shore up some legitimacy to that end. Some have also said that Peña Nieto was seeking to reclaim the PRI's role as a paternalistic and autocratic, but protectionist, party, against the technocratic neoliberal Partido de Acción Nacional (PAN), which ruled from 2000 to 2012, ushered into power with the election of former Coca-Cola executive Vicente Fox (2000–2006). But even if this were true, industry lobbyists and proxies were quite successful in blunting the tax's effectiveness at the drafting table.

It is unclear whether those who praise Mexico's efforts, like Barry Popkin, Marion Nestle, the *Guardian, Wired* magazine, and others, do so because even a small tax is a big victory compared to the uphill battle and legislative flops in the United States and other places, or because they are unaware of the ways that the advocates on the ground view it as falling short. Surely, "big soda" anticipates a coming "big tobacco" moment in which the industry might be held responsible for continuing to market harmful products well after evidence was available as to their ill effects. It's possible that the industry uses concessions like soda taxes to appear less villainous and disengaged from the public health consequences of consumption of their products, even while they double down on marketing globally. Rather than throw all their weight around defeating soda taxes and provoking negative publicity, they may simply try to blunt their impact. Ultimately, what is clear is that a small tax on sugar-sweetened beverages is a symbolic victory, but is not sufficient to stem the tide of diet-related illnesses, the industrialization of the Mexican diet, and the domination of the Mexican economy by corporations.

LIVE LONG AND PROSPER?

I am sitting in the offices of SEDESOL, la Secretaría de Desarrollo Social—Mexico's welfare ministry—interviewing Pedro, one of the architects of this agency's signature program, Oportunidades, about its transformation into Prospera. While we talk, he receives a knock on the door. "Es mi jefe" (It's the boss), he tells me. The boss comes in and with a broad smile on his face says, "¡Llegó Piketty!" (Piketty has arrived!) He holds up a freshly printed Mexican edition of the best-selling book *Capital in the Twenty-First Century,* by French economic historian Thomas Piketty.[32] Pedro and his boss discuss how this translation is said to be better than the previously released Uruguayan edition. I chime in, "There's a joke going around: that is the book that more people say they have read than any other." The boss doesn't get it—my skills at delivering a punch line are not very good—and says, "That's a lie; not everyone has read it." I lamely add, "That's why it's a joke. They *say* they've read it, which is not the same as reading it."

This somewhat surreal and awkward interruption to one of the more dynamic and engaging interviews I conducted among government officials reminds me Mexico is not like other places. Here, even though much of the federal government's policy is as unabashedly pro-business, pro-foreign investment, pro-1 percent as anywhere, the activities of the state are still often cloaked in the language of the Mexican Revolution, fought to free an exploited peasantry from the extortionist practices of an authoritarian, landed ruling class. The PRI, which ruled Mexico for seventy-one years continuously until 2000, and returned to power again with Peña Nieto, folds the revolution into its name and the institutionalization of that revolution continues to be its stated mission.[33]

But we can see a shift in orientation in Mexico's major anti-poverty program, Prospera (formerly named Progresa, and more recently Oportunidades) away from revolutionary ideals of solidarity and communal prosperity, and toward self-reliance. The program became known internationally because it is based on what is still the fairly radical concept that the best way to help the poor is to give them money. Of course, there are strings attached to these benefits, known as "conditional cash transfers." The recipients in the original model were always mothers, who, to continue receiving benefits, had to demonstrate that their children stayed in school, regularly visited the health clinic, obtained immunizations, and fulfilled other specific expectations. Since President Enrique Peña Nieto's relaunch of Prospera, the program has reduced the number of eligible beneficiaries and articulated an emphasis on nutritional and educational assistance to children and the disabled, as opposed to families as a whole. Cash transfers for adults are now oriented around credits for small-business ventures and financial emergencies, as well as *becas,* scholarships for studying or obtaining labor certifications and training.[34] Financial literacy and inclusion are emphasized, as is a gradual withdrawal of support as recipients are imagined to "graduate" from the need for benefits.

In the interview, Pedro at SEDESOL described to me all of the ways that Oportunidades was transformed to become Prospera. Even the name of the program is an indicator of the ideological inclinations of each successive government. When the PRI created the program during Carlos Salinas's presidency, it was called Solidaridad. Co-opting the words "solidarity," "progress," and its cognate "progressive" was strategic for a party whose only rival for domination in rural areas was the Partido Revolucionario Democrático (PRD), the leftist opposition party. Oportunidades, as it was rebaptized under President Vicente Fox, inserted a correspondingly neoliberal emphasis on "self-help," a bootstrap model of development premised on equality of opportunities, even amid inequality of conditions. Prospera reflects a new, leaner, meaner PRI. Prosperity—a very different objective from solidarity, progress, or even opportunity—is now the name of the game. What does this mean in terms of the content of the program?

The main goal of Prospera, I was told, is to foster financial inclusion. Rather than simply provide direct benefits, Prospera seeks to incorporate beneficiaries into productive activities through education, *capacitación* (job training and licensing), and the consumption of specifically developed financial products. Among these products are microloans. Pedro explained to me that for poor families an emergency, an unanticipated expense such as those brought by a death or illness in the family, can cause financial ruin. Beneficiaries of Prospera can now apply for small loans for up to 14.4 percent of their future cash transfers (the maximum loan is 2,000 pesos, or about $136 US).[35] The money would be automatically deducted from their transfer, and the collateral for the loan was the value of their future cash payments. This, he said, was life-changing for families without collateral who might once have incurred crushing debts to loan sharks, with their high-interest emergency funds. I nodded as he spoke. While $136 seemed minuscule (costs for burial, for example, are not that low), I thought this sounded humane and beneficial. He went on.

Prospera benefits would now be distributed electronically, deposited directly to beneficiaries' accounts and available for withdrawal from cash machines in their home communities. In communities too remote for this, a truck would come by monthly, loaded with satellite-equipped automated teller machines that would distribute cash. He touched on some of the advantages: less corruption, more security; no one can walk away with the bags of cash that previously were distributed in small towns. The cards would be linked to a bank account with all of the same features as any other, only the bank was held and managed by the federal government.

Beneficiaries would develop a credit history, and those who successfully paid back emergency microloans would be eligible for larger loans for productive activities—"enabling people to plan," Pedro said, with larger limits and longer amortization.

As convincing as it sounded, and as compelling as I found the impromptu skit performed in my presence about Piketty's book—a seven-hundred-page indictment of the ways capitalist economic policies generate and perpetuate inequality—I began to feel uneasy. What does this proliferation of credit mean for communities not previously "banked"? If I am feeling uncertain about financial inclusion as it is being defined by Prospera, would I advocate returning to some mythical Eden of cash-free rural life? Is the antonym of financial inclusion financial exclusion? I can't advocate for that. I argue with friends over dinner and find myself making distasteful assertions that sound like I would deny the poor access to the small and large streams of credit like the credit cards and mortgage I have no qualms using to manage my own household economy.

Let's examine the consequences of a proliferation of cash in rural communities in terms of the narrow focus of this book on food and diet-related illness. Loading conditional cash transfers onto debit cards that are linked to a bank heightens the surveillance of the poor by the state and also now by non-state actors. The beneficiaries of Prospera always had to perform certain behaviors and comply with certain requisites to maintain their eligibility for benefits. Now, that same process of continuous recertification and eligibility assessment would be extended: the beneficiary's lifelong profile, in the form of a credit history, would presumably follow her around indefinitely. Surveillance of welfare recipients has often been justified as the ante paid by beneficiaries for the privilege of receiving the state's largesse.[36] And the potential of negative marks on one's credit for failing to adhere to the terms of an extension of credit are assumed to be part of the price of consuming credit. Here, we see the two converge: welfare recipients now face the possibility that their consumption of state benefits can mark their lifelong credit history. Credit profiles are a measure in large part of the degree of one's consumption of credit as much as of one's reliability and discipline. In another universe, consuming *no* credit might be praised as the ultimate indicator of responsible financial behavior, but instead, managing credit—accumulating debts and paying them down—is the way in which financial citizenship is assessed. In this case, larger loans for future projects would be contingent on having demonstrated one's credit-worthiness through prompt payment of smaller "emergency" loans. Having soundly evaded *needing* an emergency loan through savings or other strategies could not, evidently, be counted as a mark of responsibility.

Responsibility and *discipline.* These are the key words that Prospera is organized around. They are words that place the onus on the beneficiary to perform her worthiness of future benefits. Education becomes the key concept for creating savvy, credit-worthy consumers integrated into the market. And what of poverty? Poverty becomes defined then as the inability to deal adequately with the anticipated and unanticipated turns of life, to overcome adverse events through strategic deployment of credit. Education and financial inclusion, as appealing and even progressive as they can be made to sound, are being substituted for a substantive state response to poverty and inequality. While no longer overtly appealing to now unfashionable and always offensive "culture of poverty" precepts, we see a "culture of prosperity" being promoted by the state agency charged with "social development."[37] Within this culture of prosperity, individuals and families are expected to "responsibly" and in "disciplined" fashion save, plan, invest, *emprender* (a verb in Spanish for the act of being an entrepreneur), and ultimately prosper. The blame for the inevitable failure to prosper of many of Mexico's most vulnerable poor—even with maximal exertions of discipline and responsibility—can be laid at their own feet, not the larger inequalities that have left the structures for the production and maintenance of crushing poverty untouched.[38]

The architects of Prospera's transformation are tweaking a program that has been widely praised and replicated. When he was mayor of New York City, Michael Bloomberg visited Mexico and came back with plans to implement a copycat program called Opportunities NYC. This was a bit ironic, given the decades of retrenchment of welfare benefits witnessed in the United States, where the trend was to limit and discontinue benefits. Oportunidades seemingly demonstrated the effectiveness of quite simply throwing cash at the problem of poverty. Even though the transfers were "conditional," the idea of giving poor people cash was distasteful for many and ultimately was not extended in New York beyond a limited pilot. But, as that program and so many microloan and cash transfer programs have shown around the world, it can be effective and necessary to simply (and often quite minimally) increase the monetary wealth of the poorest and most marginalized.

But did Oportunidades succeed in its stated aims? Many studies of the program have been conducted and published by researchers, showing mixed results. According to those I interviewed at SEDESOL and the documents they showed me, Oportunidades did not drive down the rate of poverty. This was part of why they argued a reform was needed. In their own published documents and slide presentations discussing the revamping of Oportunidades into Prospera, they admit that the rate of poverty has not budged in thirty years, including the seventeen years since the launch of the program, and may have gone up a few percentage points to about 45 percent.[39] It is impossible to glean from the data whether the program may have prevented a further heightening of poverty than might have been expected with the recent global recession. In addition, if migration has tapered off, but poverty has not, it is possible that those who are not migrating or who have returned are swelling the population, but not swelling the poverty rate as much as might be expected—indicating a stabilization of the economy for the most vulnerable since the mid-1990s.

If assessments of the effectiveness of Oportunidades at alleviating poverty are mixed and the changes brought with the switch to Prospera are too new to assess, what do we know? Conditional cash transfers in Mexico since the mid-1990s have been successful at increasing market integration of the poor, especially rural poor, and accelerating the transition from subsistence agriculture and reciprocity-based local economies to a market economy premised on the exchange of cash for goods and services.[40] What this means is that people who previously relied on a combination of subsistence strategies and consumption of goods available for cash, are shifting more toward exclusively cash-based participation in the economy. Thus, anti-poverty programs accelerate the rise in dominance of cash in the countryside and the further decline of small-scale agriculture. Because the foods most affordable and readily available for purchase are highly processed, consumption of these has risen.

As a result, we have what some have called the "growing pains" of demographic and economic transition.[41] As Mexico moves from an agricultural economy to a service and manufacturing economy, temporary imbalances and displacements are perhaps "to be expected."[42] But increasingly, the promised rewards of the resulting social and economic upheaval are not reaching those who have been most abruptly displaced. Without having entered the middle class, their consumption—even of the most basic elements of life: food, water, education, health care, and services—is commoditized and privatized, with multinational corporations best situated to rake in the proceeds.

Thus, aspects of life that were not market driven in a subsistence economy increasingly succumb to market logics: health, welfare, food procurement, production, and processing. These require expanded spheres of distribution, marketing, and sales. Then, to address the logical outcomes of hyperconsumption, companion industries flourish with products for weight loss, fitness, wellness, and living with chronic illnesses: medications, medical devices, and products for diagnosis, treatment, prevention, record keeping, and more.[43] Good citizenship is ever more closely associated with "good" consumption, with ideas about market insertion increasingly serving as proxies for assimilation, framed against its opposite, marginalization. Thus, the state is less concerned with demonstrating that it is addressing poverty, providing educational and occupational opportunities, health care, and other social services, and more concerned with expanding market participation. Indeed, some formerly basic aspects of governance are obliged to be "reformed" and "privatized" as quid pro quo for participation in trade pacts that demand adherence to minimalist trade, labor, environmental, and occupational health protections. All of this has public health consequences.

THE CRUSADE AGAINST HUNGER

Prospera is designed as a long-term strategy to stem poverty and promote development. But, the "double burden" of malnutrition and obesity in many low-income households in Mexico requires short- as well as long-term strategies.[44] In its efforts to close the gap between persistent malnutrition and hunger and the diet-related illnesses of "abundance," Mexico's social service ministry SEDESOL initiated the Cruzada contra el Hambre (Crusade against Hunger). In this program, families living in extreme poverty are given a *canasta básica,* a basic allotment of staple foods.

Following FAO guidelines, regulations dictate that such food be "sufficient, nutritious, and high quality." Recent scholarship and investigative reporting have demonstrated that it fails on all counts.[45]

The basic food allotment is comprised largely of processed foods, including canned sardines, powdered eggs and milk, and soy protein. Those who receive food baskets and cash transfers from the Mexican government are more likely to demonstrate excessive weight gain than those who do not.[46] Interviewed by a reporter, a recipient of the food benefit in the mountainous region of Guerrero state, one of the most economically marginalized areas in the country, said about the goods she receives, "We are not used to eating this way. If we eat eggs, it's from the hen, not from powder. This soy protein, what is it called? We are not used to that." When asked about the rationale for providing ultraprocessed foods higher in sodium, sugar, and fat than recommended by the national strategy for minimizing risk of chronic disease and obesity, Omar Garfias, charged with implementation of the Crusade, said, "Well, it's a problem we must try to solve by giving information to the cooks so they can make the necessary changes in their food behavior." He went on, "It's all about culture. The home cook [*cocinera*] is accustomed to cooking with too much fat and salt."[47] Garfias uses the term *cocinera,* which means cook, but a female cook, not male or the plural and gender-nonspecific *cocineros*. An evaluation team has criticized the Crusade for associating hunger with "women's affairs."[48] As described above, household food economies are still understood as a female domain where decisions made by women determine their family's health, well-being, and the size of their waistlines, which rise and fall along with their "education" or "culture." This is in spite of evidence of changing demographics and labor force participation by women. The administrators of the food benefits program who make decisions about what kinds of food to distribute to millions of program participants are exculpated; use of the food by undereducated home cooks is framed as the problem.

ASSUMPTIONS

Perhaps most troublesome, the thrust of the public health interventions and their implementation as envisioned by the anti-obesity strategy's architects are premised upon a set of assumptions about target populations. Implicit in ideas about "*el buen comer,*" or "the correct diet," are norms that are influenced precisely by corporate interests, but also draw on long-standing stereotypes about the inadequacy of peasant diets and the persistent ignorance of the poor. In this framing, Mexican food is inherently unhealthy; to be healthy requires eating differently from the imagined norm among working-class and rural populations. Missing in official and even many civil society approaches to nutritional support and education is acknowledgment that the typical diet of a campesino in most regions of Mexico historically and until quite recently offers sound nutrition, accessibility, and affordability. Instead, people are fed nutritional advice that implies that to be healthier, one must *learn* to eat healthfully, adopting new styles of cooking as well as ingredients. This is what I call the "salmon and broccoli approach," in which specific "diets" and recipes are promoted rather than an inductive, culturally specific, foodways-oriented approach. Salmon and broccoli are not some exclusive pathway to health (especially if salmon are raised on farms and fed with soy feed, and if broccoli is grown with pesticides and transported long distances from industrial farms). Making people feel that their own handed-down practices and ideas about food are inadequate destabilizes their own knowledge about food and nutrition, but also fosters the creation of a consumer market for new products marketed as "healthy" or "functional." Creating desire and demand and destabilizing contentment and satisfaction with what one already has are strategies covered in Marketing 101.

González writes in *Zapotec Science,* "Maize, beans, and squash (the so-called Meso-American Trinity), when combined with small amounts of other foods and animal-based proteins, provided the nutritional base for the development of complex societies like those of Monte Albán, Mitla, Tenochtitlán, Chichén Itzá, and others."[49] Nixtamalization of corn increases its bioavailability and makes it, when combined with beans, a complete protein. When beans and corn are combined with other plant foods and small quantities of animal protein, they constitute a complete and advantageous diet.[50] Further, Mexico is the place of origin of some foods recently achieving "superfood" status for their high quantity of nutrients, including quelites, amaranth, and chia. However, you will not see a government campaign promoting those foods, or the "trinity" of maize, beans, and squash, as part of the national strategy against obesity or hunger. Instead, it is common to hear critiques of "popular" eating styles and diets, as we saw with the comments by the health ministry official quoted above.

The foodways of low-income Mexicans are critiqued and slated for improvement within development rhetoric. Absent is any recognition of the fact that the diet consumed by rural Mexicans has been radically modified in the last twenty years due to shifts in Mexico's economic policy. Ironically, while indigenous and rural people were historically criticized for being insufficiently modern, today the critique is inverted, and they are characterized as overly enthusiastic in their embrace of the excesses of modern lifestyles, consuming soda and snacks wantonly, lacking sufficient self-discipline and education to moderate their consumption.

These critiques are related to long-standing themes in Mexico's developmental discourse. One is that rural and indigenous people's diet and lifeways have always been backward, and continue to be obstacles to development in the ways they always have been. This rather simplistic mode of analysis characterizes even ancestral ways of eating in Mexico as unfavorable to health and presumes that solutions—this time to obesity and diabetes, but in the past to underdevelopment, poverty, malnutrition—come from outside and from projects of "modernization" or "improvement." This overlooks that elements of campesino foodways—a plant-based diet, high fiber, with little or no processed foods—are broadly recommended and probably sound and appropriate for any lifestyle. In this strand, some critique peasant diets as a relic that should be retired, not considered appropriate for today's more urban and sedentary lifestyles, which, by the logic of the country's development and entrance into the first world, Mexicans are already living or aspire to live.

A second strand of critique condemns colonial and postcolonial influences alike, and sees the influx of processed foods made by multinational corporations as a threat to Mexico's food landscape and cultural sovereignty. While this perspective sometimes corresponds to radical social justice projects, it also can spill into portrayals of poor and indigenous Mexicans as needy of protection and guidance, vulnerable to the influences of marketing and hyperavailable processed foods. In this paternalistic vision, the poor and indigenous have existed in isolation for millennia, marginalized from such influences and only recently, because of television, roads, trucks, the internet, supermarkets, and mass marketing, are able to purchase and consume manufactured goods. Within these conceptualizations, the poor, left to their own devices, are wont to consume indiscriminately and in excess, and are powerless against the marketing ploys of processed food manufacturers and soda bottlers. They are viewed as so ill-prepared for this influx that they must be protected until they can be sufficiently educated to be responsible consumers.[51]

Both of these strands presume that the root of Mexico's current epidemic of diabetes is in the behavior, or even genetics, of those afflicted. This obscures the integration, even centrality, of rural and indigenous Mexicans in intraregional and even transnational trade and development projects dating beyond the colonial to pre-Columbian periods.[52] It also conceals the social and structural importance of the food system not only in provisioning food but also in shaping and fomenting desire for some kinds of food over others.

We see in the comment by the health ministry representative cited above that both strands are present in her lamentation that having mothers prepare snacks for children at school was worse ("¡Era peor!"). For her, a sope with beans, sour cream, cheese, and lettuce, is not and never could be healthy, and the confidence with which she exclaimed this indicates that for her this is an objective fact. If options are between the packaged muffins, cookies, sweets, and soda sold at stands outside of school and what the mothers prepared, she has little faith in the mothers' capacity to provide a healthier option. In this framing, the handmade, unprocessed foods of the ancestral milpa-based diet—a sope with beans on top—is not superior to ultraprocessed foods. In fact, her comments imply that not only she but anyone should share in appreciating how obviously unhealthy a fried sope might be. In her view, and consonant with the policies of the health ministry, the mothers of schoolchildren, unless aggressively educated, are incapable of providing a healthy snack because of their own poor instincts in assessing the quality of or meeting recommended guidelines for both prepared/processed and home-cooked foods. At the same time, it is mothers who are charged with the overall health of their children and families, and the idea that it is their role, duty, and in their capacity to do so is the last assumption I will explore here.

The same health minister confided in me, "When it's late, and I've just gotten home from work, and I'm exhausted and stressed, all I want is a Coca-Cola and my little bag of Doritos." Here, she makes two assertions. First, she implies that no one can be blamed for making "unhealthy" food choices when they are tired and stressed—everyone can be expected to do something they know is not good for them when their tank is empty. Even someone whose full-time job is precisely the stewardship of the health of the nation can be expected to fall into temptation from time to time—human beings are weak, and/or, Coca-Cola and Doritos are simply too easy and tempting to resist. Second, she implies that people, including herself, should do better most of the time; a small lapse may be insignificant, but day-to-day expectations should be higher. In other words, people should be expected—when they are not tired, stressed, or short on time—to hold themselves to higher standards, to be, in fact, more like her, a fair-skinned, blonde, thin, privileged, highly educated, sharply dressed professional woman whose supper is presumably not Coca-Cola and Doritos every day. In this framing, the etiology of obesity can be traced to people willfully, or out of ignorance or exhaustion, not doing what is good for them, not making appropriate choices in consumption, allowing themselves not occasionally, but regularly, to be tempted by junk food. It also overlooks that increasingly being tired, stressed, and short on time is a condition of everyday life not only of highly paid female professionals in the capital, but of people from all walks of life who today are more likely to work outside the home, commute, and lack extensive family support than in the past.[53] Here, we see her begin to define the role of the health ministry that is implied by this framing: to educate the population to make better choices, to know that Doritos and Coca-Cola are an occasional surrender to temptation, not a regular source of nourishment. The implication is that people simply do not know how to make healthy choices; they cannot be trusted.

The very same anecdote about fried sopes would be repeated to me—more than a year later and while I sat talking in New York, not Mexico City, with a high-ranking professor of epidemiology at Mexico's largest university, who shook her head as she talked, at the ignorance, the lack of commonsense knowledge about nutrition of the Mexican population. This framing of the relationship between a "healthy" diet and the general public, who are portrayed as overweight, poor, and uninformed, echoes the historical framing of those of lower socioeconomic status by elites. Those who are thin are framed not only as aesthetically appealing within global elite cultural norms, but also as smarter, more sensible, and more responsible.[54] Historically, thinness has not been idealized among poorer sectors of the Mexican population, who were more likely than the rich to suffer from the effects of inadequate nutrition and to associate plumpness with having enough to eat, and with vigor and health. As anthropologist Elizabeth Roberts puts it: "Thinness has little purchase when more is more . . . a relational world where food is love and more food is more love and more existence."[55] In the United States, critics of healthism have traced the ways that having a body that matches the elite preference for thinness is not only aesthetically idealized but also conflates social status, lifestyle, wealth, race, health, and moral superiority in ways that are biased, racialized, and that ignore the privileged access those who are white and wealthy may have to "healthist resources": high-quality food, exercise, and protection from poverty, violence, and toxins.[56]

But in Mexico, and many other parts of Latin America, contemporary elite discourses, even when they are quite easily linked to globalization and neocolonial economic relationships with the United States, cannot be divorced from the region's own long and elaborate methods of generating race, class, and status hierarchies. How ironic that overconsumption is so confidently associated today with impoverishment—both economic and educational deficiency—when gout, a kind of arthritis historically associated with gluttony, was the archetypical disease of the wealthy in medieval and early modern times. In other words, we have to think about Latin America's legacy of colonization and the ways that colonial social hierarchies divided those of white European stock from the indigenous, black, and mestizo lower classes. Status was deciphered from and reinforced by skin color, occupation (including eligibility for slavery and servitude), and residence, but also by consumption and body type. Unwillingness or inability to conform to certain European aesthetics around whiteness, height, thinness of nose and of waist, shape of rear end, and so on were used constantly to classify, separate, and police different social groups.

In the colonial period, sumptuary laws and social norms made it not only unaffordable, but even illegal for the poor to consume like the rich, whether wearing velvet that was reserved for nobility or eating foods imported from Europe and reserved for the elite.[57] Later, we see other legal and extra-legal mechanisms for regulating consumption by the poor and nonwhite. Within Mexico's idea of itself as a progressive democracy after the revolution, education and acculturation were framed as the means for preparing the lower classes for citizenship, including norms of appropriate and responsible consumption.[58]

Such hierarchies and social controls on consumption depend wholly on theories of difference that associate social groups with disparate distribution of intelligence, democratic capacity, moral principles, and other assumed characteristics. In fact, the only possible justification for the maintenance of rule by the white sons of the European-born colonists after independence in most Latin American countries was a theory of race that posited that they were better suited to rule, better positioned to make decisions for all, than the numerical majorities they saw as morally, physically, and intellectually inferior.

Dietary theories of racial superiority and bias against rural and low-income communities' foodways preceded the revolution, even if they took on a more robust "scientific" character in the twentieth century. During the Porfiriato, analysts, *los científicos* who advised Díaz, attributed Mexico's underdevelopment to the centrality of corn in the typical family's diet, and promoted wheat as an alternative.[59] This should not come as a surprise from the Eurocentric and elitist Porfirians. It is more surprising, perhaps, and contradictory, when the same idea reappears after the revolution, from self-avowed pro-Indian anthropologist Manuel Gamio, among others.

Mexico's revolution sought to rupture the some of the hierarchies carried over from the colonial period to the postindependence period by advancing a notion of a singular Mexican identity that was Mestizo, a bronze race equipped to rule precisely because of the strength it gained by combining the nation's European and indigenous stock.[60] Even so, the idea of mestizaje fed off racialized hierarchies in which the indigenous could only achieve their potential if "improved" by being mixed with the Europeans.

It was not coincidental, then, that the economic and political program that emerged from such a vision included as a very urgent task the conversion of Mexico's staple diet away from corn and toward wheat. The "progressive" *científicos* who drove the country's domestic policies viewed corn as an inferior source of nutrients, an explanation for what they saw as the languid Mexican capacity for work, while wheat, more heavily consumed in the industrialized northern nations, was thought to be conducive to greater productivity. Warman writes, "Elites used corn as a contemptible object subject to discrimination . . . It shared the fate of the poor, those of mixed race, the unchaste."[61]

In 1935, Gamio, Columbia University–trained student of Franz Boas and a founder of Mexican anthropology, published *Hacia un México Nuevo,* where he argued Mexico's economic vitality was hindered by a lack of "essential" foods in the typical Mexican diet, by which he meant meat, bread, and eggs.[62] A few years later, in the journal *América Indígena,* he published a series of articles in which he lamented the "monotonous" diet of indigenous Mexicans, who subsisted on maize, chile, and beans.[63] This "malnutrition," he surmised, led to high mortality rates, an unproductive countryside, and peasants' purported inability to withstand strenuous physical labor, posing a threat to Mexico's potential for development after the revolution.[64] The radical nation builders of the revolutionary government insisted on indigenous Mexicans as a noble, powerful "race" wanting only a better diet, more protein, and perhaps a little more out-marriage to achieve their full potential and compete with the powerful nations of the north. Gamio's perspectives were part of an overall approach that celebrated indigenous peoples' contributions to Mexico's composite mestizo identity while identifying specific obstacles they were understood to pose to future development that would have to be corrected in the name of the revolution.[65]

Cultural studies scholar Gabriela Méndez Cota notes that both the Porfiriato and postrevolutionary governments conflated the indigenous with the rural and viewed both as "backward" and ill-prepared to advance the national project of modernity. The main difference between them was whether they viewed that inadequacy as innate or behavioral.[66] The latter opens space for "education" as a key role for a state interested in modernizing. As visible and quotidian manifestations of behavior, diet and hygiene were objects of sustained attention. Foods like *chapulines* (grasshoppers), maguey worms, *pulque* (fermented maguey sap), algaes, and other foods were looked down upon as irredeemably "Indian" foods.[67] If, for the revolutionary government, the indigenous were the stuff of which Mexico's prosperity would be built, their fuel had to be bettered to overcome what was imagined to be centuries of malnutrition and lethargy of the body and mind.

Later versions of this, what Pilcher calls the "tortilla discourse," insisted that it was not the nutritional quality of corn, but its low productivity that recommended its replacement by wheat. As discussed earlier, the supposed efficiency of large-scale, industrial cultivation of corn and wheat was used as an argument against subsistence farming. Corn would never actually be replaced by wheat, but wheat consumption was still indelibly associated with progress, whiteness, upper-class status, and city dwellers.[68] Of course, the idea that Mexico's indigenous people were in any way lacking a strong work ethic when it was they and working-class mestizos, not the Spanish colonizers and their descendants, who did virtually all of the physical labor in New Spain and independent Mexico is patently absurd. Nonetheless, the "tortilla discourse" proposed a rationalization and industrialization of Mexico's food system toward certain favored staples. Wheat, along with greater mechanization of all agriculture, as well as the insertion of Mexico's labor force into urban sectors, would liberate them from the tyranny of malnutrition and poverty thought to be endemic to the rural sphere. Such an emphasis on production and not social organization took attention away from inequalities and discrimination that persisted through and after the revolution, and to the present day. These views enable later generations of "revolutionary" leaders who assumed leadership of the ruling political party and stewardship of its legacy to explain persistent poverty not as a consequence of structural inequalities but of cultural anachronisms and inefficient archaic systems, to be solved by an ever more determined march into modernity.[69]

WOMEN'S LABOR

Bundled with ideas about indigenous, rural, and poor people's readiness for modernity are ideas about women and the value accorded the labor roles they have been given or assumed. It is clear that women's increased labor force participation in both Mexico and the United States, in different ways and different periods, is inseparable from dietary transition. Schlosser, among others, has thoroughly explored the association between futuristic technology and women's liberation forged by corporations in the United States in the 1950s. In the Jetsons-like home of the future, women would simply push a button and out would pop steaming hot meals for their families. The US industrialized food system cannot be separated from a utopian (even Marxist) vision of a future without labor.[70] This vision emerged from a specific political and historical context in which the chemical and manufacturing industries searched for new activities after the boom of weapons-making in World War II. In Mexico, as we've seen, the sequence and timing is different, and the rise in importance of transnational food corporations and prepared foods followed different paths; nonetheless, some of the associations carry over.

In Mexico City, in 2014, when I asked whether it was safe to assume that with the elimination of kiosks and carts selling processed foods outside of school, children would bring food from home instead, the health ministry representative told me quite confidently, "There's always a mom." Perhaps in response to a skeptical expression on my face, she then added, "Or another woman." In other words, nutritional health, and by extension prevention and maintenance of diet-related illness in Mexico, is in the hands of women. Boero writes, "One does not have to dig far below the surface to find a distinct trend of 'mother blame' in common sense and professional understandings of both the causes of and interventions into this 'epidemic of childhood obesity.'" As they are usually charged with the preparation, regulation, and purchase of food for their children, mothers—working mothers in particular—are held responsible for children's "poor" eating patterns and their assumed-to-be related "obesity."[71]

This is not a new concept. We can go back to Mexico's 1908 education law, just before the revolution, which posited that it was "indispensable to modify the diet to which [the lower classes] are accustomed" by mandating cooking classes aimed at improving and refining popular diets as the minimum—and sometimes maximum—recommended education for young women.[72] Hygiene campaigns were common in the early twentieth century—offering a socially acceptable domain for women's activity outside of the home while reinforcing their "expertise" and "natural" relationship to home and healthful habits.[73] Social hygiene campaigns in the 1920s and 1930s were designed to "'modernize' and 'civilize' the poor, but also to equip them with the attitudinal wherewithal to manage their own destinies, 'free' of state dependency but subordinated to the discipline of the market."[74]

In her analysis of Oportunidades, sociologist Maxine Molyneux describes the program's "capabilities approach," in which the "no longer passive recipients of state handouts become active participants in meeting the costs of development." This "co-management of risk" assumes "the individual has to make responsible provision against risks (through education and employment)[;] the family, too, must play its part (through better care), while the market (through private interests) and the community (through decentralization 'co-responsibility' and the voluntary sector) are all involved in the decentering of expectations of welfare from the state."[75] Underlying the assignation of responsibilities are gendered and maternalistic notions of the appropriate distribution of responsibility and locations of need.

Within this model, driven by market logics and neoliberal economic and social policy, citizens are imagined to be empowered and capable (both economically and in terms of skills) to choose the best solution to their financial, health, social, labor, and other challenges.[76] Even though Mexico's social, economic, and political structure has been radically altered since NAFTA, solutions to the current problem of diet-related illness are ostensibly still to be found in an old-fashioned and patriarchal distribution of labor that assumes that it is mothers who have the time, the availability, and the ability to control every bite of food their families consume.

LIZARDS AND TORTILLAS

There is a small, horned lizard endemic to the arid region of the Mixteca region in Puebla state that likes to sit in the shade cast by desert plants during the heat of the day. It is said that a girl who can hold one of these lizards in the palm of her hand without it escaping will make a good wife, with hands well-suited to the art of making tortillas from ground corn masa. Making tortillas is the archetypal role of Mexican housewives. The task is seen as so monotonous, repetitive, and labor intensive that it requires someone who is not afraid of work—implying that more than skill, tolerance of tedium and willingness to be tethered to the kitchen are required. But making tortillas is historically so crucial to everyday life and the basic diet of households that it is imbued with tremendous symbolic value and esteem. Zapotec research participants refer to the daily preparation and consumption of household meals as *mantenimiento,* describing both the value of sustaining the physical organism of family members and the role that meals play in bonding family members to one another and within cultural norms, values, and practices.[77]

Even though, as in most patriarchal societies, men in Mexico have historically been credited with doing the "hard" work, while women's labor is viewed as involving less skill and stamina, women's labor has traditionally been plenty strenuous. The production of tortillas for an average household prior to mechanical grinding of corn required about forty hours of labor per week, including nixtamalization of corn with mineral lime, grinding of corn, kneading of masa, and hand shaping and cooking of tortillas. This does not include all of the other aspects of production and procurement of food (women often were in charge of vegetable gardens, chickens, etc.), and cooking, which are often labor intensive, including daily preparation of fresh and cooked salsas, soups, stewed vegetables, meats and beans, and more.

For wealthier families, social status has historically been associated with having sufficient domestic help to accomplish these basic tasks, along with the elaboration of sophisticated multicourse menus. When humble families comment about a girl's ability to "make tortillas" to assess the marriageability of a son's love interest, they refer to tortillas literally, but also to a woman's ability and willingness to do housework generally. Historically, most populations in Mexico have been patrivirilocal, with women joining the household of their husband's families upon marriage. So, the heavy domestic labors of a multigenerational extended family household have typically rested on the shoulders of unmarried daughters and daughters-in-law, with the mother-in-law as administrator and often taskmaster.

The mechanization of tortilla production was a linchpin for the imagined liberation of middle-class women, who were at the time still expected to make tortillas by hand for their family's midday meal, a factor perhaps as consequential as any other in explaining the slow pace of women's workforce integration. Wealthy women never really made their own tortillas, but the centrality of tortillas and ideas about them needing to be fresh still governed notions of what constituted a meal and determined many of the labor arrangements within households.[78]

Industrial grinding of corn and later the invention and proliferation of tortilla factories partially freed women from the servitude of household food preparation. But even with machine-ground corn widely available, making fresh tortillas or buying them fresh from a local tortillería to accompany a hot family meal implies a level of labor and availability at home that is incompatible with most paid labor outside of the home. As in many other industrialized nations, in Mexico, women's labor participation has changed faster than cultural norms about women's roles. In Mexico today, while women's labor force participation (at 45 percent) is lower than the international median, about 50 percent, and the United States at 55 percent, many moms are working, with 25 percent of them single heads of household.[79]

But we see that even when women work outside of the home and often commute long distances, there is still an implicit assumption that women are in charge of and responsible for the diets of their families. Such assumptions rest on increasingly rare patriarchal family structures not fully compatible with contemporary living and working arrangements. Families are less likely today to include a multigenerational team of women engaged full time with household maintenance. Even though society has changed around them, it is still mothers who are held responsible for any effect those changes may have on their children's health.

In an article entitled "A Plea for Culinary Modernism," Rachel Laudan argues that the contemporary hankering for a preindustrial food utopia relies on romantic and invented assumptions about the past, when only the rich could be sure to have enough, and the poor led short, undernourished lives, limited to the monotonous and often insufficient diet available locally and subject to all of the vagaries of weather, politics, land tenure, and more.[80] Processing of food has been key to human survival and flourishing, with technologies like fermentation and pickling allowing foods to be preserved and eaten long after fresh foods would rot. Further, while once only nobility could consume products brought from far away—whether chocolate, spices, wines, preserved fruits, or coffee or tea sweetened with sugar—advances in industrialization certainly democratized consumption in ways few of us would be willing to give up. For those of us living in temperate climates, would we be willing to eat only food that is grown locally without olive oil, coffee, pepper, vanilla, or chocolate brought to us from other latitudes?

If a line is to be drawn marking the sweet spot on the spectrum between preindustrial and industrial food, when and where? When Mexican women kneeled over *metates* for several hours a day, hand grinding corn? Or when the corn could be industrially ground, but tortillas were still made by hand, one by one? If buying freshly made tortillas fresh out of a tortillería's electric press is OK, is it only when the corn is no longer freshly ground but comes from a sack of ground corn flour, Maseca, that we draw the line? What is gained and what is lost in the march toward the industrialization of food?

In the rural community of Santo Tomás Tlalpa, women queue up at one of four corn mills before dawn to grind corn for the day's tortillas, but Elena is not one of them. Sometimes, as the sun rises, she can be found having breakfast at a truck stop in northern Mexico, Texas, or Louisiana. Other times, she might be at her sister-in-law's Bronx, New York, apartment, or at home rushing to get her younger children off to school. Elena and her husband Samuel possess visas enabling them to routinely enter the United States. The visas enable them to enjoy a degree of mobility relatively unparalleled in their rural community. Talk to anyone in this community, and they will tell you that they have a close family member in the United States, probably the Bronx, and often they have themselves spent time there. Elena's neighbor Ana and her daughter Sonia returned just a couple of years ago to Santo Tomás Tlalpa. Sonia was born in New York City, compelling her classmates to call her "La Gringa," and not affectionately. Their neighbor, Estela, has five brothers in New York, and she herself returned several years back, leaving her ex-husband there. Estela's younger sister, Beatriz, has not migrated, but she is able to continue studying in a professional institute at the age of nineteen because her migrant brothers pay the tuition for her. Samuel's sister, María, married to Beatriz and Estela's brother, lives in the Bronx and has two children, Santiago and Lorena.

Elena and Samuel, like everyone else in Santo Tomás Tlalpa, work onyx, a stone that occurs in shades of pink, vanilla, or black, and is endemic to this region. Some dig up the crude rocks from a mine at the top of the hill that lies behind the town. Others work the onyx after it has been mined, crafting an infinite variety of objects, from expensive countertops and tables, to lamps, candleholders and chess sets, to roughly hewn little figurines of dogs or frogs that are popular among children. Others in town engage in marketing and sales, and have showrooms along the main road, competing for the business of the few tourists who come through. Elena and Samuel have a workshop in their home, and they also have a store down on the road, but they hire workers for most tasks, because more often than not Samuel is away, traveling to or from the Bronx. Samuel's main enterprise is a *paquetería* business—once a month, or so, he puts a sign on his front gate and a post on Facebook announcing his next departure for New York. His neighbors bring their homemade *mole,* bread, chiles, cheese, dried herbs, onyx handcrafts, and other items and he packs them all in large suitcases. He flies to New York, staying with his sister; the relatives of his customers in Puebla know to find him at her apartment, and they gather there to receive their care packages from family members back home. He usually has been asked to purchase a vehicle, often a used pickup truck, for someone who can't travel, so after a week or two, he drives back, taking three to five days to make the journey. Sometimes, the vehicle needs to be rushed, or occasionally he needs to bring two vehicles, and that is when Elena will join him in the Bronx; together, they drive back home, taking turns driving around the clock, or driving in a caravan, with Elena leading the way.

When Samuel makes the trip solo, Elena holds down the home front and takes care of their five children. Their eldest daughter is away at culinary school in Acapulco, to the west in the state of Guerrero. The eldest son is in high school, and the next daughter is in middle school; they travel daily to Tehuacán, about thirty minutes on a regional bus. The two youngest children are still in the elementary school in town. Before Samuel's mother passed away in 2014 due to diabetes-related kidney failure, she did most of the food preparation. As I described in chapter 1, I sat in her kitchen and watched her roast chiles and tomatoes over an open flame, smash them in a stone molcajete, and serve the freshly made salsa with a delicious assortment of meat, beans, vegetables, tortillas, and cheese. Elena states that she's not a good cook (although I beg to differ) and tells me she avoids it when possible. As her marriage is based on rather egalitarian values of shared labor, her reluctance to cook is not an issue in their relationship. Like a growing number of mothers in Mexico, she does not spend every day standing at the stove, although when she can, she makes a hot meal of stewed zucchini and tortillas, or eggs and *tetechas*, a local edible plant, for her children to eat as their midmorning meal at the primary school. She is utilitarian in her cooking, she tells me; it does not give her much enjoyment, and for her, tortillas may be an afterthought—picked up at the local mill or forgotten with many meals. As a family, they enjoy driving to Tehuacán to do their weekly shopping, stopping for a meal at a restaurant on the way home. Like many Mexican families today, the older model of a multigenerational extended family living under one roof is no longer their reality. As a result, what constitutes a meal for them may not be "traditional."

With more money than time, they often rely on prepared foods. The children grab milk and cereal or a granola bar as they head for school. This family has devised a routine and division of responsibilities that works for them and is based on mutual respect and commitment, as opposed to patriarchal divisions of labor. Still, according to ideas prevalent in Mexican policy and public discourses, Elena is the one who determines the health and well-being of her family. Whether or not she likes cooking or her schedule permits the time to do it, it is her responsibility to make sure not only that her children and husband are well-nourished, but also that they are healthy and avoid chronic disease. This centering of the responsibility for the well-being of her family—in the day-to-day and in the long term—on the shoulders of Mexican mothers decenters the role of the state in supporting families amid shifting economic and social roles.

Charging mothers with the responsibility for correcting problems in diet for their children, themselves, and other family members, but at the same time implying that the same mothers are not capable of such interventions without extensive education in nutrition and the "correct" diet, is not an effective strategy for confronting obesity. On the contrary, the market-oriented reforms of Mexico's economic and political system have made traditional, if patriarchal, family structures ever more precarious. International and regional migration, the deskilling of manufacturing jobs using the labor of young women (for their presumed dexterity, docility, and relatively lower wages), and an overall restructuring of the economy away from subsistence agriculture mean that fewer families than ever before have a mom at home as is thought to be required to take charge of the task of stemming the spread of diet-related illness.[81] Like most people facing a surfeit of availability, Mexicans have demonstrated an appetite for hyperpalatable processed foods and sweetened beverages, even when they cost more or buying power is reduced.[82] Individual behavior clearly plays a role at the level of the shopping cart and the plate: while it is clear that no one is literally forcing shoppers in the supermarket to select sweetened cereal and high-fat chips and crackers, it is also true that the available choices are constrained.[83] Policies that do not address the systemic changes that have increased the availability and lowered the cost of sugar-sweetened beverages and high-energy, high-calorie foods, while decreasing the availability and raising the cost of unprocessed basic foods and small-scale agriculture, are unlikely to succeed in stemming the rise in chronic diseases—although they may succeed in deflecting the blame.

6 Diabetes

THE DISEASE OF THE MIGRANT?

Mis hermanos, la mayoría están allá, y pues mi jefecita está enferma porque son mis hermanos y de ella son sus hijos. Y le digo, "Mamá, pues si te hablan por teléfono, no te sientas mal. Porque tú estás acá con nosotros, acá nos ves. Pero ellos, te imaginas cuantos años están allí."

Le digo, "Bueno, no, tú, por mis hermanos, también mis hijos están allí. Y pues, debe uno de pensar si se fueron es porque algo van a hacer." Entonces, mi jefecita, se ha enfermado ahorita más de lo debido porque pues busca a sus hijos, a mis hermanos. Y aunque le hablan, y aunque le mandan dinero, para nosotros como padres lo más hermoso es ver a un hijo presente . . . Pero yo lo veo que es más bonito tener a los hijos o verlos aunque sea cada mes, cada dos meses. Y estos que se han ido ya tienen más de quince años.

Y supuestamente, aunque los oímos por teléfono no es igual. No es igual porque pues, nada más les oímos de palabra. Y los que están acá pues, aunque no están con nosotros, están casados pero cada ocho días o en la semana: "Qué haces, Papá?

"Aquí estoy, pásele, hijo." Comparte uno aunque sea un taco, aunque un abrazo se da uno, aunque sea un saludo, y los que están lejos, se saluda uno pero es de diferente manera. No es igual como tenerlo de cerca.

Y todo eso, a nosotros, no, pues, a mi esposa al principio, sí, le afectó también. A mí también me afectó un poco, pero fuimos buscando la forma de sobrevivir esa pena.

> Y ahora que ya pasaron los años, pues nos hablan, nos marcan, nos hablan, pues ya vivimos en otro modo diferente. Porque nos vamos acoplando a que de por sí no están. Cuando se fue el segundo de mis hijos, se llama Juan, llegaba de trabajar y era todos los días que cenábamos juntos. Y me decía mi esposa, "Vente. Vamos a cenar."
>
> "Espérate . . . que llegue Juan."
>
> Y este llegaba con su bicicleta, "Ahorita vengo."
>
> "¿A dónde vas?" "Ahorita vengo, cinco minutos." Se salía a la calle, se iba, y regresaba a los cinco minutos.
>
> Y cuando se fue, yo llegaba en la tarde, "Vamos a cenar."
>
> "Espérate." O sea, se hace una costumbre entre hijos y padres de que hay que cenar juntos, que hay que platicar, aunque era nada más como nosotros decimos aquí en el pueblo, nada más platicamos puros chismes. Pero sirve de mucho porque hay convivencia entre los hijos y padres. Pero cuando se fue, se quedó un vacío.
>
> "Vamos a cenar."
>
> "Espérate, ahorita."
>
> Se acordaba y decía, "No viene."
>
> No, es que ya se fue.[1]

In this interview, Don Alberto discusses the cycle of migration in his family and in his town, Malacatepec, Puebla. His brothers left, and his mother, he reports, became sick waiting for them. When sadness overcomes her, he tries to reassure her, but his sons have left, too, living in North Carolina for the past decade. He has grandchildren he has never met. He speaks to them on the phone, but they do not speak Spanish fluently and it is as frustrating for him as he knows it is for them. He reported that both his mother and his wife have suffered health consequences as a result of the separation from their children and grandchildren. The changes brought since NAFTA to Mexico are not simply economic and political. The rise in diet-related illness has not occurred just because the food system has been altered.

FATHER GUSTAVO'S THEORY OF DIABETES

"Diabetes is the disease of the migrant . . . Not just because migrants change the way they eat, but because it is the somatization of pain, trauma and depression." These were the words of Father Gustavo, the so-called *padre de los migrantes* in the state of Puebla, when we sat down to discuss migrant issues and his views gathered from forty-one years of pastoral labor.

Father Gustavo is a tall and imposing man, but he tends to hunch slightly, in the manner of tall people concerned with being at eye level when talking to shorter people. He has an open and friendly face, with gray hair and big, nerdy glasses. He carries a *morral.* This is a term that can be used for a satchel or knapsack. His is woven, handmade, from sheep's wool, the kind of simple bag, sewn on three sides with a simple string strap, sold at every craft market in Latin America. He later sent me his book, *Desde el Morral: Apuntes de un Pastor Popular,* a collection of reflections on his life as a rural priest, and now, representative of migrant affairs for the Puebla diocese. His use of the morral as the organizing principle of his book describes his pastoral philosophy. He writes, "El morral. . . . recoge lo que se necesita para el camino, el tequío, la faena, pero también reparte la semilla. Sólo lleva lo necesario, siempre lo indispensable, lo que puede ser útil" (El morral carries what one needs for the journey, collective work, chores, but it also is used for spreading seeds. It carries only the essentials, what can be useful).[2] In his assertion of the connection between diabetes and sorrow, Father Gustavo is on to something.

Health research has begun to document and investigate the role of cumulative stress and trauma in health outcomes. Whether this stress is framed in terms of social indicators of health, allostatic load, or the body/mind connection, health researchers have begun to document the ways that socioeconomic disadvantage manifests in the body and eventually expresses itself in poor health outcomes. Gabor Maté, a physician who found his conventional Western medical training insufficient for tracing the relationship between the body and the mind, writes and speaks publicly about "when the body says no," the idea that the onset of diseases may be related to unaddressed emotional stress and trauma.[3] He describes a career in primary medicine in which many of his patients reported an onset of chronic disease that coincided with trauma or extreme stress. He notes that having unrushed and unscripted conversations with patients about their current emotional state, roles in their families, histories of trauma, and other significant life events, and interpersonal dynamics revealed connections relevant to their physical ailments. He argues that those connections offer better ways to understand and treat his patients' illnesses than the isolated and symptom-oriented method of inquiry recommended by his medical training.

Moving the lens beyond the individual to social groups, scholars have tried to trace the effects of "weathering," or cumulative stress produced by the experiences of disadvantage and discrimination faced by groups.[4] Allostatic load is the concept of the sum of the physiological consequences of exposure to chronic stress.[5] Scholars examining these connections seek to identify how it is that stress gets into the body, and what the effect of it is when it takes up residence over a long period of time. Health researchers at Rutgers University, led by Karen D'Alonzo, note: "Mounting evidence suggests that a key factor in the genesis of chronic illnesses among disadvantaged minority groups may lie with cumulative exposure to chronic psychological and physiological stressors through the biobehavioral process of allostatic load."[6]

While it is well established that there are socioeconomic and racial disparities in chronic disease, research into how disadvantage gets into the body is still emergent. In this chapter, I explore the ways that NAFTA contributed to traumas and family separation in its triggering of a mass wave of migration. Then, I will connect trauma and propensity for diabetes with references to recent research on allostatic load and syndemics. I will also trace the debunking of some of the previously dominant theories about a disproportionate genetic risk of diabetes among Mexican populations. The potential migrants have of facing violence on their journey or being disproportionately exposed to violence before and after migration correlates to social inequalities. In that way, when I propose that we think about diabetes and diet-related illness as a kind of structural violence, I am not simply referring to the unfavorable access poor and marginalized communities have to "healthist" resources like fresh, affordable food, exercise, and clean water. I am referring also to the disproportionately high exposure of those communities to trauma. Migration is another consequence of the political and economic restructuring of Mexico after NAFTA, and chronic disease is inseparable from its dynamics.

I came to this study having researched the "immigrant paradox"—the better-than-expected health outcomes of recently arrived immigrants in the United States. Even though recent migrants often have favorable health outcomes in spite of disadvantage, leading often to celebration of their "resilience," longer duration of settlement in the United States is associated with poorer health outcomes, with a decline in outcomes beginning within a few years of immigration.[7] Within immigrant groups, the protective shield of recent immigration and preservation of social ties and lifeways drawn from communities of origin can be challenged by heightened exposure to damaging and dangerous life experiences.

Trends in border control and enforcement, including the closing of avenues previously available for migrants to enter the United States legally or via less hazardous land routes, have meant that unauthorized migrants are often funneled into the most dangerous regions of the border and face risks from organized crime syndicates, exposure, exhaustion, and more.[8] Before experiencing risk in transit, many women cite poverty and violence as reasons for migrating in the first place.[9]

In her book *Syndemic Suffering,* Emily Mendenhall asserts that diabetes is syndemically associated with the trauma of migration. The term "syndemic" "conceptualizes the intersection of multiple epidemics including those both of diseases and epidemic social problems such as poverty."[10] She constructed the VIDDA framework to illustrate the five core dimensions of health and social well-being among the Mexican immigrant women in Chicago with whom she worked: violence, immigration-related stress, depression, diabetes, and abuse. In her study, she found that more than half experienced physical abuse, and one in four experienced sexual abuse. The abuse they experienced was compounded and in some cases precipitated by the structural violence of migration, including labor precarity, poverty, and isolation.[11] She argues that "increasing wealth disparity within our globalized, neoliberal world contributes to the profoundly disparate distribution of burdensome chronic diseases among the poor."[12] Large studies of immigrants and their children have demonstrated the burden and stress of living in fear of deportation and family separation, as well as the attendant everyday stressors of discrimination, workplace exploitation, and poverty that are ubiquitous in immigrant families.[13] Women are highly likely to face sexual violence on the border.[14] As such, migrants, especially women, are disproportionately exposed to trauma and risk. This pioneering work has since been expanded into a proposal for addressing global health inequalities, especially the disproportionate burden of chronic disease in low-income populations.[15]

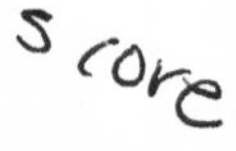

Others point to metabolic and epigenetic responses to stress and trauma. For example, periods of food scarcity in childhood may affect the way the body metabolizes foods, contributing to obesity in adulthood.[16] There are some who believe that Mexican populations are genetically predisposed to diabetes. These theories rely heavily on the "thrifty gene hypothesis" developed by James Neel. He proposed that past experiences of famine change the genes of groups and contribute to higher susceptibility to diabetes mellitus. Later, he came to renounce this hypothesis, even though it continues to influence etiologies of the disease.[17] Neel later concluded that it was rapid "lifestyle changes" that led to higher susceptibility to diabetes—a "thrifty phenotype" perhaps, rather than a "thrifty genotype." As we have established in earlier chapters, "lifestyle changes" are typically driven by structural shifts in the economic and political landscape, making some kinds of behavior and consumption more accessible than others. Neel's retraction of the "thrifty gene" hypothesis points us back to structural violence, in which the inequitable accretion of disadvantage or advantage according to social status, racialization, residency, and more, contributes to some groups experiencing a higher disease burden. A generation ago, such a construction of "groupness" begged a genetic explanation, but today we have a large body of research indicating that the social construction of inequality confers biological consequences, as inequality gets into the body and manifests in disease.

After all, there is no historically stable continuity, genetic or otherwise, in Mexican populations, even those assumed to correspond to "indigenous" groups, as historically national and cultural borders have been drawn and redrawn according to the demands of empire and nation. Anthropologist Michael Montoya debunks assertions of "groupness" in the diverse amalgam of Mexican and Mexican American populations, demonstrating that the categories genetics labs utilize draw more from social than biological conceptualizations of difference and similarity.[18] Changes in lifestyle driven by political and economic factors that marginalize some Mexican and Mexican American communities and place them at higher risk for nutritional transition, stress, and exposure to environmental toxins, for example, may go further to explain chronic disease than shared genetic heritage. It's possible that being treated as Mexican in the United States is as detrimental to health as any potential genetic predisposition, as time in the US is a predictor for onset of disease.[19]

Further, irrespective of population-level consequences of prior food scarcity, individuals' experiences of food scarcity may impact their approach to food. Megan Carney, in her book *The Unending Hunger*, describes the ruptures and the continuities in women's experiences of food insecurity before and after migration.[20] Material scarcity and its association with difficulty in securing what they understood to be a healthy diet were constants even after the women migrated from different parts of Latin America to affluent Santa Barbara, California. Greenhalgh and Carney argue that blaming a lack of education for high rates of obesity among racialized minority groups in the United States obscures structural violence and health disparities.[21]

It is also clear that migrants' diets change when they come to the United States.[22] Their family members who do not migrate also experience dietary change, as they often have increased buying power and access to consumer goods, including processed foods and beverages, and fewer hands dedicated to small-scale agricultural production in rural communities. What is less clear is the complexity of the reasons why and how changes in diets intersect with heightened stress and sometimes trauma to possibly accelerate onset of disease. Migration changes family dynamics and migrant lives in multiple ways. While many people seek through migration to better their own and their children's life chances, looking to improve their financial situation and enable greater access to education, migration has significant costs.

In all of these ways, migration can be both a result and a cause of trauma. The cumulative stress faced by many migrants and their families can affect the ways that their bodies process food and may predispose them to chronic disease. Further, with lower rates of health insurance coverage, chronic diseases among immigrants may be less likely to be diagnosed or treated at onset, instead being detected at more advanced stages, when treatment options are more limited and prognoses less optimistic.

CHANGES IN FOOD HABITS

Migration erodes many social supports migrants may have enjoyed in their communities of origin. Extended kin in many of the households in Mexico that migrants grew up in provided much of the labor associated with meals. No longer is there a base for pooled collective labor to prepare food to be consumed at the family table, or, if many members of a migrant's family have also migrated, they often are working just as many hours and commuting long distances. Conflicting schedules can make it difficult to share meals. Even though many people do eat meals prepared by hand, from scratch, following norms that are sometimes shared across cultural groups, the distance between consumer and producer is often longer.[23]

Migradollars are a key factor in the shift of foodways of migrants and even their families back home who receive remittances. Increased purchasing power can result in an increase in the quantity of food available, but it can also contribute to the consumption of larger quantities of retail and processed foods and fewer homegrown and unprocessed foods. In her 2013 study, anthropologist Marisa Macari found that the routines and rhythms of the lives of Latino migrants in Queens, New York, were largely shaped by work schedules.[24] Many migrants interviewed worked more than eighty hours per week. It was difficult for them to find the time to cook, and many people lived in shared apartments and houses where they did not have easy access to a kitchen or adequate storage facilities to store ingredients or leftovers.[25] Many relied on prepared foods for the bulk of their meals, or ate in a "disordered" way, grabbing a bite on short breaks or even while in transit to work or home at unpredictable times of day.

When I asked migrants to talk about how they navigate life in the United States and tried to care for their health, a vast majority described McDonald's as emblematic of poor food options in their new place of residence. In my study on the experiences of Mexican immigrant women in the public prenatal care system of New York City, I came to refer to this as the "McDonald's hypothesis."[26] Women told me that they observed that the health of people they knew declined with greater duration in the United States (in keeping with scholarly studies finding the same), and said that it had to do with the surfeit of fast-food options, while eating in the ways they did before migration was challenging given their budgets, living situations, work schedules, and the ingredients available in their communities. Public health scholar and anthropologist Peter Guarnaccia and his colleagues found that Oaxacan migrants in New Jersey reported that they ate "meat every day," with increases in consumption of meat following migration related to the hyperavailability and low cost of meat as opposed to the relatively high price of fruits and vegetables.[27] Similarly, one woman told me that in Mexico she was accustomed to feeding her children "*fruta, fruta, todo el día*" (fruit, fruit, all day), but found the prices prohibitive in New York City. When I asked how they defined "healthy" food, many women evoked advice from their mothers and other female kin in their home communities: not too much grease, avoid "cold" foods like pork (referring to humoral properties, not temperature), and eat a lot of fruit.[28] Women with significant experience in the United States health care system echoed advice I heard nutritionists give patients in the prenatal care clinic: roast or steam rather than fry foods, consume low-fat dairy, avoid carbohydrates, and avoid sweets. One woman described a chaotic routine in her home, with one child eating pizza on the way to soccer practice from school and another child demanding the chicken fingers his classmates ate. She said she ended up buying a lot of prepared foods for her children and said this was "typical" of life in New York City, where, she told me confidently, "no one cooks!"

In New York City, migrants are not free from the ideas that influence health messaging in Mexico. Many people—both Mexicans and non-Mexicans—told me that "Mexicans have a big sweet tooth," and that learning to avoid sugar was especially important and difficult for Mexican immigrants. The wife of a Mexican diplomat stationed in New York City volunteered in the prenatal clinic where I conducted research. While I was in the middle of an interview with a woman who was telling me about her daily routine, typically involving a soda at lunchtime, she interrupted to say, "Soda is a sin, a sin of gluttony!"[29] Ideas about the need for Mexicans to constrain their outsized appetites for sugar and about "education" being a solution echoed discourses in Mexico that I discussed in earlier chapters. The structural features of Mexican migration—for example, the fact that few paths to authorized migration have been available to Mexicans since the 1990s, when the bulk of those who migrated to New York City arrived—are overlooked. Migrating without authorization means that much of the population works off the books, with little recourse to minimum wage, meal breaks, sick days, health insurance, and other health-sustaining privileges.

Access to Mexican products was limited in the early days of Mexican migration to the New York area, when fresh tortillas were hard to come by and markets might only stock processed foods that could weather the journey to the northeastern United States from Mexico or be mass-produced here, like candy, snacks, cheeses, and preserved meats. Finding fruits and vegetables to be costly and relatively unappealing, without aroma or flavor, contributed, for many, to a decline in the consumption of fresh foods. Separation from extended family networks and living in crowded conditions with limited or shared access to refrigerators and stoves also may contribute to a decline in home cooking. Knowledge about cooking may not have been fully transmitted by the time the migrant left home, leading to frustrating efforts to make food resembling that which was remembered.

Further, for many migrants, migration was precisely part of an effort to free oneself from the constraints of traditional patriarchal living arrangements. So, eating prepared food, eating out, purchasing instead of preparing food, were sometimes metonyms for making "progress" in one's migration project. All of these contribute to changes in foodways that migrants experience and often accelerate. María Pacheco contrasted the fruits and vegetables available to her in the Bronx supermarkets and corner stores where she shops with the outdoor market where her family bought fresh food in Santo Tomás Tlalpa, Mexico.

> Las verduras no son de temporada, por ejemplo, las naranjas, las sandías, y todo el tiempo hay esa fruta aquí. Y en México, no, porque nosotros a la plaza que íbamos—le decíamos así, plaza—adonde venden todas las verduras y todo eso de temporada, solo había un tiempo que había esa verdura, esa fruta y no había hasta el próximo año que se cosechaban.
>
> Y aquí no. Aquí todo el tiempo uno ve las manzanas bien grandes. Las naranjas. Las sandías, el melón. Todo el tiempo hay.
>
> Entonces yo pienso que eso, son como, que están con químicos todo el tiempo y allá en México no, es totalmente diferente.[30]

María Pacheco's migration story was one of transitions and shifts. Changes in her approach to cooking and eating did not derive only from differences in food availability between the Bronx and her rural Mexican community. When she migrated to New York City to join her teenage sweetheart, he secured her a job at first in a soul food restaurant where he worked filleting fish. Without knowledge of English, she relied on her partner to help her understand the instructions she was given about how to make collard greens and macaroni and cheese. Eventually, when she became pregnant with her first child, she found the work of lifting and carrying the industrial-sized pots to the stove and the sink to be too strenuous, so she left the job.

In each of María's two pregnancies, she was diagnosed with gestational diabetes. She had never heard of anyone suffering from this disease before she migrated, so she depended entirely on guidance from the health care personnel at the public hospital where she received prenatal care. She was given a strict diet by a nutritionist that she followed to the letter. Among other guidelines, she was told to eat a half-cup of cold cereal with a half-cup of milk for breakfast, to eat no tortillas, to bake or steam, not fry, all of her cooked foods, and so on. Then, when she lost weight—during the second trimester of her pregnancy—she was scolded for "endangering" her fetus. Apparently, the diet she had been given was not intended to be followed strictly but more as a series of "guidelines." Even though she was told that her gestational diabetes was because of excessive weight gain and overconsumption of sugar and carbohydrates, when she dramatically decreased her food intake, she was told she had gone too far. In my 2011 book on the experiences of Mexican migrants in New York City's public prenatal care system, I analyze this as an example of "subtractive health care," which treats low-income women as incapable of properly caring for themselves and their pregnancies, and provides guidance that is dangerously diluted and simplified.[31] If we analyze this, too, in light of our understandings of diet-related illness, we can see that María's gestational diabetes is framed and treated as a product of her own behavior and failure to properly care for herself. The facts that her life had been completely transformed by migration, and that the food landscape in which she found herself living was profoundly different from what she had grown up with, were not taken into consideration. Even less remarked upon by health care professionals is the trauma of migration, which separated her from her mother and sister, who would have cared for her in her pregnancies.

She described shopping at a market in her home community featuring local and seasonal produce. If something was not available, such as oranges or melons, it was because it was out of season and would not return until the next harvest. In contrast, she finds all kinds of fruits and vegetables available for sale year-round in the Bronx (even though she lives in an area repeatedly noted to be a "food desert"), but in her view, they lack flavor and are suspiciously unaffected by the season. She surmises that the food must be full of chemicals, and is also wary of the packaged meats and cheeses that seem not to spoil as quickly as they should. For her, the foods available to her in New York are not as appetizing as the foods in her home community, and may be harmful to health, but when she consulted with the nutritionist, it was tortillas she was told to avoid. She was told tortillas (both corn and wheat flour) convert directly into sugar. She described suffering the months of her pregnancy, warming up tortillas for her partner but not eating any herself and feeling that she was never full while she followed the diet she was given. In spite of her efforts, her entire first pregnancy and second pregnancy were treated by the prenatal clinic as "high risk," subjecting her to a higher level of intervention and supervision at every stage. In fact, after the gestational diabetes and bouts of postpartum depression she experienced with both pregnancies, she and her partner decided another pregnancy would be too risky.

If you ask María whether she finds it easier to be healthy in the Bronx or in her home community, she says there is no question. In her home community, she described a lifestyle built around fresh, seasonal foods and home cooking. In New York, one cannot find the same foods, and fruits and vegetables are not as fresh. Meats in New York look good, she said, wrapped in plastic in the supermarket, but lack flavor. One wonders how long they've been sitting there and what chemicals were put on them to keep them from going bad, she said. Schedules, resources, and the appeal of novel foods mean that since migrating, she and her partner ate more snacks, sweets, and take-out, and also followed less predictable schedules of meals. Unlike her home, where her siblings, their spouses and children, and her mother would gather for meals, in New York City, she and her partner, and later, their children, found it difficult to eat together because of conflicting work and school schedules. She blames her gestational diabetes on all of this, and her later efforts to maintain what she considers a healthy weight after having been what she described as effortlessly thin before migration.

But diabetes is not only, or even primarily, a disease faced by migrants. When María had been in the United States about five years, her mother was diagnosed with diabetes. An activist from the same community as hers told me that every third person there suffers from diabetes, and a walk around town indeed reveals many community members who have lost their eyesight, limbs or digits, or walk with canes, signs of damaged toes, feet, or legs due to nerve damage, foot ulcers, and poor blood circulation associated with advanced or untreated diabetes. I already discussed the changing dynamics in María's hometown, in which Walmart and other chain stores have come to dominate. In the case of María's mother, diabetes led to kidney problems, and she required dialysis several times a week. The family paid for this with remittances from María and her family in New York. Luckily, María's sister had moved to Tehuacán, the midsized city a half-hour from Santo Tomás Tlalpa, so their mother moved in with her and could avoid the tiring and expensive regional bus ride every few days for dialysis. The sister also had studied to be a nurse, so the family saved on some routine procedures, like injections, changing bandages, and wound care. But the relocation of María's mother to the city also impacted Samuel and Elena's family back in Santo Tomás Tlalpa, because when she was well, she cooked all of the family meals. When she became ill and eventually moved to Tehuacán, no one had time or inclination to do this, and the five children and two adults left in the home turned more to prepared and processed foods for their meals.

If you ask María why her mother became sick, she will attribute her illness to a broken heart. María describes her relationship with her mother as a symbiotic one, in which they depended on each other. Phone calls helped bridge the distance, but not enough for either of them. When her mother eventually died in 2014, from complications following an amputation and kidney failure, María took to her bed and said she contemplated following her mother to the grave. María's undocumented immigration status made her unable to travel freely, producing a fifteen-year separation between mother and daughter.

While research into the syndemic connections between stress and the body's ability to metabolize and regulate sugar is emergent, these embodied etiologies of migrants and their family members assert connections between heartbreak and diabetes that influence the ways they view the onset of disease, its treatment, and its prognosis. It is incumbent on agencies and public health administrators to expand their approach to noncommunicable disease beyond the narrow confines of diet and exercise and to take into consideration structural factors, including the separation of families by borders and the cumulative effect of stress, discrimination, labor exploitation, poverty, and other kinds of structural violence when addressing chronic disease. In these connections, we can see that the ripple effects of the political and economic restructuring following NAFTA changed more than Mexico's food system. While the rise in availability and affordability of ultraprocessed foods and beverages and the decline in milpa-based foodways are crucial to an understanding of the rise in diet-related illness, we must also take into consideration that the shifts in people's lives are not superficial. NAFTA has not just brought down the cost of a Coca-Cola or extended the distribution networks into the countryside, it has altered the viability of rural ways of life and produced a massive wave of migration, with the corresponding consequence of family separation and trauma. Stress, violence, and trauma have bodily effects that a truly comprehensive understanding of the rise in diabetes must take into account.

7 Nostalgia, Prestige, and a Party Every Day

WATERCRESS

I am standing next to a colleague in my academic department. For an event, we have requested a catered lunch from the college's food service. My colleague is from the Dominican Republic, and as she serves herself salad, she leans over to me and whispers, "There must be a Dominican on the cafeteria staff." She points to the leaves of watercress in the salad: "Only a Dominican would put watercress in the salad." She tells me that watercress is considered a very typical food of the island's countryside, and while you do not see it often in New York, she read it as a coded message, from one compatriot to another: we are here.

Dominican food, like Mexican food, is woefully misunderstood and stereotyped. Dominican restaurants in New York specialize in strong coffee and roasted chicken, stewed beans and fluffy rice, and sweet or savory plantains. A lot of items are fried, and you'd be hard-pressed to find anyone, even a Dominican, who would tell you that Dominican food is "healthy." But when I was teaching a course entitled Latino Health and discussing food and nutrition with my students, one young woman told me that her grandmother travels to New York City from the Dominican

Republic for Christmas with a suitcase full of sweet potatoes and squash. She needs these foods as part of her daily eating and cooking, and she does not trust US-grown sweet potatoes and squash, preferring to pay excess baggage fees so she can bring her own. That anecdote and my colleague's reception of what she took to be a secret message from a Dominican cafeteria worker made me wonder how many people's foodways are cheapened, stereotyped, transformed, and then maligned for their "unhealthiness" in the process of assimilating to the United States. Why, when health advice changes with the seasons, do the diets of people whose food traditions date to long before the current epidemic of noncommunicable disease continue to be reflexively slated for "improvement"?

For me, watercress will always remind me of my Michigan-born grandmother, who as the eldest child of six, was put in charge of family meals as soon as she could reach the top of the stove. I found watercress to be too bitter as a child, but I vividly remember standing at the kitchen counter with my grandmother in Southern California as she made salad every night. For her, there was no dinner without salad, and no salad without watercress. While she chewed on stems of watercress, she would recall walking along the streams in the woods behind her family home in the 1920s, picking the watercress that grew on the banks in the shade.

I was surprised when years later, in a South Bronx apartment, I interviewed a Mixtec-speaking woman from the state of Guerrero, Mexico, as she sat at her kitchen table eating watercress. She was tucking into a bowl of chicken, stewed in a spicy red chile sauce, using her teeth to soften the meat for her toddler, as he sat on her lap. Between bites of chicken, she plucked and ate leaves of watercress from a bunch standing in a bowl of water on the table. I was impressed to see watercress—I think I'd forgotten it existed in the years since eating my grandmother's salads—and I asked her what it was called in Spanish. "*Berro,*" she told me. I asked her if she ate it a lot. She looked at me like I had holes in my head.

How many people would call to mind watercress when asked about "Mexican" or "Dominican" food? How many humble but clearly significant foods are forgotten in the transition to more urban lifestyles or with migration? How impoverished are our conceptualizations of regional and national cuisines without these foods? How much does watercress figure in food nostalgia? Which are the foods we feel nostalgic for? Why?

In Western European literature, the emblematic text on food nostalgia is Proust's meditation on a madeleine, the small pastry his mother gives him with tea that transports him back to his childhood in the French countryside and the home of his aunt.[1] Sense memory is described by Proust as transporting one past logical thought and recollection into something more subconscious. All of his childhood is wrapped up in the small, unassuming pastry, and it washes over him with a single bite, only to retreat beyond his grasp with the second and subsequent bites. But the madeleine, like tamales, discussed below, is a creation of labor and skill. Watercress, in contrast, grows without human intervention at the edge of freshwater streams and rivers in certain climates and contexts. How much of our nostalgia for specific foods is also nostalgia for the contexts in which they were produced? And is nostalgia a product of complicity—what Renato Rosaldo called imperialist nostalgia, a tendency to mourn that which we ourselves have changed?[2] Some date the embrace of corn as a nostalgic symbol of "authentic" Mexican culture to the 1940s, when industrial agriculture expanded the cultivation of sorghum, wheat, and other crops for animal feed at the expense of corn.[3] The bundling of notions about skills and knowledge, especially knowledge that is transmitted across generations, may give more value to one's grandmother's mole or tamales than to the watercress, avocado leaf, or verdolagas served along with them or used in a recipe. The specificity of a complex social context for food production—cultivating and harvesting ingredients grown nearby, sharing labor among family members, embedding food production within ritual calendars of festivals and feasts—can be obscured when a food is decontextualized. It is precisely decontextualization that enables food to be appropriated and commodified. Then, somehow, it does not matter who has made the food, or where, or even what specific ingredients it contains, as long as it evokes, through other means, such as flavor profiles, feelings of nostalgia.

Those of us more than a generation removed from elaborate handmade food traditions may have nostalgia precisely for the processed foods and beverages I've been critiquing in this book. I experience food nostalgia for my grandmother's watercress salad (which I eventually grew to love in spite of my childhood aversion to bitterness) and her "Spanish rice," but also for Kraft macaroni and cheese, Fun Dip candy, and A&W root beer.

Some are willing to spend $5 on a small bottle of "Mexican Coke" in the United States because it's made with "real sugar" as opposed to the high-fructose corn syrup that replaced sugar in Coca-Cola manufactured in the United States sometime between my childhood and my adulthood. "Mexican" Coke tastes, for some of us, like "American" childhood. The standards and criteria we use to rate and value food and foodways are acquired over a lifetime and are socially constructed, so what we remember enjoying as children may be very different from what we come to appreciate as "good" food as adults.

The rupture of connections between the production, preparation, and consumption of food means that we can long for food separate from the contexts of its preparation, and thus may crave foods that will not or cannot be prepared by the same people in the same contexts in which we remember them from the past. Alternatively, we can appreciate a home-cooked meal, of any kind, because it is the connection we crave, not any particular ingredients or recipes. In this chapter, I look at the role of nostalgia in eating practices. Eating has never been entirely about availability and scarcity. Instead it is a repository for cultural expression, and for aspirations. I examine the efforts people are willing to make to eat the foods they long for in the ways they remember. Then I will examine the ways that food and beverage corporations use nostalgia as yet one more marketing tool to locate and appeal to specific demographic niches, to cultivate desire for their products, and to mitigate countervailing information when peddling products that people have been told are bad for their health.

Paqueteros, the bustling microindustry of small-scale package shippers, like Samuel, described in the last chapter, deal in a brisk trade that is characterized by the south to north shipment of mole, bread, and herbs, and the north to south shipment of electronics, sneakers, and other consumer goods. In Mexico, people insist that each village has its own typical salsa, mole, or other sauces. People who migrated to the northeastern United States from Mexico thirty years ago describe being unable to find tortillas, except occasionally in cans. Today, in most metropolitan areas in the United States, it is possible to find fresh tortillas and many of the basic ingredients for Mexican cooking. Often niche markets have developed so that one can buy even not-so-basic ingredients like mole paste, fresh cheese, countless varieties of dried chiles, limes, and tomatillos. So, paqueteros are not transporting mole or salsa because none can be found, but rather transporting a client's mother's walnut bread, or a grandmother's mole because of sense memories that give these specific items value and because they offer a means of connection to distant people and places. Knowing someone made a food while thinking of family members who migrated can bring value to those who live too far away to sit down at the same table.

Migration intensifies nostalgia for specific places and tastes, especially when immigration law prevents free circulation between places of origin and destination, and immigrants invest no small amount of effort in obtaining or re-creating their preferred foods. Medical sociologist and anthropologist Anahí Viladrich has found in her research that "nostalgic inequality" leads to feelings of nostalgia for some Hispanic migrant women manifesting in the consumption of staple foods that are not conducive to health but seen as more expressive of sentiments and easier to access than fruits and vegetables.[4]

But the opposite of nostalgia may be aspiration, and we can also see that efforts to achieve economic prosperity and the trappings of middle-class respectability have their own tastes and smells. Mechanization and industrialization of food production have always been associated with aspirations for modernity and development. The march of "progress" has continued, and in Mexico today, being a "modern" person for many is associated with shopping in supermarkets, buying prepared and processed foods, and eating fast food. Convenience may be king not just because of its association with modernity, but also because demanding work schedules or split shifts make it necessary. Economic changes have transformed food items like soda, cookies, and cakes from the occasional splurge to everyday staples. Smaller families, faster paced lifestyles, and migration have made the "Standard American Diet" (SAD) a norm for families in and beyond the United States.

WILLIAMS-SONOMA TAMALES

The ad in the Williams-Sonoma catalog circulated in time for the holidays. Order by December 20th for Christmas Eve delivery. Thirty-six chicken tamales from Texas Tamale in Houston, for only $54.95, plus

Figure 10. Williams-Sonoma tamales. Ad from webpage.

shipping and tax: "The perfect balance of soft masa and tender chicken with a bit of a kick from piquant chilies." The whole package of frozen tamales weighs in at eighteen ounces, total, meaning that they must be bite-sized, even though the description does not indicate it. Social media erupted in a roar of derision. Snarky tweets and Facebook rants followed. Meanwhile, in New York City, street vendors sell full-sized tamales (approximately eight ounces) at about $1.50 each.

Many of the complaints about the Williams-Sonoma tamales centered on co-optation. Williams-Sonoma appropriates a humble ethnic food item and, at a significant markup, profits by it in ways that defy some of its core associations. Tamales are labor intensive to make. The laborious and time-consuming process of making them is often shared, with the communal production of tamales an aspect of holiday celebrations in and of itself.

While *abuelitas* are often credited with holding the key to secret recipes or techniques for making their masa fluffier, or their filling tastier, the assembly of tamales allows for many, even small, hands to have a role in their production.[5] They are also supposed to be plentiful, and seasonal. Today one can buy fresh, hot tamales from two different vendors at the east and west entrances of the subway at Ninety-Sixth Street and Broadway every morning, among hundreds of other locations in New York City alone. Like *habichuelas con dulce,* sweet beans, eaten by Dominicans on the island around the Christmas holidays, tamales have become an everyday food, available year round. But, they still are associated with skill and technique, "know-how" that is passed down through matrilineal lines of kinship.

For many Mexican families, migration and the division of families by the border has meant that many people are no longer able to have their mother's or grandmother's foods at the holidays. Some families no longer hold the knowledge for making foods like tamales, and must purchase them if they wish to eat them. To find someone who grew up in the same region and sells tamales made by hand can be a substitute—not quite the same, but better than nothing. However, the next step, to buy frozen bite-sized tamales from Williams-Sonoma at a massive markup is a step too far for many in terms of the appropriation and commodification of the tamal. The language in the advertisement assumes a certain degree of knowledge—referring to masa, instead of dough—but an Anglophone, not Hispanophone audience, as chiles are referred to as "chilies," and tamales are glossed as "a real Tex-Mex treat."

Tamales are, then, severed from the family labor economy that has long produced them. Those of us living in places with large Mexican populations can buy homemade substitutes and avoid the anonymous, boutique, elite version offered by Williams-Sonoma at a premium—not plentiful, not abundant, not made by someone whose face we can see. How far can food be taken out of its social context and retain meaning? Like Redzepi's space-age tortillas, discussed in the second chapter—made by hand on ancestral equipment, but otherwise cleaved from all socially specific meaning—expensive bite-sized tamales sold on the internet make it so anyone with the means can access tamales, but the meaning historically imbued by their production is lost.

TAMALE-GATE

On February 2, 2015, McDonald's Mexico managed to offend an entire country with one Facebook post. A Facebook post promoting the McBurrito featured a picture of the food item, accompanied by text that read "Tamales are a thing of the past" and a status update that read, "If it's your turn to make the tamales, you know what to do." The status update refers to the celebration of Candlemas (La Candelaria), a feast day celebrated on February 2, and a traditional end to the Christmas season in Mexico and some other Catholic-majority countries. In Mexico, the person who gets the *muñequito,* or little plastic doll in the *rosca de reyes,* the sweet eggy bread eaten on Three Kings' Day, January 6, has to make tamales for Candelaria. The status update reveals that McDonald's Mexico was not simply being flat-footed in timing its critique of tamales for February 2; it simultaneously called on cultural tradition and offended it.

Social media and news media exploded. *Sin Embargo,* a progressive news source, headlined "McDonald's Eats Its Words." Fusion network posted on Facebook, "Tamales are a go-to comfort food. Don't mess with Tamales, McDonald's."[6] Twitter exploded with critiques, many of them threatening that whoever critiques tamales picks a fight with all of Mexico. English-language media, including the Associated Press, the *Guardian,* and ABC News hopped on board. But this post, which was almost immediately removed and followed by a speedily issued apology, touches on the issues at the heart of changing food practices in Mexico. It implies a sobering state of affairs summed up by the actual caption of the post: Tamales are a thing of the past.

Marketers advertise fast and processed food using multiple strategies, sometimes alternating between tradition and modernity. Williams-Sonoma evokes festivity and tradition, at a markup, with high-priced tam-

Figure 11. McDonald's Mexico Facebook post, February 2, 2015.

ales that are, in many ways, just as far from the modes of production of traditional tamales as a McBurrito. McDonald's, in contrast, paints tamales as an anachronism. Even though McDonald's references the feast calendar of the Catholic Church by advertising McBurritos on Candelaria, the post implies that it is unnecessary to celebrate with foods "from the past."

Tamales may have been eaten as long ago as seven thousand years. Tamales and tortillas are among the most archetypal uses of corn. Both are based on corn that has been nixtamalized, and ground to make *masa*, or corn dough. The root *tamal-* in Nahuatl means "unformed corn." Tamales are a cornhusk-wrapped bundle of masa filled with meat, cheese, beans, chiles, and other combinations of savory or sweet fillings, and are eaten throughout Mesoamerica. But their far-reaching history does not diminish their contemporary popularity.

They are labor intensive, requiring the preparation of the corn masa, the fillings, the lard that keeps them from falling apart, and the corn husk that is used to wrap the bundle, all of which have their own multistep preparation, before the wrapped bundles are steamed. Purists insist on freshly ground locally sourced corn, home-rendered lard that has been vigorously beaten to a fluffy texture, and carefully prepared and arranged fillings.[7] Preparation of tamales for a feast (Christmas and Candelaria being the most prominent in Mexico, although they are now a staple for Thanksgiving for many in the United States) can be a multiday affair involving multiple cooks.

Tamales are associated with festivities. Scholars of festival have long theorized that communal celebrations offer "time out of time" in which people are able to step out of their day-to-day, mundane existence, and live momentarily in another space-time dimension.[8] Tamales—with their labor intensiveness, collective preparation, and association with feast days—should, by definition, never be "a thing of the past." But McDonald's Mexico in its post suggests that they have gone out of fashion, that even for the customary celebration of Candelaria, a "McBurrito" is not just a satisfactory, but a desirable, modern alternative.

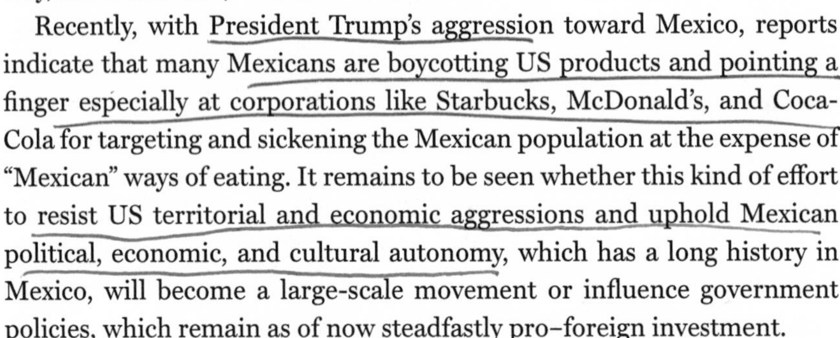

Recently, with President Trump's aggression toward Mexico, reports indicate that many Mexicans are boycotting US products and pointing a finger especially at corporations like Starbucks, McDonald's, and Coca-Cola for targeting and sickening the Mexican population at the expense of "Mexican" ways of eating. It remains to be seen whether this kind of effort to resist US territorial and economic aggressions and uphold Mexican political, economic, and cultural autonomy, which has a long history in Mexico, will become a large-scale movement or influence government policies, which remain as of now steadfastly pro–foreign investment.

POZOL AND AMARANTH

When the Spanish arrived in what is today Mexico, they noticed the frequent use of amaranth by the Mexica people. The seeds were popped and with the syrup of the agave plant as glue, shaped into effigies that were consumed in homage to the dead during festivals. While the Spanish had their own attachment to food symbolizing the body of their religious icon, the Eucharistic host was Christian, and amaranth effigies were cast by them as pagan and diabolical. Nonetheless, the consumption of amaranth continued, eventually becoming associated with the Day of the Dead, Mexico's celebration of the All Souls and All Saints feast days of the Catholic religious calendar. Amaranth effigies, sugar skulls, and *pan de muertos* (bread of the dead) are representations of the deceased and part of ritual offerings on altars. Amaranth is still frequently eaten in *alegrías,* the molded cakes of the popped seed with agave that are ubiquitous in Mexican street fairs. Amaranth is a high-protein, low-carbohydrate seed that costs little in Mexico, prompting some to promote it as a "superfood." Granted, the idea of a superfood is problematic because, like narrow dietetics, it reduces complex foodways to single nutrients and products that can somehow, on their own, be divorced from the social contexts of production and preparation, conferring health and well-being. But amaranth is surely better than ultraprocessed snacks made of simple carbohydrates and lots of chemicals. Without government assistance or promotion, a few are seeking to make it more widely available and to diversify its use in other preparations as a response to highly processed sugary snacks.[9]

Likewise, activists and researchers are promoting the resurgence of traditional beverages like *agua de limón con chía* (chia-seed lemonade), and *pozol,* a drink made from fermented corn masa. The project entitled Más Sanos Comiendo como Mexicanos (It's Healthier to Eat like Mexicans), launched in San Juan Chamula, near Zinacantán, Chiapas, seeks to raise the popularity of traditional foods and awareness of the health benefits of eating them and avoiding sugar-sweetened sodas and other industrial foods and beverages.[10] Promoting food sovereignty as a means of cultural preservation and a way to improve health, the project seeks to displace soda's claim to being a beverage of choice, promoting the flavor, healthfulness, and cultural relevance of pozol. It's possible that nostalgia can be a vehicle for promoting such efforts and countering the mainstream marketing of processed foods. While exciting and innovative, so far these kinds of campaigns have not been taken up or promoted by the federal government, which continues to emphasize that solving Mexico's diet-related illness epidemic requires multifaceted solutions, without actually investing in a different kind of food system.

ANACHRONISM AND RITUAL

We see throughout Mexico, in the early twenty-first century, an effort by corporations and the public sectors they influence to characterize "traditional" food as anachronistic, out of step with today's lifestyles. If we imagine a similar ad in the United States suggesting that instead of turkey, families consider serving McDonald's burgers, or any fast food, on Thanksgiving, we can perceive the absurdity of this effort to attack tamales even as a festive, special-occasion food. Not only are Mexicans being urged to shift their day-to-day routine toward processed and prepared foods, foods purchased in supermarkets, and take-away, but they are also being influenced to shift the way they celebrate.[11]

McDonald's has been identified as the most recognizable brand the world over, more well known than Coca-Cola, even.[12] But what is the significance of McDonald's in the story of changing foodways and food systems? Schlosser chronicles the development of McDonald's business practices in Southern California in the post–World War II period. The company revolutionized food preparation, seeking to minimize worker training, costs, and skills; create an affordable and appealing product that would be the same at every store in which it was purchased; and spread geographically through the selling of franchises. It is the corporation most named when one discusses globalization—and depending on one's perspective, it signifies the best or the worst of business practices. It is also wildly popular. According to survey data, in the United States, 66 percent reported going to McDonald's in the prior week, and no other organization feeds more children daily.[13] Further, it is perhaps the corporation that has had the most significant impact on the restructuring of food systems in Mexico and other countries, within the model of "vertical integration," through which transnational food companies seek to "bring together the entire process of producing, distributing and selling a particular food under its control by buying and contracting other companies and services worldwide."[14] In this way, Schlosser notes, "Instead of importing food, they import entire systems of agricultural production."[15] Corporations like McDonald's influence not only the food that people eat but also the entire food system in the countries in which they do business. Perhaps this is why Bolivia recently ejected McDonald's, becoming only the second country, after Cuba, in the hemisphere without a franchise.[16]

Food systems scholar Corinna Hawkes argues that globalization's impact on food systems has to do with both dietary convergence and dietary adaptation. Convergence: we all eat McDonald's. Adaptation: McDonald's is not the same everywhere. While Big Macs and Happy

Meals might appear on all the menus, burgers topped with avocado in Chile, with chiles in Mexico, and made with vegetarian patties in India are variations and adaptations to local tastes. In the United States, McDonald's and other fast-food chains are associated in food justice discourses with "food deserts," and research has shown that their marketing to minorities and the poor implicates them in the rise in chronic disease.[17] Density of McDonald's is associated by US analysts with socioeconomic marginalization. But in Latin America, and in many other countries around the world, eating at McDonald's is considered prestigious, and is a measure not of marginalization but of economic and spatial integration. Located typically in wealthier sectors of urban centers, McDonald's appeals to desires for upward mobility. It also posits a lifestyle in which family members "eat on the go," with peers, rather than at home, together. Anthropologist Sidney Mintz, in his book *Tasting Food, Tasting Freedom,* writes, "For many people, eating particular foods serves not only as a fulfilling experience, but also as a liberating one—an added way of making some kind of a declaration. . . . this act of choosing to consume apparently can provide a temporary, even if mostly spurious sense of choice, of self, and thereby of freedom."[18] Corporations play on these ideas. McDonald's motto "I'm loving it" and Coca-Cola's "Destapa la felicidad" (Uncap happiness) seek to evoke feelings of contentment, excitement, and fun. They promote a "lifestyle" that is associated with leisure, abundance, and enjoyment. In doing this, they seek to distract both from the negative health consequences associated with their products and from the transformation of the social landscape in which people are working longer hours, struggling to get by financially, and perhaps separated from extended family because of regional or international migration.

In December 2015, Coca-Cola in Mexico released and then retracted a commercial premised on tolerance and celebration of diversity.[19] The ad opens with a statistic: 81.6 percent of Mexico's indigenous people have felt "rejected" for speaking their languages; the ad then states that a group of young people wanted to give them a different message. Filmed in Totontepec Villa de Morelos, in Oaxaca state, the commercial features a group of mostly white young people with European features, dressed in fashionable and wintry clothing (red scarves, knit hats, flannel shirts, blue jeans, and ankle boots), arriving to town in sporty cars. They construct a massive Christmas tree in the town plaza with wood slats that they paint red, and then decorate with plastic red Coca-Cola bottle caps. When the tree is illuminated, the visitors link arms with local youth with indigenous features, and the tree's message, in Mixe, the local language, reads "Tökmuk n'ijyyumtat," translated as "Permanezcamos unidos" (Let's stay united). Big smiles and warm embraces abound.

Critics, including El Poder del Consumidor and other members of the Alliance for Nutritional Health, vociferously attacked the ad for presenting a colonialist, elitist, and patronizing vision of Mexico's indigenous people and for implying that soda—among those products blamed by consumer advocates for Mexico's public health crisis of diet-related illness—could somehow solve Mexico's social problems of inequality and marginalization of indigenous communities. The ad was retracted, and Coca-Cola cravenly sought to deflect the criticism by arguing that the critics were the patronizing ones.

In a playbook honed over a few decades in the United States, soda companies have found success in combating regulations by implying that they constitute an attack on the autonomy and free will of citizens. Marion Nestle shows in her book *Soda Politics* that through decades of grant making to organizations that serve communities of color and low-income communities (such as the NAACP), Coca-Cola managed to subdue potential critiques of the predatory marketing of health-damaging products and high rates of noncommunicable disease in the same communities.[20] When New York City sought to pass a soda portion control law, soda distribution trucks in the Harlem neighborhood where I live were emblazoned with posters that read, "Don't let bureaucrats tell you what size beverage to buy" and featured an image of a black man in silhouette with his fist raised (holding a soda cup) in a gesture evocative of the Black Power salute. Other ads portrayed then mayor Michael Bloomberg in a floral muumuu and called him "the nanny."

We can see that in very visible and less visible ways the soda companies seek to protect and expand their market in Mexico's rural and indigenous communities by promoting the idea that Coca-Cola has a sacred place in culture and ritual, that it is somehow an element of intangible cultural patrimony that is worthy of respect and preservation. While anthropologists have documented the use of Coca-Cola in ritual practice in places throughout Latin America, along with whiskey, cigarettes, and other products made available through capitalist market expansion, it is a distortion to imply that such use is an argument for a pious respect toward those products as ritual implements, much less an endorsement of the everyday consumption of those products. Through an erroneous application of the anthropological concept of cultural relativism, beverage corporations imply that expressing concern about consumption patterns of soda among indigenous communities constitutes an attack on the sovereignty and cultural autonomy of those communities; to question or critique ritual elements is tantamount to disrespecting the culture itself.

Many of the elements used in rituals are precisely those items associated with power in given historical contexts.[21] Further, at the time of their adoption, many ritual elements would be reserved for special occasions and festivities due to cost or limited availability, precisely the opposite of everyday items of consumption. To appropriate and utilize products associated with colonial, imperial, or neocolonial invaders in ritual can be a means for acquiring social capital and mediating the influence and violence those invaders bring. It is problematic to invert that into an argument that somehow those products now are an untouchable and sacrosanct emblem of cultural heritage. It also overlooks the efforts by the beverage companies to expand and corner the market in rural and indigenous communities by selling soda at a lower price in rural communities than in cities. Ironically, one of the reasons for a rise in soda consumption in some indigenous communities may be that health officials and missionaries concerned about alcohol consumption actively sought to promote the substitution of soda for liquor in rituals from the 1960s through the 1980s.[22] Further, the expansion of consumption of processed foods and beverages into rural communities is part and parcel of the expansion of capitalist markets and modes of production. Coca-Cola, like coffee, tea, and sugar in the industrial revolution in Europe, is a cheap form of energy, providing sugar and caffeine to fuel people working long hours. The day laborers I spoke to in a field outside of Tehuacán, Puebla, told me as much as they harvested onions while sipping from 1.5-liter bottles of Coca-Cola.

But the idea that poor and indigenous people have a "cultural" attachment to Coca-Cola circulates in elite and urban circles. Just like the fried sope story told to me multiple times in different contexts, it is a convenient means of deflecting attention away from the concerted and continuous efforts by transnational food corporations to extend the reach, appeal, and frequency of consumption of their products. I was told in diverse settings, in the United States and in Mexico, that reducing consumption of soda would be difficult in indigenous communities because of "ignorance" and the "belief systems" of indigenous people, who, they said, think Coca-Cola has religious properties or is medicinal and therapeutic. The last was always accompanied by a somewhat horror-stricken repetition of the idea that indigenous mothers give their children Coca-Cola in baby bottles. The destabilization of rural subsistence economies; the delegitimation and often prohibition of *parteras,* the lay midwives who historically helped mothers in the postpartum period with breastfeeding and infant nutrition; the lack of potable water in many communities; a rise in promotion and subsidies of infant formula; industrial food aid to the poor; and more, are forgotten or overlooked. So, the proliferation of soda into many aspects of life, including and beyond ritual, is repackaged and sold as a "cultural" problem. This creates space for the marketing of soda and processed foods as counterpoints to "traditional" ways of life for the modern-minded, and paradoxically, as a tie to "tradition," exploited by marketers to associate their products with nostalgia and cultural significance for "traditional" communities.

8 Conclusion

CONNECTING THE DOTS, AND BRIGHT SPOTS

Edgardo Martínez grew up in a rural community in the state of Puebla. He could not afford to study, so he helped his parents to work their *milpa.*[1] Like many people, they had to walk several hours into the countryside to get to the land they had rights to, so they would often sleep in the field, in a rustic shelter, *una morada.*[2] Being able to tolerate sleeping in the fields was good preparation, he said, for his future livelihood, making him strong and capable. When he was sixteen, in 1984, his family needed income and their small-scale farming was not providing enough, so he moved to the capital, Mexico City. He worked there for a fruit wholesaler, at the Central de Abastos, specializing in fruits like cantaloupe, watermelon, limes, and papaya. Eventually, he began his own business in the market, specializing in the same fruits. For seventeen years, he was able to make a living for himself, and eventually his four children, who, he notes, "grew up in the market." But by 2001, a slow decline in prices and difficulty in supply channels had him at his wits' end. He accepted help from a cousin to migrate to the New York City area.

Now, he has lived in Staten Island for thirteen years. He has worked in restaurants, construction, and in a full-circle twist, now finds himself cultivating vegetables on land he rents in Staten Island and Pennsylvania.

Among the products he specializes in are what he calls typically Mexican products: papalo, cilantro, verdolagas, tomatoes, tomatillos, jalapeños, calabazas, and sweet corn, as well as products he says are more often requested by his non-Mexican customers: bell peppers, cabbage, beets, broccoli, and cauliflower. His customers seek him out because while he has not been through the organic certification process, he uses no chemicals on his crops, using compost and relying on the richness of the soil to provide all his plants need. He describes the emotion of his customers as contagious when they find produce they remember from their homelands. He told me an immigrant from Thailand exclaimed that it had been twenty years since he had seen lemongrass that was not dried, chopped to bits, and wrapped in plastic packaging. For all immigrants, he said, food can be a connection to home.

He gained guidance on northeastern planting cycles, how to rent land, and accessing the green markets in the New York City area from a nonprofit called GrowNYC, which helps immigrants become farmers. He acknowledges, though, that most of what he knows he learned from his family, working on their milpa. From corn farming in rural Puebla to corn farming in Staten Island, Edgardo's story is unusual, but it is, just as much, an illustration of the flows of capital and trade with NAFTA. Displaced twice, to the city and then to the United States, he has found his way back to the land.

IT'S THE CAPITALISM

The historical phases of capitalism are mapped out on the territories of the world. Pursuit of profit drives capitalists to pursue low-cost materials, cheap labor, and expanded markets. When one market is saturated, spatial expansion allows access to others. Marketing and product diversification are strategies corporations use to foster desire and keep people interested in what comes next. The basic exploitation and inequality inherent in capitalist economic formations and the vacuum capitalist political formations leave in place of a social safety net produce a continual tension created by the fact that those depended on and often exploited for their labor and consumption must still somehow cooperate with the whole arrangement. As inequality grows globally, marketing is even more intensively focused on the cultivation of aspiration, so that even those most disadvantaged by their place in the economy can imagine that they will one day be able to afford to consume the products so continually offered them. Pushing the spaces in which these dynamics occur farther out from capitalism's global epicenters into places historically marginalized from policy making and excluded from access to consumer markets provides a "spatial fix" that keeps capitalist formations viable.[3]

In Mexico and the United States, capitalism's search for fixes to its inherent problems have locked the two countries' food systems, agricultural sectors, and populations together in an awkward embrace. Anthropologist Julie Guthman proposes that "fast and convenient food is a triply good fix for American capitalism" in that it super-exploits labor, provides cheap food (which facilitates the downward dive in wages), and absorbs agricultural surpluses so that the farm sector remains viable.[4] While her focus is on the US, this is doubly true for Mexico, where we can see how NAFTA has enabled US corporations to look across the border for underpaid and mobile labor whose vulnerability is produced by the failure of the United States to authorize sufficient labor migration to meet the demand. And it has opened up new markets for an ever-diversifying array of consumer goods. People in the United States can access fresh fruit year round, while shelf-stable packaged and processed foods reach all locations, displacing other ways of eating.

With NAFTA, US consumers have become able to afford and access a year-round bounty of fresh produce because so much of Mexico's farmland has been converted to industrial-scale, export-oriented agriculture.[5] We eat berries, avocados, tomatoes, and cucumbers—foods broadly linked to good health—to our hearts' content.[6] Meanwhile, US corporations reap a bonanza in terms of expanding their export markets for processed foods and beverages, commodities, chemicals, and more. Mexican citizens pay the price—absorbing US surpluses, products, and even the side effects of pesticides, herbicides, and endocrine-disrupting chemicals used in the production and processing of foods.

While expanding possibilities for consumption, trade and globalization also distract citizens from the democratic limits of capitalism. The US population has shown a limited appetite for cuts in existing entitlements and the outsourcing of jobs when economic contractions hit. Trade operates on a supranational plane and provides an out for governments lacking a solution to the untenable economic conditions they have built. Trade deal negotiators and an executive branch privileged with "fast track" authority to develop trade deals behind closed doors keep the gnawing and voracious violence of markets out of sight and out of mind, transferring it to other countries. Foreign workers and workers outsourced abroad provide a scapegoat for the decline in jobs in the United States due to automation. The United States uses its role as dominant trading partner to constrain the politics of the possible—reducing the power of organized labor, regulating the mobility and economic stability of workers, displacing the ugliest abuses and exploitation, and providing a market to absorb the excesses of production in the north. All of this, paradoxically, provides a buffer from market forces for US industrial agriculture. Who pays? The Mexican people literally pay with their lives. First, they pay as workers, valued for their labor power, with the risks of their mobility carried on their own backs, with limited scenarios for empowerment and civic participation. And increasingly, they pay with their bodies—targets for ever increased consumption, until the very limits of the human body have been pushed to extremes.

NAFTA has produced and heightened the visibility of "surplus bodies," and bodies as repositories of surpluses, storing the products of overproduction and uneven trade negotiations. Migration was the tool of choice for dealing with surplus workers for most of the twentieth century in Mexico. While the trade agreement resulted in an initial flood of new migration, especially between 1995 and 2005, since then, as migration has tapered off, other changes have been wrought, leading to the precipitous rise of noncommunicable chronic diseases.

When the efforts of "surplus" people—to make a living, to manage the food landscape, to eat enough to work—result in illness, it is presented to them as their own fault, their inability to manage and consume the "proper" amounts of the "right" foods. In this book, I have proposed that the rise of diet-related chronic illness in Mexico is not an unintended consequence or a side effect of the economic and political changes wrought by NAFTA. Rather, it is a logical result of the prioritization of foreign direct investment, industrial agriculture, theories of comparative advantage, and a specific notion of development that sees no role for small-scale agriculture. Processed foods and beverages have flooded the Mexican market, becoming ever cheaper and more available in all communities not simply because corporations are ever in search of new markets, but because the space has been created for them to do so, and the logistics of their market expansion have been facilitated by specific government policies.

Ancestral diets, simultaneously, become more difficult to maintain as rural people have seen their access to land chipped away, along with a strategic push toward the consolidation of landholding in private hands, automation and industrialization of farming methods, a shrinking of the supports for farmers to get their products to market, local markets themselves, and a decline in people willing and able to work the land using traditional methods.

Paradoxically, this has made milpa-based cuisine newly available for "elevation" and "redemption" by Mexican and foreign chefs who rationalize their stratospheric prices as the cost of their salvage of methods and ingredients that would otherwise be unappreciated and in the process of slipping away. Less able to easily and affordably access traditional foods, low-income people turn more toward processed and packaged foods. ← more available

When consumption of such products, as it has been shown to do all over the world, contributes to a rise in diet-related illness, this is framed as a problem requiring more "education" so that people can be more "responsible" consumers and better custodians of their health. Meanwhile, the state role in ensuring health—including adequate and healthy food, and the conceptualization of these as rights that correspond to citizens—is receding, amid a turn toward self-care. Constructing those most marginalized and made most vulnerable by the neoliberal economy as those most in need of intervention is convenient for the transnational food corporations that are intent on blurring the connection between their products and illness. It takes pressure off of a state less engaged than ever in its citizens' well-being. But it also draws on a reservoir of long-standing ideas about rural people and the countryside, who have continually been constructed as backward, in need of modernization, development, education, and guidance.

In the construction of citizens as consumers who need to be educated to consume responsibly, the market is reinforced as a site for solutions.

While it was the market expansion of ultraprocessed foods and chemically intensive agriculture that led to the rise in diet-related illness in the first place, the market is also framed as the site where solutions will come from with diet and light foods, pharmaceuticals, medical devices, and other products. Julie Guthman calls this "a political economy of bulimia" that differently affects individuals, according to class and social position: "On the one hand consuming is encouraged and on the other deservingness is performed by being thin no matter how that is accomplished."[7]

Historians of capitalism have long acknowledged the need for capital to reproduce labor. But in an increasingly automated economy, not so many workers are needed. When this happened previously in Mexico's history, migration to the larger labor market in the United States provided a safety valve, releasing the steam of an underutilized workforce. While today demographic changes have meant that there are not as many workers entering the labor force each year, there are still too many for an economy that needs ever fewer. Chronic disease provides a way for the government to be off the hook for its failure to produce sufficient jobs and educational opportunities.[8]

Consumers "choose" to consume what and how they want. Today, their right to consume is upheld, even when such consumption, and the products consumed, pose risks. Instead, the buying power of consumers is framed as a right, utterly inalienable. No one can tell empowered citizens what to do with their bodies, even though the options available to them—to eat differently, to protect themselves from toxic chemicals, or to use their energy in pursuits of their own choosing in safe and clean environments—are ever more limited. The body is newly expanded market territory, but also one's own responsibility for its care has expanded in ways that are unprecedented.

When consumer advocates in Mexico, like El Poder del Consumidor and their allies in the Alliance for Nutritional Health, advocate for structural changes to the food system, such as better product labeling and taxes on sugar-sweetened beverages, corporations strike back with marketing campaigns urging consumers to fight for their autonomy against the nanny state. Consumer advocates and nutritionists have received anonymous death threats, and their emails and text messages are hacked using sophisticated spyware.[9] The role of the state to protect its populace from abuse and exploitation by external threats is forgotten. Also forgotten is the customary responsibility of the state to protect national industries, food supplies, and health.

NEOLIBERALISM AND THE "OBESITY" EPIDEMIC

In 1975, a PepsiCo vice president said, "There are 800 million gullets in China and I want to see a Pepsi in every one of them."[10] This quotation coincided with a strategic shift away from a model of every corporation for itself to a concerted collaboration between corporations, government, and multinational lending and development institutions to foster foreign direct investment, minimize regulation, and integrate the global economy. Since the 1970s, we have seen the articulation of a more aggressive model of corporate autonomy and market-based economic policy, poised to promote and profit from globalization. The path for neoliberalism was paved by "a theory of political economic practices that proposes that human well-being can best be advanced by liberating individual entrepreneurial freedoms and skills within an institutional framework characterized by strong private property rights, free markets, and free trade."[11] That theory informed policies at the national level in the major economic powers of the United Kingdom and the United States, most notably, but was propagated around the world by World Bank and International Monetary Fund policy in international aid and lending.

In spite of the ostensibly free market emphasis of neoliberalism, it is in fact largely a set of assumptions and cultural inclinations on the part of a specific set of elite actors and the institutions they populate and manage. When in power to make policy, they routinely contradict some of their stated principles, such as efficiency, unfettered trade, and comparative advantage.[12] While neoliberalism as an idea rests on the free market, it was an idea hatched in places that have never had a fully market-based economy, but instead have had robust periods of state-led and interventionist economic policy that shaped the conditions of production and competition.

For the purposes of this book, the most relevant place to see this is in agricultural policy, in which government subsidies have propped up and protected the growers of select commodities from the vagaries of the market. Without subsidies, the United States could probably never have dominated the world commodity market in corn and other commodities the way it has for so long. Nonetheless, the dominant financial institutions and nations have had an easier time prescribing the bitter medicine of neoliberalism than taking it themselves. This prescription included structural adjustment, austerity, and market-oriented political reforms. It is telling that in 2016, scholars affiliated with the International Monetary Fund itself published an article poignantly entitled "Neoliberalism: Oversold?" indicating the realization of at least some that neoliberal policies since the 1980s have contributed to cycles of economic crises and the growth of inequality around the world, and have not been the unmitigated success they promised to be.[13]

Mexico's recent history provides a compelling illustration of the promises and the pitfalls of neoliberal models of development. Today, labor migration is no longer a safety valve for Mexico's surplus population. While demographically Mexico is a changed nation, and some economists and certainly many elite financiers and investors say it is booming economically and NAFTA is working exactly as it should, inequality and poverty have risen.[14] Many families continue to be divided by the US-Mexico border, separated for years, even decades, by a failure of the United States and Mexico to regularize migration. There has been a shift toward consumption, and indeed hyperconsumption, not only as a business strategy but as a strategy for social control. It is an extension of the cultural values of neoliberalism into the pantries and onto the plates of everyday people in both countries, with tremendous public health consequences. Meanwhile, Mexican people's "bad bio citizenship" acquits the government of its complicity in creating a food system that harms its people.[15] Neoliberal economic and political ideals hold citizens responsible for their own health. Self-care is not just expected to minimize one's consumption of public health resources, it is good citizenship. It removes the onus from the state to provide the conditions for good health, including treatment and prevention of disease and want. Systemic failure is magically transformed into individual failure.

Critical theorist Lauren Berlant calls the global rise in obesity "globesity," a "shaming sickness of sovereignty, a predicament of privilege and of poverty, a crisis of choosing and anti-will, and an endemic disease of development and underdevelopment."[16] It produces a "slow death: a condition of being worn out by the activity of reproducing life." Those "whose appetites are out of control" can be targeted for intervention, labeled as irresponsible biocitizens, and left out of the fruits of development and economic expansion. Obesity and diet-related diseases provide a convenient excuse for the state's failure to better protect its citizens from the negative effects of NAFTA.

It is important for us to see the growing public health crisis of noncommunicable diseases in Mexico not only as a consequence of trade and food policies in the NAFTA signatory countries, but also as a transnational cultural coup on the part of corporate strategists. It converts a binational strategy for trade and economic development that has generated massive instability, exacerbated poverty, and displaced millions into a problem suffered by—but ostensibly also produced by—the very poor most impacted by it. It changes the debate into a question of "personal choice" and "responsibility." So, instead of seeing a larger discussion between the two countries about the need to regulate hyperpalatable foods, which now, ever closer to their "big tobacco moment," are unequivocally associated with deleterious health consequences, we see public promotion and sponsorship of yoga, Zumba, meditation, and nutrition education to "teach" the poor to be healthy.[17]

At the same time, Mexico has been engaged in a protracted struggle with organized crime syndicates that operate with increasing impunity and visibility. The complex bilateral relationship between the United States and Mexico has been reduced to a conversation about security. Plan Mérida provides support to the tune of $2.5 billion to Mexico to combat organized crime, drug trafficking, and money laundering in the region. Foreign aid to Mexico from 2012 to 2014 reached $819.7 million (with military aid constituting about half of the total aid to the country).[18] The spectacle of violence has enabled a further shrinking of the role of the state in social welfare and provided a distraction while the economy has been restructured.

While some have characterized the relationship between Latin America and the United States (especially its corporations) as neocolonial, I argue it is actually more innovative than that. While, as in colonialism, current economic relationships between the United States and its neighbors to the south are based on unequal relationships and exploitation, the ideologies and even the basic premises of economic activity have shifted. What we are seeing is an economic model no longer premised on productivity; it is a model that is post-labor and post-migration. It is a capitalist structure premised instead on consumption. Profit is generated from the very bodies of those "surplus" workers who no longer have a place in the economy and have stopped migrating.[19] By consuming ever larger quantities of imported goods, processed foods, and soda, the poor and marginalized generate profit. The bodily (not to mention social) malaise of unproductive citizens that are increasingly sick is solved by still greater consumption—of specialty, "functional" foods (low-cal, low-fat, low-carb, gluten-free, sugar-free, artificially sweetened) and eventually consumption and use of pharmaceuticals and medical devices (blood sugar testing kits, syringes, circulation hosiery, etc.) to treat the diseases of "abundance" from which they increasingly suffer. Such consumption is aided both by migrant remittances (Mexico's top source of revenue today) and by poverty mitigation programs that place funds for purchase of processed foods and beverages in the hands of the poor, as well as the goods themselves in grocery rations.

The ways that the economy and food systems have been transformed to produce a rise in noncommunicable chronic diseases is a kind of structural violence. As Paul Farmer has argued, we must be attentive to structural violence and social suffering because "suffering is 'structured' by historically given (and often economically driven) processes and forces that conspire—whether through routine, ritual, or, as is more commonly the case, the hard surfaces of life—to constrain agency."[20] The narrowing of possibilities and ways of life for low-income Mexicans has paradoxically limited their ability to live how they lived in the past and perhaps may wish to today. At the same time that the current economic and political program has removed the structural supports that made small-scale agriculture and small-town life feasible, it has bestowed on them more responsibility than ever for their own health.

This dismal and dystopian rendering of Mexican lives today is depressing. But there are alternatives. Some of them are David and Goliath-esque fables of regular people taking on enormous multinational corporations and global trade policy, and they offer a glimpse into an alternative reality. Some are well known, like ethical eating and fair-trade campaigns. Others are less widely known but work in very specific niches, connecting cultural sovereignty, personal fulfillment, and wellness to food. These include the "decolonized diet," advocated by Chicanx scholars and food activists Luz Calvo and Catriona Rueda Esquibel, who argue that health and culture are best served by eating foods that pre-date the arrival of Europeans to this hemisphere.[21] Related to this are broader movements that promote food as medicine. We can also see peasant movements that promote a return to older foodways, as in Sin Maíz, no Hay País (Without Corn, There Is no Nation), a food movement in Mexico working to preserve corn's biodiversity and opposed to patenting of seeds and GMO corn.[22] Finally, there are interesting initiatives that build on the transnational context of migration, such as GrowNYC, which encourages migrants with agricultural backgrounds to rent land and grow produce for the city's green markets. These alternatives provide a glimpse of an alternative future in which people will neither be obliged to nor prevented from working the land; small-scale farming would be supported and celebrated; people will cherish and sustain ancestral foodways and refuse the "supermarketization" or "McDonaldization" of food; and health and well-being will be improved.[23] This alternative would involve different kinds of transnational flows—not of commodities, but of cultural practices, heritage, and the joy of conviviality.

These bright spots in an otherwise depressing food landscape provide glimpses of alternative scenarios. Rather than medication and increased consumption of functional foods that promise weight loss or appeal to "lifestyles," they demonstrate ways that an approach that weds social justice, resistance, and resilience to the everyday necessities of preparing and eating food can heal the body and the spirit. Eating in a way that does not erase or erode but builds our connections to each other and to land and culture in a continuum between the present, the past, and the future can be restorative and therapeutic. When René Redzepi crows about the tortilla being "the perfect food" he may be right, but not for the reasons he thinks. The tortilla does not need to be elevated or made more sophisticated—it is and has been enough all by itself. The key is not to increase its use in elite global kitchens but to restore its relationship to the people to whom it historically belongs so that they can eat tortillas if, when, and where they want them.

I am not arguing in this book that it is feasible or desirable to return to preindustrial food systems or that we should all grow and grind our own corn, a kind of romanticized "peasant essentialism." I do not think many of us want to give up our daily activities to spend hours each day bringing our food from the fields to the table by hand. For women, especially, much of our struggle for equality has been centered precisely on getting out from under the tyranny of patriarchal distributions of domestic labor. But we can envision today a not distant moment when what we eat could be completely disconnected from people and place, and I do not think we want that, either. I wish to ask us to consider alternatives.

Currently, high numbers of people suffer the physical, social, and psychic consequences of an economic and political system not built for them. In it, their flexibility, mobility, and responsibility for themselves, including both their health and their economic survival, are not bestowed on them in acknowledgment of their rights as autonomous citizens, but rather as an abdication of the responsibilities of government to protect and provide. "Consumer choice" and the risks associated with it—the health consequences of eating the products that the economy rests upon—are elaborate schemes to evade blame and accountability on the part of corporations and the politicians with whom they collude. Binational trade agreements ostensibly designed to ensure a fair and equitable playing field have produced, instead, a landscape in which citizen-consumers are ever less protected. To strive for more equitable and just solutions is going to require more than consumer activism narrowly defined at the local level; attention to the inherently binational nature of the situation we are in is required. As Father Solalinde, quoted in the preface, said, we are intertwined and inseparable, and our fates will rise and fall together.

CODA: LORENA'S CANDY

Lorena was nine when she traveled from the Bronx to her parents' hometown, staying alternately with her maternal and paternal grandmothers for the summer between fourth and fifth grades. Her parents had tucked some money in her pocket when they sent her with her uncle, early on a summer morning on a flight to Mexico City, to be followed by a few hours on a bus to Santo Tomás Tlalpa, Puebla. Her aunts, uncles, and grandparents would not dream of accepting her money for routine expenses in their hometown: it was their privilege and honor to provide her with meals and everything else she needed during her stay. So, she found herself with money to spend, and—in contrast to her life back in the Bronx—freedom to spend it. "Oh, Lorena loved walking over to the corner store and buying candy," her uncle told me, when we chatted about her visit. All summer long, she would enthusiastically walk out of her aunt and uncle's gate to the corner store and buy candy for herself and her cousins. The freedom to move around town independently is one of the most frequently named differences between childhood as experienced in the United States by the children of Mexican migrants and by their parents in Mexico. Many parents lament that their children grow up in the United States "inside four walls."

Assessing the vast array of choices in even the smallest rural stores among candy, chips, crackers, muffins, sodas, and other cheap and colorful options requires a lot of knowledge. Children advise one another on which candies are a good buy, which are too spicy (candy with chile powder predominates), and other important criteria. Children are understood—by store owners and by manufacturers—as consumers with a small but significant amount of spending money to be used at their exclusive discretion. For Lorena, this was completely novel, and she relished it. When her uncle brought her back to the United States, they had to pass through Mexican customs, submitting the tourist permit she had been given when she, a US citizen, had entered the country. The agent, an expert in just this kind of journey, the end of summer return exodus of the children of immigrants, leaned over his counter and smiled at Lorena, asking, "How much candy did you eat this summer?"

Acknowledgments

This book, like each one that I have written before, owes a great debt of gratitude to Manuela Fuentes and her family, including her husband, Saúl, her brother, Moisés, and his wife, Pilar. I have had the privilege to meet and spend time with each sibling in Manuela and her husband's families, as well as their parents, children, and many of their cousins. It seems that no matter what topic emerges in my research, Manuela has a personal experience that is highly relevant and also has connections to family members, friends, and neighbors with relevant professional expertise or lived experience in the area. I cannot imagine doing research in Mexico or with Mexican communities in the United States without their generous guidance, assistance, and most importantly, two decades of friendship.

This book is a result of years of research, discussion, writing, and feedback in which I have been aided by colleagues and students at Lehman College and the City University of New York, and many beyond. At Lehman College, David Badillo, Licia Fiol-Matta, Daniel Fernández, Milagros Ricourt, Teresita Levy, Mila Burns, Sarah Ohmer, Veronica Mason, Stephanie Rupp, Michelle Augustine, Yasmin Morales Alexander, Mary Phillips, Kenneth Schlesinger, Rebecca Arzola, Yini Rodríguez, and Orquidia Rosado Acevedo have provided moral support and collegiality. David Schwittek has been a lively interlocutor on this project and collaborator on the related documentary film we made. I am grateful to internal resources, including a Book Completion Award, a PSC-CUNY Research Grant, and a Fellowship Award. Generous administrators like Ricardo Fernández, José Luis Cruz, Harriet Fayne, Melissa Kirk, and Deirdre Pettipiece facilitated leave and resources for me to do this work. I am thankful to Nick Freudenberg and his colleagues, especially Anabel Perez Jimenez, Karen Flórez, Melissa Fuster, Ashley Rafalow, Elene Murphy, and Janet Poppendieck at the CUNY Urban Food Policy Institute at the CUNY School of Public Health, for providing me with a writing nook and collegial support.

The Jaime Lucero Mexican Studies Institute at CUNY was my professional home for five years and also provided me with a tremendous network of contacts in and outside of Mexico that fostered this research. I am particularly thankful to José Higuera López, Marlen Fernández, and Alonso Gorozpe for their direct support at the institute, as well as to external partners Sandra Fuentes Berain, Alexia Nuñez Bachman, Jorge Suárez Vélez, Mariana Sánchez de Ovando, and others who answered my questions or connected me to people who could.

In a study like this, which required me to depart from familiar territory into fields that are new to me, I am grateful to my academic guides, mentors, and advocates, especially Judy Hellman and Peter Guarnaccia. Colleagues who weighed in with feedback, citations, and suggestions include Elizabeth Roberts, Irwin Sánchez, Marrisa Senteno, Victoria Stone Cadena, Deanna Barenboim, Dana-Ain Davis, Natali Valdez, Daisy Deomampo, Eunice Georges, Abril Saldaña Tejeda, Emily Yates-Doerr, Megan Carney, Xanat Camacho, Miriam Bertrán Vila, Rafael Meza, Mara Tellez Rojo, Ulla Berg, Susan Coutin, Alison Lee, Robert Smith, Angelo Cabrera, Alexandra Délano, Michael Montoya, Amalia Pallares, Miguel Díaz Barriga, Diana Taylor, Eric Manheimer, Marcial Godoy, Patricia Clark, Renato Rosaldo, Luz Calvo, and Catriona Rueda-Esquibel. Several students and former students who are now colleagues, including Emily Vasquez, Yamil Avivi, Cesar Andrade, Andrea Maldonado, Luis Saavedra, Nelson Rodríguez, Kathryn Chuber, Ruth Fuster, María Hernández, and Shabel Castro, were helpful and inspiring at key junctures. I am especially grateful to Marisa Macari for guidance and resources, as well as for connecting me to the work of El Poder del Consumidor in Mexico, and her colleagues, Alejandro Calvillo, Jimena Camacho, Rebecca Berner, and Denise Rojas. Thanks to invitations from Winifred Tate (to whom I am also grateful for connecting me to UC Press), Patricia Barbeito, Jennifer Hirsch, Elizabeth Roberts, Eleana Kim, Carlos Decena, R. Scott Hanson, Vania Smith-Oka, and Agustín Fuentes, I was able to present portions of this project at Colby College, the Rhode Island School of Design, the Mailman School of Public Health at Columbia University, the University of Michigan, UC Irvine, Rutgers University, the University of Pennsylvania, Notre Dame University, the Trade Justice Alliance, and the Wenner-Gren Foundation. These opportunities afforded me valuable feedback on the project at key stages of its development. Friends who provided moral support and encouragement include Kelly Collins, Elizabeth Frankel Rivera, Alicia Carmona, Michael Casey, Karen Rojas, Karnit Gefen, Jessica Ritz, Sherine Hamdy, Anahi Viladrich, Evangelos Calotychos, Marika Lynch, Natalia Méndez, Marco Saavedra,

Franziska Castillo, and Melissa Escano. I am grateful to the anonymous peer reviewers recruited by UC Press, who gave me detailed and helpful feedback on the manuscript at multiple stages and agreed to have their identity revealed to me: Roberto González, Margaret Gray, and Ed Morales. This book exists because Kate Marshall at UC Press believed in it from the start and brought formidable vision and encouragement to midwifing it into reality, along with her team at the press (with special thanks for the attentive copyediting of Sue Carter and indexing by Joan Shapiro). I cannot imagine this project being completed without the constant support and encouragement of Nara Milanich, whose expertise in Latin American history, society, and politics is matched only by her clear-eyed insights into the highs and lows of academic life, and her friendship and solidarity when all of it can be too much.

Finally, I dedicate this book to Elías, Lázaro, and Carlos, the loves of my life, who have had to deal with me being distracted and sometimes physically distant as I made room for this project in an already overly full day-to-day existence. While they got to eat really good food as a perk of this research, that was not enough to compensate for their forbearance, patience, and support.

Notes

PREFACE

1. I use pseudonyms throughout this book for all people and places with the following exceptions: (1) I use the real names of people who have been named and portrayed in roughly the same context in mass media sources or other published texts, and (2) I use real names for mid- to large-sized cities.

2. The Pan American Health Organization lists diabetes as the top cause of death for women in Mexico. The INEGI report lists diabetes as the first cause of death for men and women after heart disease, and the first cause of death and disability combined. Pan American Health Organization 2012; INEGI, Causas 2015.

3. Gleijeses 1992, Gonzalez 2011, Grandin 2006, and Striffler 2001 document some of the many chapters of US intervention in the Americas.

4. The confluence of neoliberal economic policies and US hegemony have been discussed thoroughly in Klein 2007 and Harvey 2005. See Ostry et al. 2016 for a critique of the overreach of such philosophies by former adherents.

5. Freudenberg 2014.

6. Clinton 1993.

7. There is disagreement among economists about whether trade deals actually accelerate the outsourcing and decline of manufacturing, or whether the primary driver of shrinking industrial jobs is automation.

8. Office of the US Trade Representative 2017.

9. Perot and Choate 1993.

10. Weisbrot et al. 2017, 2. See also Zepeda et al. 2009.

11. Weisbrot et al. 2017, 2.

12. Interview with Mario Garcia, SEDESOL offices, Mexico City, Dec. 8, 2014.

13. Fox and Haight 2010, Zepeda et al. 2009, 8.

14. Ahmed and Malkin 2017.

15. This figure includes naturalized and dual citizens, and authorized and unauthorized immigrants. González-Barrera 2015.

16. Passel, Cohn, and González Barrera 2012.

17. Whether and how this might be connected to NAFTA has been debated, but Paley 2014 argues that the drug war provides a "fix" to capitalism's shortcomings that has economic benefits for powerful parties in Mexico and beyond.

18. Talk at Leaders of Mexico Forum, Columbia University, May 5, 2015.

19. Green 2011, 367. Green mainly refers to CAFTA (Central American Free Trade Agreement), but her words are generalizable to people in the NAFTA countries as well. Also see Magaña 2008; Ahmed and Perlroth 2017.

20. Small-scale farming can occur in rural or semi-urban areas and can be as simple as having chickens and a planter with herbs or as complex as access to a small plot of land where corn and other crops can be grown, and domestic animals raised. Historically, families that migrated to the capital often retained some food production activities, such as keeping chickens, growing fruit trees, and bringing back a bag of dried corn or other bulk food supplies after visits with relatives in rural areas.

21. Diabetes mellitus is not a single disease but many, and is associated with elevated blood glucose triggered by poor insulin production, insulin resistance in skeletal muscle or lipid tissue, or both. Gómez-Dantés et al. 2016; Montoya 2007.

22. Abajobir et al. 2017.

23. Gómez-Dantés et al. 2016.

24. Gómez-Dantes et al. 2016.

25. World Bank 2017.

26. Secretaría de Salud 2014; Statistics Canada 2015; World Health Organization 2016.

1. INTRODUCTION

1. Laudan 2001; Mintz 1986; Pollan 2007; Flandrin and Montanari 2013.

2. See, e.g., Gray 2013; Pollan 2007.

3. Nestle 2015; Blanding 2011.

4. Moran-Thomas 2017 criticizes the categorization of chronic disease as "noncommunicable."

5. Frieden 2010.

6. Farmer et al. 2006, 1686.

7. Farmer 2004, 7.

8. My colleagues in anthropology have critiqued notions of tradition and modernity in useful ways. Ideas about what is traditional frame culture as static and unchanging. Essentialized visions of tradition both underestimate the amount of change in the past (because change is a constant), but also often involve a power dynamic in which keepers of tradition call on visions of the past to constrain possibilities for the future. Nevertheless, I use the terms "tradition" and "traditional" to refer to foodways in this book because it is the way many of the people I spoke to in rural and urban communities refer to foods centered on *milpa*-based agriculture. Modes of food preparation have changed over time (e.g., from grinding corn by hand on a *metate* or blending ingredients with a *molcajete,* to wide use of industrial corn grinders and electric blenders; more consumption of wheat and meat, and less consumption of foraged greens and insects, but the ingredients and their combination into specific kinds of dishes have changed less. The stark shift in diet to more processed foods produced with industrial methods far from the site of consumption has occurred relatively recently. So, for purposes of this book, traditional diets and traditional foodways refer to foods prior to this most recent shift, in all their variety.

9. Arellano, *Taco* 2012.

10. O'Neill 2013; Suárez Vélez 2011; Zahniser et al. 2015.

11. Today, fewer Mexicans are migrating to the United States than leaving, but as many as 11.4 million people born in Mexico continue to reside in the United States, close to 1 in 10 of Mexico's total population (Passel et al. 2012). For more on the risks and costs of migration by land, see De León 2015; Marcela Ibarra, presentation at conference on Mexican migration, New York University, May 6, 2003; Magaña 2008.

12. CONEVAL 2012; Flores 2014; Jordan and Sullivan 2003; Garcia 2014; Public Citizen 2014; Weisbrot et al. 2017; Zepeda 2009.

13. Secretaría de la Salud 2013; Friel et al. 2013, 2015; Mazzocchi, Shankar, and Traill 2012.

14. See World Bank database, "Data: Mexico," 2014, https://data.worldbank.org/. See also Beaubien 2017; Secretaria de Salud 2013.

15. Weisbrot et al. 2017. Also Wilson and Silva 2013.

16. Barclay 2006.

17. I largely leave out consideration of the third partner in the trade deal, Canada. This omission suggests space for future research.

18. Guthman 2009; Osterweil 2014.

19. See, e.g., Lender et al. 2014; Alang and Kelly 2015; Ridaura et al. 2013.

20. Moss 2013.

21. Moss 2013.

22. See Moran-Thomas 2016; Guthman 2011. In Mexico, I observed an increasing variety and visibility of advertisements for medical devices related to chronic disease, including blood sugar monitors, compression hosiery, and artificially sweetened foods and beverages marketed to encourage their users to forget their disease, or live in uninhibited ways in spite of it. Diet soda has consistently been advertised as a product that allows "pure" enjoyment without the health consequences of sugar (while remaining silent on emerging data on the health consequences of the consumption of artificial sweeteners). See Nestle 2015. For a critique of the use of the term "lifestyle," see Cannon 2005.

23. Nestle 2015; Blanding 2011; Poder del Consumidor 2015; SugarScience, http://sugarscience.ucsf.edu.

24. President Carlos Salinas, in advance of NAFTA, asked the legislature to revoke Article 27, which stipulated communally held land by rural communities, clearing the way for private ownership and sale of lands that had been redistributed according to the constitutional provision after the Mexican Revolution. This was overwhelmingly approved by both houses, clearing the way for conglomeration of lands into large industrial farms held by multinational food and beverage firms (Kelly 1994).

25. Harvey 2005; Vivas 2009; Hawkes 2006.

26. Harvey 2005, 29; Keshavjee 2014, xxi.

27. Williamson (1990, 1993) coined the term "Washington Consensus" as shorthand for policies emerging from Washington, DC, the place that happens to be home to international lending institutions like the World Bank and the International Monetary Fund in addition to the US federal government, while noting that the United States did not take the same medicine it endorsed for others. Later on, Williamson (2000) strenuously objected to the use of the term as a shorthand for neoliberalism, but it is precisely as a catch-all term for the market-based reforms accompanying structural adjustment and neoliberal political and economic turns in globalizing economies throughout the world that the term is most commonly used in interdisciplinary Latin American studies contexts. See Harvey (2005, 54–55), for a thoughtful history of the convergence of the ideas associated with neoliberalism in the United States and in a different fashion in the United Kingdom.

28. Import substitution, described later, is a strategy by which countries with smaller economies produce their own goods, rather than import them. If, for example, blue jeans were no longer imported, local blue jean production would be fostered. Harvey 2005, 29; Cameron and Tomlin 2000, 56–59; Schanbacher 2010.

29. Cameron and Tomlin 2000.

30. Cameron and Tomlin 2000.

31. Luis Ernesto Derbez, former foreign minister of Mexico, personal communication, Columbia University, New York, 2006. See Bello 2008, and also Barkin 2005.

32. Passel et al. 2012.

33. Fox 1993.

34. Reardon and Berdegué 2000.

35. Talk by López Obrador, Columbia University, 2014.

36. Asad 1994; Briggs 2005; Hacking 1986, 2007; Maynard 2006; Scheper-Hughes and Lock 1987; Yates-Doerr 2012, 2015; Yang, McDaniel, and Malone 2012.

37. Carney 2015; Greenhalgh 2015; Greenhalgh and Carney 2014; Guthman 2011; Rothblum and Solovay 2009; Wann 2009.

38. At the population level, higher BMI may be correlated with higher incidence of noncommunicable disease, but BMI by itself does not facilely translate into increased risk for an individual, absent analysis of other factors. Data-driven models for anticipating risk may be promoted as neutral and empirical, but they are an inexact science and are too often misappropriated to imply that they can be used to predict an individual's likelihood of experiencing particular outcomes. On the contrary, as Osterweil writes, "body weight is an almost sublimely arbitrary, politicized, and medically indeterminate measure of health" (2014; see also Tomiyama, Ahlstrom, and Mann 2013; Mann, Tomiyama, and Ward 2015). Obesity researcher Traci Mann has questioned whether there even is an "obesity epidemic."

These critiques remind us that while classifications and metrics can be clinically useful in assessing potential risk for certain health conditions or population-level analysis, they are often based on problematic or ill-defined categories that fail to capture the diversity of human experience, allow for errors and variation in measurement and interpretation of criteria, technological variance in instruments of measurement, and conceptual problems of bias. Further, discussions of obesity are inseparable from cultural constructions of fatness and its historical association in the West with vice and slothfulness (even while most human societies have historically valued plumpness over thinness) (Kulick and Meneley 2005, 17). The construction of a physical condition, even when done within the realm of scientific biomedicine, is a social process that can be tainted with moral opprobrium. While the public health challenge posed by the sets of conditions collectively referred to as "metabolic syndrome" (Sadikot and Hermans 2010) and "noncommunicable chronic diseases" should not be underestimated, it is important to acknowledge critiques of these categories, even while there may be justification for their continued use.

In concert with the Health at Any Size movement, fat studies scholars advocate for discussion of weight in health-neutral ways and health in weight-neutral ways, arguing that health can be associated with any size, and that thinness is not necessarily more soundly correlated with health than fatness (Rothblum and Solovay 2009, 272–77; see also Mann, Tomiyama, and Ward 2015). What Rothblum and Solovay call a witch hunt, cultural anthropologist Susan Greenhalgh calls a "war": "a critical cultural shift in our concern about fatness, from 'self-control' (or virtue) to 'health'" (2015, 5). She describes fat talk and fat shaming as principal strategies in that war, serving to discipline people into a model of "thin, fit biocitizenship," no matter their size. She argues that this is not only ineffective, and sometimes achieves the opposite of its stated aim, but also that it is based on myths, including the assumption that weight is under the control of individuals.

While Greenhalgh's emphasis on structural, social, and genetic contributors to body size is important, her conclusion that individual efforts might be completely useless may be too deterministic for many. An overly structural view can overlook the decisions and indeed the pleasure that many people take in shaping their bodies in all kinds of ways as they strive toward or away from cultural, societal, and also personal preferences, aesthetics, and norms. As powerful as fat talk and healthist norms may be, individuals make choices every moment in response to their own embodied experiences of wellness and they do not do so only in response to "fat talk" or in pursuit or avoidance of externally imposed norms of beauty and health.

39. Greenhalgh convincingly demonstrates that the pervasiveness and violence of fat talk, and the coercion that accompanies it, do little to help people alter or achieve the body images that are transmitted to them as ideal.

The scholars mentioned here make clear that definitions of overweight and obesity change all the time. Far from "objective" scientific facts, they are culturally specific and fluid, with no universally accepted definition, metric, or correlation with general or specific health and disease (Kulick and Meneley 2005). Guthman writes, "'Health' can be used to police body conformity and can be code for weight-related judgments that are socially, not scientifically, driven" (2009, 277). Western medicine has associated overweight with health consequences such as diabetes, heart disease, and a shortened life span, but obesity was not classified as a disease until 2014 by the American Medical Association, and even then, as discussed in a later chapter, it was more in response to its members' desire for reimbursement from health insurers than a clinical assessment of risk or a specific scientific classification. The classification of obesity has been subject to recent and vociferous debates. For example, "metabolic syndrome"—a cluster of risk factors including obesity—is not accepted everywhere as a diagnosis, even though in Mexico it is a commonly used term. In 2013, the American Medical Association appointed a committee to determine whether obesity should be classified as a disease. While the committee unanimously opposed the classification, the membership voted to do so anyway. While the classification was lauded by the AMA as a way to draw attention and resources to a growing "epidemic," others critiqued the classification as economically motivated to boost reimbursements (see Frellick 2013; also Douglas and Wildavsky 1982; Douglas 1985, 1992; Rapp 2000; Bridges 2010; Guthman 2011; Maraesa and Fordyce 2012; Mann, Tomiyama, and Ward 2015; Martin 1992; Osterweil 2014; Rabinow 1992; Rothblum and Solovay 2009; Sesia 1996; Susser 1973; and Tomiyama, Ahlstrom, and Mann 2013).

40. Wann 2009, x. See also Berlant 2007.

41. Weismantel 2005, 51.

42. Greenhalgh 2015.

43. Less frequently used in English, *tamal* is the singular counterpart of *tamales,* plural. *Paletas* are popsicles.

44. Marcus 1995.

45. Ethnographic research methods included participant observation and interviews, forty-eight in all, semistructured and unstructured. In addition to speaking to people in various states in Mexico and Mexican communities in the US about their own life experiences, I was able to conduct interviews with people at the federal ministries of health, foreign affairs, and social welfare, as well as with state government offices of migrant affairs and health, and with the governor in Puebla as well as staff and academics at think tanks, universities, and foundations. I had institutional review board approval for the study and prefaced every formal research interaction with a consent procedure, but I also found that even my day-to-day administrative work of directing a research institute provided me with valuable data that made its way into the book.

46. Berlant 2007.

2. PEOPLE OF THE CORN

1. Gordinier 2014.

2. Her taquería, Hija de Sánchez, opened in Copenhagen the following year.

3. Gordinier 2014. When I show this video to students, many are appalled that someone can claim to pay homage to tortillas and then throw one across the room because it failed to soufflé. They also always note that only Redzepi speaks—his female, Mexican assistant chef is silent and assenting in the video, except for a few words in response to his questions.

4. Gordinier 2014.

5. Gordinier 2014.

6. Noma 2017.

7. Leatherman and Goodman 2005, 833–46.

8. Easton 2015.

9. Leatherman and Goodman 2005.

10. Zimmet 1997.

11. Leatherman and Goodman 2005.

12. In this book, I use the word "citizen" in the social sense, someone who lives in a place and invests time, energy, and resources there. Many of the people in this

category may not qualify for juridical citizenship, but that does not lessen the depth of their attachment to a place or the legitimacy of the claims they make on the state and their neighbors. While Mexico and the United States allow dual citizenship, neither government fully acknowledges the rights of many who have migrated and live their lives invested fully in one or more places, and both countries have large undocumented populations lacking a path to regularization or citizenship. Further, in both places full juridical citizenship has not ensured access to the full scope of benefits of citizenship for low-income and ethnic minority communities.

13. Sutton 2014.

14. Vines 2017.

15. Bruni 2012; also Stupak and Rothman 2015. Moskin 2012.

16. There are countless examples of Mexican and foreign chefs celebrating "authentic Mexican cuisine," such as Rick Bayless, the Chicago-based chef and owner of Frontera Grill, winner of Top Chef Masters, and author of the best-selling cookbook *Authentic Mexican: Regional Cooking from the Heart of Mexico.* Bayless has based his career, as an anthropologist turned chef, on translating for US eaters a purist and reverent approach to traditional Mexican cuisine. For every milestone achieved by such chefs, some critics argue that their high-end cooking is an example of cultural appropriation. See Arellano 2016.

17. Gordinier 2014.

18. By the time this book went to press, Isabel and her children had moved back to her hometown. While her children's education was disrupted by the move (her town does not have a secondary school, and the move itself caused a lengthy interruption in attendance for her younger children), raising her children alone in Playa del Carmen was too difficult without family support.

19. Rosaldo 1993, 69. See also Méndez Cota 2016, 132–39.

20. Vasconcelos 1948; Méndez Cota 2016, 23–33.

21. UNESCO 2010.

22. See Fabian 1983 for a discussion of the ethnographic present.

23. González 2001. Also, Warman 2003, 5.

24. González 2001.

25. Calvo and Rueda Esquibel 2015.

26. Full disclosure: the copresident of a foundation with which the research institute I directed collaborates regularly praises Cosme verbally and on Facebook. When I couldn't get a reservation, I asked if he had any tricks, and indeed, he graciously secured the reservation for us. We paid for our own meal.

27. Wells, "Top" 2015.

28. Wells 2012.

29. Arellano, *Taco* 2012, 100.

30. Wells, "Curious" 2015. See Gálvez 2006 for a discussion of who the "you" constantly referenced in the *New York Times* might be.

31. Stevenson 2005.

32. Sorvino 2015.

33. No relation to Roberto González, of the University of California, Santa Cruz, author of *Zapotec Science,* or Roberto Gonzales, of Harvard University, author of *Lives in Limbo,* both cited elsewhere in this book. See Arellano, "Five Reasons" 2012.

34. Burnett 2016.

35. Burnett 2016.

36. As I finished this book, David Brooks (2017) wrote a column in the *New York Times* critiquing the exclusionary ways elites reproduce their own social status through their children. More than thirty-two hundred reader comments were posted within two days on the paper's website, and many more comments and discussions appeared on Twitter and Facebook—most of them not about the column as a whole, but about one anecdote in which he relates taking a friend with only a high school education out to lunch. She is, he guesses, intimidated by words like "sopressata," "caricola," and "baguette" on an Italian sandwich place's menu, so they leave, deciding instead to "eat Mexican." One reader commented: "I am Mexican and I find the characterization of Mexican food as the food of the uneducated very odd." Other readers marveled that their grandparents' foods, treated as lowly upon first arrival from Italy, were now considered elite. At least one reader called Brooks out for "casual culinary racism."

37. See Schlosser for more about why previously unheard of consumption levels of cheese in the United States were a direct response to the FDA's policy of subsidizing dairy farms and employing its power to promote heightened consumption of dairy products to use up the surplus, rather than allow supply to ebb and flow with unmanipulated demand.

38. Wells 2016.

39. Barber 2014.

40. Barber 2014, loc. 166.

41. Bourdieu 1984.

42. According to Barbara Sibley, a pioneer in her own right as chef/owner of La Palapa in New York City, gender plays a role, too, as a given style of cooking typically achieves prestige only after a prominent male chef singles it out. Sibley 2016.

43. Interview with Gaviria, 2016.

44. Blythman 2013.

45. Small 2013.

46. "*Amor al arte*" is a sardonic phrase for something one does purely for love, even if it is economically unviable.

47. The Free Library 2004.

48. Mexico Ministry of the Economy 2012.

49. The Free Library 2004.

50. Mexico Ministry of the Economy 2012; Patel and Henriques 2004. Note that during the period research for this book was conducted, the Mexican peso fell in value from 12.5 to 22 on the US dollar.

51. Fanjul and Fraser 2003.

52. Office of the US Trade Representative 2017.

53. Fanjul and Fraser 2003, 3.

54. Fox and Haight 2010; Polaski 2004; Wise 2014; Zahniser et al. 2015.

55. Wise 2010; Zahniser et al. 2015.

56. Wise 2012.

57. Wise 2012.

58. Environmental Working Group 2015.

59. Some US corn farmers describe the bulk of their labor as administrative—processing paperwork for subsidies—since so much of corn growing in the United States is now large scale and industrialized, with very little physical labor involved. Schlosser 2012; Pollan 2007.

60. Yuñez-Naude 2003.

61. Patel and Henriques 2004; Hernández López 2008.

62. Fanjul and Fraser 2003, 16.

63. Mexico Ministry of the Economy 2012. Also, Fitting 2011, 17.

64. Siegel 2016, 202.

65. Siegel 2016, 208.

66. See also Clark et al. 2012.

67. See Mexico Ministry of the Economy 2012.

68. A partial list of corn-derived ingredients used in many processed foods, according to Rosen 2010:

Baking powder
Caramel
Cereals
Confectioner's (powdered) sugar (many contain corn starch)
Dextrin or maltodextrin
Dextrose, glucose, or fructose
Golden syrup (treacle)
Glucona delta lactone
High-fructose corn syrup
Invert sugar, invert syrup
Zein (protein from corn, sometimes used in time-released medications
Malt, malt syrup, malt extract
Modified food starch (may be corn)
Mono- and di-glycerides
Monosodium glutamate (MSG)
Polenta

Sorbitol
Starch, food starch
Sucrose (may derive from corn)
Vanilla extract
Vegetable mixes (may contain corn)
Xantham gum

69. Recent archaeological evidence, however, suggests that the first cultivation of corn may have been elsewhere, Fitting 2011, 7. Also MacNeish 1972; Méndez Cota 2016; Pilcher 2012.

70. Socolow 2000.

71. "Criollo" is a term that was widely used in Latin America during the colonial period to refer to people of Spanish ancestry born in the Americas. Criollos were the primary instigators of the wars of independence. They viewed their whiteness as a mark of deservingness of privileges and power, although colonial social structures held them inferior to the *peninsulares,* or *gachupines,* born in Spain. Today, "criollo" can mean different things. In Mexico, in rural contexts, it is used to refer to "native" as opposed to "hybrid," or newly developed strains of livestock and plants.

72. Ejidos are communally held and worked lands; families have been able to pass down access to the land to heirs when they retain documentation of membership in the community that holds the title. Problems with paperwork are a frequent reason for people losing access to such land.

73. Quelites are wild greens that grow spontaneously in some conditions, but can also sometimes be cultivated. They include huauzontle, papaloquelite, and verdolaga. As many as one hundred species of quelites grow in Mexico. Aguilar, Illsley, and Marielle 2005, 87; Calvo and Rueda Esquibel 2015.

74. In this town, I was told the legend of the founder of the major egg company established there. According to local lore, he was an indigenous man who started off with a bicycle, selling eggs at the city's markets from his family's home coop. Eventually, he bought out others and sold on an ever larger scale, growing his business without seeming to attract a lot of attention. In a parable that illustrates the local social structure, he eventually went to the town's industrial vehicle dealer, looking to buy three hundred trucks. He wanted to buy the trucks, the legend says, in cash, and carried with him a sack of paper bills. He walked into the dealership, and the person at the front counter laughed at him and ejected him back onto the street, allegedly because of his indigenous appearance. Apparently, the dealership owner came out and, realizing what had happened, scolded the employee for not recognizing one of the wealthiest people in the region and, worse, for rejecting his money.

75. In *Zapotec Science,* González writes that in the Zapotec community he researched, "in all of the stories maize appears as a living being, a plant-person

who can help humans meet certain moral obligations and responsibilities toward kin and neighbors" (2001, 106). In *Up, Down, and Sideways,* Stryker and González write, "Maize is no ordinary plant, but may more accurately be called a plant-person with a heart, a soul, a memory, a strong will, and the ability to punish people" (113).

76. See González 2001 for more information on long-standing practices for supporting criollo maize stalks with dirt mounds, preventing their collapse in the wind.

77. Fitting 2011, 41 and 48; Méndez Cota, 2016, 39.

78. Judy Hellman, personal communication, 2015. Also Barkin 2005.

79. See, e.g., Hollingsworth, Schmitter, and Streeck 1994.

3. LAYING THE GROUNDWORK FOR NAFTA

1. We could trace these ideas further back. Certainly, early modern Spain had elaborate notions about the relationship between modernity and urban civilizations, as well as the role of the countryside in their vision of prosperity and development. An urban-centric ethos informed Spanish colonial settlements in the New World, as did a disdain for people who worked with their hands (see Kagan and Marías 2000), but I begin with the Porfiriato due to space concerns and because of its more direct linkages to NAFTA.

2. Méndez Cota 2016, 30.

3. Patel and Henriques 2004.

4. Patel and Henriques 2004; Mexico Economic Ministry 2012.

5. Patel and Henriques 2004.

6. In his book, *Tacos,* Alex Stupak, chef of Empellón Cocina, states that sweet corn is a different plant than grain corn and that grain corn cannot be eaten fresh. He makes a strong argument that for anyone interested in making quality Mexican food, freshly nixtamalized and ground corn is the only way to go, but he does not differentiate between landrace corn and maíz híbrido the way the farmers I spoke with in Mexico do. In Mexico, elote, esquites, and corn masa all are produced from the same species of corn and it is time on the stalk, not breed, that determines applicability for different uses.

7. Foley 2013.

8. Fetishism, as a concept, was a product of orientalism and the colonial encounter. The idea of fetishism is what Europeans saw as non-Europeans' over-investment of material objects with supernatural powers. Europeans had notions of "acceptable" boundaries between the material and spiritual world. Ironically, early modern Europe was a heyday for relics, saint worship, and the advent of one of the most spectacular examples of investment of meaning in a material object—the eucharistic host. But after the Reformation, the use of objects within reli-

gious practice was endorsed simply as a mnemonic for abstract spiritual concepts or as vessels of faith; the objects were not to be imbued with any power in and of themselves. Early anthropological accounts of non-Western cultures were quick to mention fetishism and animism. While such primitive/modern dichotomies were largely purged from the discipline in the latter part of the twentieth century, more recent anthropology and pop culture have, following Marx's notion of commodity fetishism, applied the concept also to decidedly Western practices, such as the fetishization of wealth, status symbols, celebrity obsession, and so on.

9. González 2001.

10. Gálvez 2010.

11. This kind of aesthetics of resourcefulness was memorably elaborated in relation to Chicano art by Tomás Ybarra-Frausto in his essay on *rasquachismo* (1989).

12. Hellman 1978. See also Fitting 2011.

13. Hewitt de Alcántara 1976, 1.

14. Hewitt de Alcántara 1976.

15. Hewitt de Alcántara 1976, 5.

16. Hewitt de Alcántara 1976, 6.

17. Hewitt de Alcántara 1976, 12–16.

18. Hewitt de Alcántara 1976, 12.

19. CONASUPO would be dismantled in 1999, during the presidency of Ernesto Zedillo. The project of liberalizing Mexico's markets ushered in the end of CONASUPO, which had for six decades controlled prices of staple crops and controlled distribution through government-managed stores (Yuñez Naude, 2003; also Barquera, Rivera-Dommarco, and Gasca-García 2001; Ochoa 2000).

20. Hellman 1978, 57.

21. Schanbacher 2000; Hellman 1995; Lind and Barham 2004.

22. Lind and Barham 2004, 55.

23. Lind and Barham 2004, 56.

24. Méndez Cota 2016, 26.

25. Lind and Barham 2004, 51.

26. Fox 1993, 27 and 3.

27. It is important to note that all of the successive governments after the revolution and until the 2000 presidential elections were of the same party. The PRI (Partido Revolucionario Institucional) ruled Mexico for seventy-one years, winning every election, albeit not always transparently.

28. Perkins 1990; Hewitt de Alcántara 1978.

29. Fox 1993, 69.

30. Fox 1993, 72.

31. Ricardo 1821.

32. This experiment was seen as a failure, as a skirmish over tomatoes had shown that the United States was willing to use food as a bargaining chip to influ-

ence oil policy, Mexico's most important natural resource and source of wealth. Oil's importance to Mexico's economy declined only recently, when remittances surpassed oil revenues as the first source of Mexico's GDP. Harrup 2016.

33. Fox 1993, 71.

34. González Alejo 2016.

35. A high-end tequila bottler had sponsored the reception and in exchange was able to spend a few minutes promoting the product and telling "the story" of the tequila. During this recounting, another party guest whispered in my ear the price of the bottle we were sipping from, and I confirmed the price later.

36. Grayson 2007.

37. Grayson 2007, 44.

38. Rabo Research 2013.

39. Grayson 2007.

40. Grayson 2007, 8.

41. Torres 2016. In the article, Aspe uses the term "competitive advantage," which seems to sometimes be used interchangeably with "comparative advantage," but the latter is the term used by Ricardo in his 1817 book, which has been so influential to modern economics. See also Fitting 2011, 4.

42. Cortés 2003; Hellman 1995; Rivera Sanchez, personal communication, 2000; Smith 2005; Gálvez 2009.

43. Ferdman 2015. Sales of salsa and tortillas have also passed burger buns and ketchup. Hirsch 2014.

44. Fort 2017.

45. United Nations 1974. Also, Falcon and Naylor 2005; Fitting 2011.

46. Holt-Giménez 2009. See Gray 2013 for more on the food justice movement.

47. It is important to note that "food security" is a term used by anti-hunger advocates to measure a household or individual's capacity to meet basic food needs. In that context, it has retained a progressive valence, lost when the term is used to refer to nations.

48. Ostry, Loungani, and Furceri 2016.

49. Cardoso and Faletto 1970; Wallerstein 1974; Prebisch 1963. See also Biel 2016.

50. These are ubiquitous phrases in global economics. For example, they were used by several of the presenters at the Congressional Hispanic Leadership Initiative's "CHLI Trade and International Affairs Symposium," Washington, DC, Sept. 9, 2014.

51. NAFTA and subsequent trade agreements have been channeled through Congress with "fast track authority," ostensibly a mechanism of efficiency, in which Congress grants authority for negotiation and amendment to the executive branch and presidentially appointed negotiators, leaving Congress only an opportunity to give an "up or down" vote at the end of the process.

52. Carlsen 2011.
53. Marosi 2014.

4. NAFTA

1. Gansitos are snack cakes produced by Bimbo brand (now owner of Entenmann's and Arnold, among other US brands) and the largest bakery brand in the world. Sabritas are potato chips, a Mexican brand now owned by Frito-Lay, a Pepsico division.
2. GRAIN 2015.
3. Puebla is reputed to offer a safe haven from drug violence. Rumor has it the cartel leaders send their wives and children here—it's a college town with more than a dozen universities—because they can be kept safely out of the fray. But, increasingly, grassroots reports and anecdotal evidence indicate rampant drug violence in rural communities and even in the city, with kidnappings, extortion, "virtual kidnappings," human and sex trafficking, and other related symptoms of organized crime on the rise. See Palou 2010.
4. Harvey 2005.
5. Mintz 1996; Blanding 2011.
6. Mintz 1996, 27.
7. Even while the militarization of the border is not a fully funded mandate, the US-Mexico border is where vast quantities of decommissioned military equipment are repurposed. Further, US security interests are advanced by investments in training, financing, and arming of Mexican law enforcement agencies tasked with combating organized crime and stemming migration to the United States (currently originating largely from Central America).
8. This is according to the author's initial investigation analyzing data from CEPAL 2016 and World Bank 2017.
9. Mintz 1996, 27.
10. Striffler 2001; Gleijeses 1992.
11. Harvey 2005; Freudenberg 2014.
12. Mazzochi, Shankar, and Traill 2012, 2.
13. Traill 2006, 163.
14. Hawkes 2006.
15. Hawkes 2006.
16. Agencia Andaluza de Promoción Exterior 2012.
17. USDA 2005.
18. GRAIN 2015.
19. Clark et al. 2012, 60.
20. Hawkes 2006; Siegel 2016.

21. Hawkes 2006; Samb et al. 2010; Yang, McDaniel, and Malone 2012.

22. Hawkes 2006; Friel 2017; Handley et al. 2013; Yang, McDaniel, and Malone 2012.

23. Popkin 1998, 6. See also Cordain et al. 2005.

24. Popkin 1998; Wise 2014.

25. Kroker-Lobos et al. 2014. See also Singh et al. 2015.

26. Hawkes 2006; also Labonté, Mohindra, and Lencucha 2011; Stuckler et al. 2012.

27. Hawkes 2006.

28. Kennedy, Nantel, and Shetty 2004.

29. Kennedy, Nantel, and Shetty 2004.

30. Hawkes 2006.

31. Of course, it's more complicated than that, as long as the wealthy still enjoy truffles and caviar. But today, more than in recent decades, the "local" has come to signify value in ways it did not always. See Finn 2017 for more on class and food preferences.

32. Popkin 1998, 7.

33. Popkin 1998, 11.

34. Fox 1993; González Alejo 2016; Yuñez-Naude 2003.

35. Hernán Cortés's letters, Fray Diego Durán's *History of the Indies of New Spain,* Bernal Díaz's *The Conquest of New Spain,* and conquest-era codices such as the Mendoza and Florentine Codex, include descriptions of Moctezuma's banquets and the popular marketplaces of the Mexica capital at the time of the arrival of the Spanish.

36. Sociologists DiMaggio and Powell 1983 developed the notion of institutional isomorphism to describe the coercive, normative, and mimetic pressures that result in a high level of similarity between different institutions competing in the same environment.

37. Freudenberg 2014.

38. Freudenberg 2014.

39. Nestle 2013; Pollan 2007; Schlosser 2012.

40. Douglas 1992.

41. McMillan 2012.

42. Moss 2013; Avena, Rada, and Hoebel 2008; Hamblin 2014.

43. US Department of Commerce 2004.

44. Center for Responsive Politics 2015.

45. González Castro et al. 2011; Godoy 2011; Peretz et al. 2011.

46. Schlosser 2012; Guthman 2011.

47. Research on health effects of chemicals, including kidney problems, is growing around the world, with a lot of evidence that herbicides like glyphosate pose particular risk to agricultural workers with high exposure to them. Hamdy 2008; Jayawardena 2017; Laws et al. 2015.

48. Shah 2015. See also Tsing 2015; Biss 2014.

49. Francino 2014; McGowan et al. 2015; Wills-Karp, Santeliz, and Karp 2001; Rook and Brunet 2002. Jhamnani and Frischmeyer-Guerrerio 2016 have recently found that small levels of early exposure of allergy-prone infants to peanuts may prevent the development of that potentially fatal allergy later in life. Biss 2014 details science-defying efforts by many contemporary middle-class and higher-income parents in the United States to boost their children's immunity without immunizations.

50. Kennedy 2014.

51. Schlosser 2012.

52. Kennedy 2014.

53. Novotny Gebauer, and Baer 2012; Hatch et al. 2010; Hectors et al. 2013; Khazan 2016; Brown et al. 2016.

54. Pontzer et al. 2016.

55. Khazan 2016; Hallal et al. 2012.

56. Perro and Adams 2017 address this.

57. Marx de Salcedo 2015 demonstrates that many of the technological developments in food production technology have been innovated by and for the US military.

58. See also Baillie-Hamilton 2002, 188.

59. Kennedy 2014.

60. Blaser 2014; Blaser and Falkow 2009.

61. Mann, Tomiyama, and Ward 2015.

62. Guthman 2011, 15–16.

63. Referred to as "leptogenic": the opposite of "obesogenic," leptogenic environments promote thinness. Guthman 2011, 66.

64. Guthman 2011, 99.

65. INEGI 2015.

66. Nestle 2015.

67. "The consensus forged in conferences and policy spaces concerning the uncertainty and complexity of obesity's determinants creates a continued deflection of responsibilities back to the purported knowledge deficiencies of individual eaters" (Sanabria 2016, 134).

68. Gálvez 2011; Harvard 2015.

69. Pollan 2008.

70. Nestle 2015, 2013; Associated Press 2015. See also Guthman 2011 and O'Connor 2015.

71. Since December 2016, revelations have emerged that spyware purchased by the government of Mexico from an Israeli firm has been used to hack the telephones and servers of civil society organizations that work in consumer protection and human rights. Ahmed and Perlroth 2017.

72. Sanabria 2016, Méndez Cota 2016.

5. DEFLECTING THE BLAME

1. El Poder del Consumidor 2015.

2. *Antojitos,* literally "little cravings," is the name given to appetizers on Mexican food menus.

3. See Arellano 2017 for a hilarious takedown of the translation of Mexican street food by hipster US chefs.

4. Secretaría de la Salud 2013.

5. The midmorning meal is typically called *almuerzo,* and the larger midafternoon meal is *comida.* See also Lomnitz and Adler-Lomnitz 1987.

6. A sope is a thick handmade corn tortilla, sometimes called a "memela." Alejandro Calvillo calls attention to the perversion of what he calls *la dieta popular,* in which patrimonial foods like tamales, which are customarily steamed, are sometimes now deep-fried in lard by street vendors competing with the mouth feel and level of satisfaction advertised by processed foods that have been engineered to satisfy, even addict, consumers.

7. Molyneux 2006, 430–31.

8. Mintz 1986, 1996.

9. Freudenberg 2014; Moss 2013.

10. Fried 2015.

11. See Freudenberg (2014, 71–88) for an analysis of this process with the processed food, firearms, tobacco, automobile, and pharmaceutical industries.

12. Hoffman 2001; Beaglehole et al. 2007, 2011; Yang et al. 2012.

13. Swinburn et al. 2011.

14. Swinburn et al. 2011. See also Bray 1998, 2015.

15. Frieden 2010.

16. Nestle 2015, 2013.

17. The following timeline has been constructed based on interviews in December 2014 and January 2015 with architects of the policy from the Ministry of Health, scholars, elected officials, and representatives of involved nonprofit and advocacy organizations and foundations (El Poder del Consumidor, la Fundación Chespirito, Fundación Mídete), as well as news media reports, published reports from nonprofit and advocacy organizations, and government documents from 2014 to 2017.

18. OECD 2012.

19. The name of the economic ministry is Hacienda, and it may have fewer conflicts of interest with the food and beverage industry than the health ministry, advocates have told me.

20. Nestle 2015.

21. Philadelphia, Pennsylvania, became the second city after Berkeley, California, to pass a soda tax in the United States, in June 2016.

22. Colchero et al. 2016; Colchero et al. 2017; Hernández-Cordero et al. 2014; Rosenberg 2015.

23. Ministry of Health of Brazil 2014; Consumers International and World Obesity Federation 2014.

24. Journalists and civil society organizations have pointed out many conflicts of interest. One example: FUNSALUD (Fundación Mexicana para la Salud), is a health-focused foundation that receives the bulk of its funding from Nestle. The health minister at the time I conducted the bulk of the research for this book, Mercedes Juan, and the third in command, Pablo Kuri, came to the ministry from FUNSALUD. Alejandro Chertorivski was another recent minister of health, appointed in spite of having only a master's-level education and no medical credentials. He is the son of the president of ConMéxico, Mexico's agency charged with promoting international investment. Multinational food corporation executives have been included at the negotiating table of all recent high-level anti-obesity discussions, while scholarly experts have been pointedly excluded from the final negotiations regarding legislation. A high-level "summit" on obesity, diabetes, heart disease, and nutrition held in 2012 at the Mexican World Trade Center was sponsored by McDonald's, Jumex, Bimbo, and Alpura, major global and national food corporations. See also Consumers International 2014 and Calvillo 2015.

25. Currently, Mexico's nutritional labeling includes a detailed nutrition facts label on the back and a front-of-package summary of a product's saturated fat, other fat, total sugar (added and natural), sodium, and "energy," or calories, but the labeling is so small as to be practically illegible (at least to my middle-aged eyes). Further, the failure to distinguish between added and natural sugars for products like sugar-sweetened fruit juices, which include, presumably, both sugars from the fruit and added sugars, indicates that officially both kinds of sugars are treated as equivalents.

26. In September 1985, Mexico experienced a massive earthquake, 8.0 on the Richter scale, with its epicenter in the center of the country. Five to ten thousand people were killed and the capital's infrastructure was devastated. Many analysts date Mexico's relationship with bottled water to that event. The water was unsafe to drink following the earthquake, and the beverage corporations met the need with bottled water. Ever since, many people tell me, the public does not trust the public water system to deliver safe, potable water. Corporations have been seen as more trustworthy than government, and thus, at all income levels, people are very likely to consume bottled water instead of tap, even for cooking. Mexico has become the largest per capita consumer of bottled water in the world, and indicators are that the number is on the rise as consumption of soda has begun to decline since 2014. Testing of Mexico's tap water indicates that it may in fact contain less bacteria than some bottled water brands, but this has not led to

most people changing their habits (Pallares and René 2015; Roberts 2015). As a result, potable water infrastructure in the country is surprisingly underdeveloped, with most public schools still lacking drinking fountains. Installation of potable water fountains in Mexico's public schools is the major investment identified to be funded by Mexico's sugar-sweetened beverage tax. It has remained mind-numbingly difficult to accomplish, even with the influx of resources since the tax went into effect (personal communication, Poder del Consumidor, 2017).

27. Freudenberg 2014, 71–72; Schmitt 2005.

28. Calvillo, personal conversations, Sept. 23, 2014, Dec. 12, 2014.

29. ConMéxico 2014.

30. López Obrador 2014.

31. Goldman 2014; Ahmed and Perlroth 2017.

32. Piketty 2014.

33. PRI 2016.

34. Many of the "scholarships" are for training and workshops that bear no credit and do not result in licensing or any other objective token of completion.

35. When this interview was conducted, this was about $136. This would be $113 with the exchange rate as of July 23, 2017.

36. Bridges 2017, 2010; Park 2011.

37. Credited to Lewis 1959, but taken up by a broad range of policy makers and highly influential in the 1960s and 1970s, such as Moynihan 1969.

38. Centeno 2001, 296.

39. This was a lower rate of poverty than that indicated by the external data I gathered, which held it to be as high as 55 percent. See Weisbrot et al. 2017; CONEVAL 2012; Jordan and Sullivan 2003; Garcia 2014; Public Citizen 2014, Rowe 2010–2011; Skoufias and Di Maro 2008.

40. Leroy et al. 2013; Smith Oka 2013. See also Barquera, Rivera-Dommarco, and Gasca-García 2001.

41. Rojas-Suarez 2009.

42. See World Bank database, "Data: Mexico," 2014, https://data.worldbank.org/.

43. Osterweil 2014; Moran-Thomas 2016.

44. Kroker-Lobos et al. 2014.

45. Cejudo and Michel 2015; Gil, Méndez, and Sobrino 2014; Montalvo 2016.

46. Leroy et al. 2013.

47. "Es un tema que hay que resolver, dar información y capacitar a las cocineras para que ellas vayan asumiendo los cambios necesarios en su comportamiento alimentario." "Todo es una 'cuestión cultural,' pues las cocineras están acostumbradas a cocinar con demasiada grasa y sal." Montalvo 2016.

48. Elizalde et al. n.d., 41.

49. González 2001, 2. On the same note, Warman writes about pre-Columbian diets in the Americas: "Nature, so lavishly bestowed with plants, was far

less well endowed with edible animals: the humble and prized turkeys, ducks, dogs, rodents, Andean ungulates—llamas and alpacas—bees, and cochineal, that is, if one can speak of the domestication of insects" (2003, 5).

50. Bertrán Vila 2010.

51. This can be seen with the "coca-colonization hypothesis" (Zimmet 1997; Leatherman and Goodman 2005). For a critique, see Montoya 2007; for an alternative case study, Vaughan 1991.

52. Wolf 2010.

53. Berlant describes this state of affairs as "where life building and the attrition of human life are indistinguishable, and where it is hard to distinguish modes of incoherence, distractedness, and habituation from deliberate and deliberative activity" (2007, 761).

54. Kulick and Meneley 2005; Guthman 2011.

55. Roberts 2015, 249; Carney 2015; Kulick and Meneley 2005.

56. Guthman 2011; Greenhalgh 2015; Firth 2012.

57. Bauer 2001. Berlant 2007 also writes about this in more general terms.

58. Vaughan 1997. See also Méndez Cota 2016.

59. Bertrán Vila 2010, 390; Pilcher 1998; Popkin 1998.

60. Vasconcelos 1948. See Méndez Cota 2016 for a lengthy discussion of Gamio and Bonfil Batalla's differing approaches to the problem of Mexican citizenship after independence.

61. Warman 2003, xiii.

62. Gamio 1935.

63. Gamio 1942.

64. Bertrán Vila 2010, 391.

65. Vasconcelos 1948.

66. Méndez Cota 2016.

67. Lomnitz and Adler-Lomnitz 1987, 178.

68. Pilcher 1998; Hernández López 2008; Ochoa 2000, 589; Weis 2012.

69. In the United States, we can see anxieties about consumption practices of nonwhite and poor people—including Mexican Americans and immigrants—manifest in all sorts of locations, including the Zoot Suit Riots in Los Angeles in the 1943. The sartorial choices of Mexican Americans who wore elegant tailored suits were viewed as pathological and excessive—too much fabric, too many lines and drapes. An aesthetic based on being over the top seemed to make white Navy sailors and law enforcement officers nervous, aggressive, and violent, leading them to punish such "excess" with brutality (Ybarra Frausto 1989, Sánchez Tranquilino and Tagg 1992). Of course, there are echoes of this in attitudes today about baggy clothing worn by Latinx and African American youth.

70. Marx 1887.

71. Boero 2009, 113. See Saldaña Tejeda (2017) for discussion of the ways that current trends in epigenetic research in Mexico have led to new kinds of mother

blame, this time implicating mothers' wombs, genetic profiles, and ancestry in transmission of propensity for obesity and diet-related illness.

72. Pilcher 1998, 62.

73. Farnsworth 2009; Hershfield 2008.

74. Molyneux 2006, 430; see also Farnsworth 2009.

75. Molyneux 2006, 430–31.

76. See Roseberry (1996, 772) on constrained choice.

77. González 2001.

78. Pilcher 2006; Lewis 1951; Mintz 1996.

79. See World Bank database, "Data: Mexico," 2014, https://data.worldbank.org/.

80. Laudan 2001.

81. Fernandez Kelly 2005.

82. Arroyo, Loria, and Méndez 2004.

83. Manheimer 2012.

6. DIABETES

1. Interview with couple in Malacatepec, Puebla. January 2015.

> My brothers, most are there [in the United States], and "the boss" [my mother] is sick because of my brothers, her sons. I tell her, "Mamá, if they call you on the phone, don't feel bad. You're here with us, and you see us. But imagine how many years they have been gone."
>
> I tell her, "Well, you feel that way about my brothers, I also have my sons there. And one has to think that they left because there's something they want to accomplish." And well, my mom is sick now, more than she should be, because she's looking for her kids, my brothers. They talk to her, they send her money. But for us as parents the most beautiful thing is that your kids are with you—even though your kids might feel bad because they drag you to the store. But the way I see it, it's the most beautiful thing to have kids and see them even if it's once a month, every two months and those that have left have been gone fifteen years.
>
> And even though we speak on the phone, it's not the same. We only hear their voices. And the ones who didn't leave, well they're here with us, they've married, but every week or during the week, they stop by: "Papá, what are you up to?"
>
> "I'm here. Come in." We share something as simple as a taco, a hug, just a greeting. But those who are far away, even though you greet them, it's different. It's not the same as having them close by.
>
> And all of this, for us, well it affected my wife a lot. Me, too, a little, but we had to find a way to get through it.
>
> And now that the years have gone by, they call us up, they talk to us, but we live in different worlds. We've adjusted to the fact that they're not here. When my second son left, his name is Juan, I would get home from work and every day we would eat dinner together. My wife would say, "Come, let's eat."
>
> "Let's wait for Juan."

And he'd arrive on his bike and he'd say, "I'll be right back." And he'd go out to the street and he'd be back in five minutes.

And after he left, I'd arrive in the afternoon. "Let's eat."

"Wait." And well, the custom between kids and parents is to eat together. You have to chat. Even if you're only chatting about what we would call simple gossip. But it's important to spend time together. But when he left, he left an empty space.

"Let's eat."

"Wait."

And then she'd remember, and say, "He's not coming."

He's gone.

2. *Tequío* and *faena* are words used to refer to the collective labor distributed between community members in indigenous communities—the word *tequío* derives from Nahuatl—and taken up as a form of labor organization by the colonial system, and again with the ejido system in postrevolutionary Mexico.

3. Maté 2011.

4. Geronimus 1992.

5. McEwen 2000; McEwen and Wingfield 2003; Arbona et al. 2010.

6. D'Alonzo, Johnson, and Fanfan 2012, 364; Tuñon-Pablos and Dreby 2016.

7. For a review of this literature, see Gálvez 2011.

8. De León 2015.

9. Brennan 2014; De León 2015.

10. Mendenhall 2012, 12. Mendenhall builds on Singer's (2009) concept of syndemics.

11. High rates of trauma and violence were also found by Gálvez and Pallares (n.d.).

12. Mendenhall 2012, 13. See also D'Alonzo, Johnson, and Fanfan 2012.

13. Gonzales 2015; Arbona et al. 2010; Suárez Orozco and Suárez Orozco 2015; Abo-Zena, Suárez Orozco, and Marks 2015; Yoshikawa 2011.

14. Green 2011; Magaña 2008; De León 2015; Eschbach and Hagan 2003.

15. Mendenhall 2017.

16. For a review, see Montoya 2007.

17. Neel 1962, 1999; Schulze and Hu 2005. See Montoya 2007 and Saldaña Tejeda 2017 for discussion.

18. Montoya 2007, 2011.

19. Borrell 2005; Chavez 2013; D'Alonzo, Johnson, and Fanfan 2012; Hayes-Bautista 2002; Viruell-Fuentes 2011 and Viruell-Fuentes, Miranda, and Abdulrahim 2012.

20. Carney 2015; Batis et al. 2011; Greder, Slowing, and Doudna 2012.

21. Greenhalgh and Carney 2014; Guthman 2009.

22. Guarnaccia et al. 2012.

23. Macari 2013 describes the *señoras,* women who may be from Ecuador or Colombia, or any other migrant-sending country, whose occupation is to cook

"home style" hot meals for Latino laborers. They may serve in their homes, from food trucks, or even from shopping carts, near the work places or residences of their customers.

24. Macari 2013.

25. Macari 2013; Rosenbaum 2003.

26. Gálvez 2011.

27. Guarnaccia et al. 2012.

28. See Lomnitz and Adler-Lomnitz 1987.

29. "¡La soda es un pecado, un pecado de gula!"

30. Interview 2014. I also cite interviews with the same person from 2003, 2005, and 2006 in this section.

> The vegetables are not seasonal, for example, the orange, the watermelon, and all the time there is fruit here. And in Mexico no, because at the plaza we go to—we say plaza where they sell all the vegetables and everything is seasonal—there is only a short time that there is that vegetable, that fruit, and when they're done, there won't be any until next year when it is harvested again.
>
> And here, no. Here, all the time anyone can see that the apples are very big. The oranges. The watermelon, the melon. All the time they are available.
>
> Then I think that it is as if they are full of chemicals all the time, and in Mexico no, it is completely different.

31. Gálvez 2011.

7. NOSTALGIA, PRESTIGE, AND A PARTY EVERY DAY

1. Proust, Pinter, and Di Trevis 2000.

2. Rosaldo 1993.

3. Fitting 2011, 95; Pilcher 1998.

4. Viladrich 2017; Viladrich and Tagliaferro 2016.

5. See Carmen Lomas Garza's *La Tamalada* here: http://decolonizeyourdiet.org/wp-content/uploads/2013/12/tamalada-cover-web.jpg.

6. McDonald's Mexico 2015.

7. Purists interested in making tamales as they were made before the arrival of the Spanish leave out the lard, which comes from large domesticated animals brought with colonization. See Calvo and Rueda Esquibel 2015.

8. Felassi 1987.

9. Kilpatrick 2015.

10. Medina 2015. Lomnitz and Adler-Lomnitz 1987 presciently proposed celebration of ancestral indigenous foods and foodways thirty years ago, as a way of thinking about food for the future.

11. In his book *Tasting Food, Tasting Culture* (1996), Sidney Mintz levels what he acknowledges to be a controversial assertion: the US has no cuisine, even while he honors the importance and unique trajectories of various "regional cuisines"

within the US. If one result of globalization is "dietary convergence," by which people the world over come to have access to the same sorts of processed and prepared foods and ingredients, then the US, it can be argued, has had less to lose. Indeed, some argue that fast food, including the rapid and enthusiastic development of the fast food that Eric Schlosser 2012 locates definitively in Southern California at the peak of the automobile age, is the closest the US comes to a cuisine. Of course, the idea that the United States does not have a cuisine is a legacy of settler colonialism, which appropriated native food traditions and ingredients, for example, turkey, ground corn, sweet potatoes, and squash, and recast them as aspects of white American culture, as in the typical Thanksgiving menu. For Mexico, where this process is still ongoing, there is arguably more to lose.

12. Schlosser 2012, 217.

13. Freudenberg 2014, 101.

14. Hawkes 2006; See also Heffernan et al. 1994; Martínez 2002.

15. Schlosser 2012, 218; Bonanno 1994.

16. Naudziunas 2013.

17. Kurland 2009. See also Gray 2013.

18. Mintz 1996, 13. See also Bourdieu 1984.

19. The video was removed by Coca-Cola, but reposted by consumer and nutrition advocates at www.youtube.com/watch?v=k9-AtfwDX5w.

20. Nestle 2015.

21. Abercrombie 1998; Bacigalupo 2016.

22. Medina 2015; Fitting 2011, 87.

8. CONCLUSION

1. Interview featured in Schwittek and Gálvez 2017.

2. González 2001 describes the rhythm and conditions of farmers who sleep near their fields with the cycles of planting and harvest.

3. Harvey 1988, 2005. See also Guthman 2009; Osterweill 2014.

4. Guthman 2011, 174.

5. Freudenberg 2016.

6. Freudenberg 2016.

7. Guthman 2009, 187–88.

8. Debord wrote that in the primitive stage of capitalist accumulation, the worker need only "be allotted the indispensable minimum for maintaining his labor power" but eventually, "commodity abundance reaches a level that requires an additional collaboration from him . . . Once his workday is over, the worker is suddenly redeemed from the total contempt toward him that is so clearly implied by every aspect of the organization and surveillance of production and finds

himself suddenly treated like a grownup, with a great show of politeness in his new role as a consumer" (2011, 43).

9. Ahmed and Perlroth 2017.

10. Nestle 2015, 200.

11. Harvey 2005; see also Keshavjee 2014.

12. See Comaroff and Comaroff 2001.

13. Ostry, Loungani, and Furceri 2016.

14. Suárez Vélez 2011.

15. Greenhalgh and Carney 2014.

16. Berlant 2007, 758–63.

17. Maldonado 2014.

18. USAID 2016; Isaacson et al. 2014.

19. Green 2011; Harvey 2005; Osterweil 2014.

20. Farmer 2004, 40.

21. Faced with a breast cancer diagnosis, Luz Calvo and partner Catriona Rueda Esquibel were confronted with a daunting path of treatment and recovery. Researching breast cancer rates, they learned that while Mexico has some of the lowest rates of breast cancer, for Latinxs in the United States, risk rises significantly with duration of residency. The two scholars investigated pre-Columbian foodways and decided that a diet ancestral to Mesoamerica and rich in plants like beans, squash, corn, wild greens, nopales, and more, could promote protection from disease as well as a feeling of connection to their *antepasados*. In 2015, they published a cookbook/manifesto that emerged from that process of experimentation and inquiry: *Decolonize Your Diet: Plant-Based Mexican-American Recipes for Health and Healing* (2015). Their book includes recipes that are mainly vegan, and except for whole wheat tortillas (inspired by Chicana author Gloria Anzaldúa), almost entirely based on ingredients that preceded the arrival of Europeans to the Western Hemisphere. As important as their recipes are for good (nutritious and appealing) eating, they propose a way of life that honors preindustrial ways of producing and preparing food that is slow, deliberate, mindful, and premised on interconnections between people, what they call "revolutionary love." Accompanying the book is a Facebook page that celebrates other efforts at decolonized eating, in which food activists argue for a return to preindustrialized and ancestral approaches to food.

This approach to microlocal food sovereignty promotes respect for indigenous knowledge, can have protective health benefits, and emphasizes resistance and resilience over assimilation. They acknowledge that for many people, knowledge about how to cook as well as ingredients may be limited, with more than one generation separating people today from a way of eating that is not reliant on processed, packaged food. They write that cooking a pot of beans is a revolutionary act. So, they provide clear and thorough instructions for everything from boiling beans to making tamales from corn nixtamalized at home. They emphasize health as well as flavor, and make a strong argument for eating a plant-based diet. This approach to food—producing, cooking, and eating—provides a recipe not only for health, but also for cultural resilience and resistance. See also Pérez 2014.

22. Esteva and Marielle 2007; Fitting 2011.

23. Reardon and Berdegué 2000; Ritzer 2008.

Works Cited

Abajobir, Amanuel Alemu, Cristiana Abbafati, Kaja M. Abbas, Foad Abd-Allah, Semaw Ferede Abera, Victor Aboyans, Olatunji Adetokunboh, et al. "Global, Regional, and National Age-Sex Specific Mortality for 264 Causes of Death, 1980–2016: A Systematic Analysis for the Global Burden of Disease Study 2016." *Lancet* 390, no. 10100 (2017): 1151–1210.

Abercrombie, Thomas Alan. *Pathways of Memory and Power: Ethnography and History among an Andean people.* Madison: University of Wisconsin Press, 1998.

Abo-Zena, Mona M., Carola Suárez-Orozco, and Amy K. Marks. *Transitions: The Development of Children of Immigrants.* New York: New York University Press, 2015.

Agencia Andaluza de Promoción Exterior. *Nota sectorial distribución alimentaria en México.* May 2012. www.extenda.es/web/opencms/fondo-documental/lectorFondo.jsp?uid=9adf8af7-1cf6-11e2-96af-87ba319ddd41.

Aguilar, Jasmín, Catarina Illsley, and Catherine Marielle. "Los sistemas agrícolas de maíz y sus procesos técnicos." In *Sin maíz, no hay país,* edited by Gustavo Esteva and Catherine Marielle, 83–122. Mexico City: Consejo Nacional para las Culturas y las Artes, 2005.

Ahmed, Azam, and Elizabeth Malkin. "Mexicans Are the Nafta Winners? It's News to Them." *New York Times,* Jan. 4, 2017.

Ahmed, Azam, and Nicole Perlroth. "Using Texts as Lures, Government Spyware Targets Mexican Journalists and Their Families." *New York Times*, June 19, 2017.

Alang, N., and C. R. Kelly. "Weight Gain after Fecal Microbiota Transplantation." *Open Forum Infectious Diseases* 2, no. 1 (Feb. 4, 2015). doi: 10.1093/ofid/ofv004.

Arbona, Consuelo, Norma Olvera, Nestor Rodriguez, Jacqueline Hagan, Adriana Linares, and Margit Wiesner. "Acculturative Stress among Documented and Undocumented Latino Immigrants in the United States." *Hispanic Journal of Behavioral Sciences* 32, no. 3 (2010): 362–84.

Arellano, Gustavo. *Taco USA: How Mexican Food Conquered America*. New York: Scribner, 2012.

———. "Five Reasons to Hate GRUMA, Makers of Mission and Guerrero Tortillas, Maseca, and Other Tortilla Evil." *OC Weekly* (blog). June 26, 2012. www.ocweekly.com/five-reasons-to-hate-gruma-makers-of-mission-and-guerrero-tortillas-maseca-and-other-tortilla-evil-6628385/.

———. "The Problem Isn't Rick Bayless Cooking Mexican Food—It's That He's a Thin-Skinned Diva." *OC Weekly* (blog). March 28, 2016. www.ocweekly.com/restaurants/the-problem-isnt-rick-bayless-cooking-mexican-food-its-that-hes-a-thin-skinned-diva-7075113.

———. "10 Mexican Dishes Hipster Chefs Need to Get Over Already." *OC Weekly* (blog). Jan. 3, 2017. www.ocweekly.com/restaurants/10-mexican-dishes-hipster-chefs-need-to-get-over-already-7706336.

Arroyo, Pedro, Alvar Loria, and Oscar Méndez. "Changes in the Household Calorie Supply during the 1994 Economic Crisis in Mexico and Its Implications on the Obesity Epidemic." *Nutrition Reviews* 62, no. 7 (2004): S163–68.

Asad, Talal. "Ethnographic Representation, Statistics and Modern Power." *Social Research* 61, no. 1 (1994): 55–88.

Associated Press. "Emails Reveal Coke's Role in Anti-Obesity Group: Company Says Exec Has Retired." *Telegraph-Journal* (New Brunswick), Nov. 25, 2015.

Avena, Nicole M., Pedro Rada, and Bartley G. Hoebel. "Evidence for Sugar Addiction: Behavioral and Neurochemical Effects of Intermittent, Excessive Sugar Intake." *Neuroscience & Biobehavioral Reviews* 32, no. 1 (2008): 20–39. doi: http://dx.doi.org/10.1016/j.neubiorev.2007.04.019.

Bacigalupo, Ana Mariella. *Thunder Shaman: Making History with Mapuche Spirits in Chile and Patagonia*. Austin: University of Texas Press, 2016.

Baillie-Hamilton, Paula. "Chemical Toxins: A Hypothesis to Explain the Global Obesity Epidemic." *Journal of Alternative and Complementary Medicine* 8, no. 2 (2002): 185–92.

Barber, Dan. *The Third Plate: Field Notes on the Future of Food*. New York: Penguin, 2014.

Barclay, Eliza. "Mexican Fast-Food Craze: Japanese Instant Noodles." *Fortune Magazine,* May 11, 2006.

Barkin, David. "El maíz y la economía." In *Sin maíz, no hay país,* edited by Gustavo Esteva and Catherine Marielle, 155–76. Mexico City: Consejo Nacional para las Culturas y las Artes, 2005.

Barquera, S., J. Rivera-Dommarco, and A. Gasca-García. "Políticas y programas de alimentación y nutrición en México." *Salud Pública de México* 43, no. 5 (2001): 464–77.

Batis, Carolina, Lucia Hernandez-Barrera, Simon Barquera, Juan A. Rivera, and Barry M. Popkin. "Food Acculturation Drives Dietary Differences among Mexicans, Mexican Americans, and Non-Hispanic Whites." *Journal of Nutrition* 141, no. 10 (2011): 1898. doi: 10.3945/jn.111.141473.

Bauer, Arnold J. *Goods, Power, History: Latin America's Material Culture.* Cambridge: Cambridge University Press, 2001.

Beaglehole, R., R. Bonita, R. Horton, et al. "Priority Actions for the Non-Communicable Disease Crisis." *Lancet, 377,* no. 9775 (2011): 1438–47.

Beaglehole, R., Ebrahim, S., Reddy, S., Voute, J., and Leeder, S. "Prevention of Chronic Diseases: A Call to Action." *Lancet* 370 (2007): 2152–57.

Beaubien, Jason. "How Diabetes Got to Be the No. 1 Killer in Mexico." *Goats and Soda.* NPR. 2017. www.npr.org/sections/goatsandsoda/2017/04/05/522038318/how-diabetes-got-to-be-the-no-1-killer-in-mexico.

Bello, Walden. "Manufacturing a Food Crisis." *Nation* 286, no. 21 (2008): 16.

Berlant, Lauren. "Slow Death (Sovereignty, Obesity, Lateral Agency)." *Critical Inquiry* 33, no. 4 (2007): 754–80.

Bertrán Vila, Miriam. "Acercamiento antropológico alimentación y salud en México." *Physis Revista de Saúde Coletiva,* no. 2 (2010): 387–411.

Biel, Robert. *Sustainable Food Systems: The Role of the City.* London: University College London, 2016.

Biss, Eula. *On Immunity: An Inoculation.* Minneapolis: Graywolf Press, 2014.

Blanding, Michael. *The Coke Machine: The Dirty Truth behind the World's Favorite Soft Drink.* New York: Penguin, 2011.

Blaser, Martin J. *Missing Microbes: How the Overuse of Antibiotics Is Fueling Our Modern Plagues.* New York: Macmillan, 2014.

Blaser, Martin J., and Stanley Falkow. "What Are the Consequences of the Disappearing Human Microbiota?" *Nature Reviews Microbiology* 7, no. 12 (2009): 887–94.

Blythman, Joanna. "Can Vegans Stomach the Unpalatable Truth about Quinoa?" *Guardian,* Jan. 16, 2013. www.theguardian.com/commentisfree/2013/jan/16/vegans-stomach-unpalatable-truth-quinoa.

Boero, Natalie. "Fat Kids, Working Moms, and the 'Epidemic of Obesity': Race, Class and Mother Blame." In *Fat Studies Reader,* edited by Esther D.

Rothblum and Sondra Solovay, 113–19. New York: New York University Press, 2009.

Bonanno, Alessandro. *From Columbus to ConAgra: The Globalization of Agriculture and Food.* Lawrence: University Press of Kansas, 1994.

Borrell, L. "Racial Identity among Hispanics: Implications for Health and Well-Being." *American Journal of Public Health* 95, no. 3 (2005): 379–81.

Bourdieu, Pierre. *Distinction: A Social Critique of the Judgement of Taste.* Cambridge, MA: Harvard University Press, 1984.

Bray, George A. "Obesity: A Time Bomb to Be Defused." *Lancet* 352 (1998): 160–61.

———. "Diabetes and Obesity: Time Bombs to Be Defused." *Diabetes Care* 38, no. 11 (Nov. 2015): 1997–99. doi: 10.2337/dci15-0008.

Brennan, Denise. *Life Interrupted: Trafficking into Forced Labor in the United States.* Durham, NC: Duke University Press, 2014.

Bridges, Khiara. *Reproducing Race: An Ethnography of Pregnancy as a Site of Racialization.* Berkeley: University of California, 2010.

———. *The Poverty of Privacy Rights.* Palo Alto, CA: Stanford University Press, 2017.

Briggs, Charles L. "Communicability, Racial Discourse and Disease." *Annual Review of Anthropology* 34, no. 1 (2005): 269–91.

Brooks, David. "How We Are Ruining America." *New York Times,* July 11, 2017.

Brown, Ruth E., Arya M. Sharma, Chris I. Ardern, Pedi Mirdamadi, Paul Mirdamadi, and Jennifer L. Kuk. "Secular Differences in the Association between Caloric Intake, Macronutrient Intake, and Physical Activity with Obesity." *Obesity Research & Clinical Practice* 10, no. 3 (2016): 243–55. doi: 10.1016/j.orcp.2015.08.007.

Bruni, Frank. "Skipping Dessert for Mexican Food." *New York Times,* Feb. 22, 2012. www.nytimes.com/2012/02/22/dining/the-chef-alex-stupak-opens-empellon-cocina.html.

Burnett, Victoria. "Oaxaca's Native Maize Embraced by Top Chefs in U.S. and Europe." *New York Times,* Feb. 11, 2016.

Calvillo, Alejandro. "¿A dónde nos lleva Sra. Secretaria Mercedes Juan?" *Sin Embargo,* March 24, 2015. Opinion sec.

Calvo, Luz, and Catriona Rueda Esquibel. *Decolonize Your Diet: Plant-Based Mexican-American Recipes* for *Health and Healing.* Vancouver, BC: Arsenal Pulp Press, 2015.

Cameron, Max, and Brian Tomlin. *The Making of NAFTA: How the Deal Was Done.* Ithaca, NY: Cornell University Press, 2000.

Cannon, Geoffrey. "Out of the Box." *Public Health Nutrition* 8, no. 4 (2005): 344–47. doi: 10.1079/PHN2005743.

Cardoso, Fernando Henrique, and Enzo Faletto. *Dependência e desenvolvimento da América Latina: Ensaio de interpretação sociológica.* Biblioteca de Ciências Sociais. Rio de Janeiro: Livrarias Editôras Reunidas, 1970.

Carlsen, Laura. "NAFTA Is Starving Mexico: Free Trade Has Starved Mexico and Stuffed Transnational Corporations." Oct. 20, 2011. http://fpif.org/nafta_is_starving_mexico/.

Carney, Megan A. *The Unending Hunger: Tracing Women and Food Insecurity across Borders.* Berkeley: University of California Press, 2015.

Cejudo, Guillermo M., and Cynthia L. Michel. "Resolviendo problemas sociales complejos mediante la integración de políticas: El caso de la cruzada nacional contra el hambre en México." *Revista del CLAD Reforma y Democracia* 63 (2015): 33–64.

Centeno, Miguel Angel. *The Other Mirror: Grand Theory through the Lens of Latin America.* Princeton, NJ: Princeton University Press, 2001.

Center for Responsive Politics. "Chemical and Related Manufacturing." OpenSecrets.org. 2015. www.opensecrets.org/lobby/indusclient.php?id=N13&year=2015.

CEPAL (Comisión Económica para América Latina y el Caribe). *Foreign Direct Investment in Latin America and the Caribbean.* 2016. www.cepal.org/en/publications/40214-foreign-direct-investment-latin-america-and-caribbean-2016.

Chavez, Leo. *The Latino Threat: Constructing Immigrants, Citizens, and the Nation.* Palo Alto, CA: Stanford University Press, 2013.

Clark, S. E., C. Hawkes, S. M. Murphy, K. A. Hansen-Kuhn, and D. Wallinga. "Exporting Obesity: US Farm and Trade Policy and the Transformation of the Mexican Consumer Food Environment." *International Journal of Occupational and Environmental Health* 18, no. 1 (Jan.–March 2012): 53–65. doi: 10.1179/1077352512Z.0000000007.

Clinton, William J. "Remarks at the Signing Ceremony for the Supplemental Agreements to the North American Free Trade Agreement." American Presidency Project. 1993. www.presidency.ucsb.edu/ws/?pid=47070.

Colchero, M. A., B. M. Popkin, J. A. Rivera, and S. W. Ng. "Beverage Purchases from Stores in Mexico under the Excise Tax on Sugar Sweetened Beverages: Observational Study." *BMJ (Clinical Research Ed.)* 352 (Jan. 6, 2016): h6704. doi: 10.1136/bmj.h6704.

Colchero, M. A., J. Rivera-Dommarco, B. M. Popkin, and S. W. Ng. "In Mexico, Evidence of Sustained Consumer Response Two Years after Implementing a Sugar-Sweetened Beverage Tax." *Health Affairs (Project Hope)* 36, no. 3 (March 1, 2017): 564–71. doi: 10.1377/hlthaff.2016.1231.

Comaroff, Jean, and John L. Comaroff. *Millennial Capitalism and the Culture of Neoliberalism.* Durham, NC: Duke University Press, 2001.

CONEVAL (Consejo Nacional de Evaluación de la Política del Desarrollo Social). *Medición de la pobreza: Evolución de las dimensiones de la pobreza, 1990–2014*. 2014. www.coneval.org.mx/Medicion/EDP/Paginas/Evolucion-de-las-dimensiones-de-la-pobreza-1990-2014-.aspx.

ConMéxico. *ConMéxico*. Accessed Sept. 23, 2014. http://conmexico.com.mx/sitio/.

Consumers International and World Obesity Federation. *Recommendations towards a Global Convention to Protect and Promote Healthy Diets*. May 2014. www.consumersinternational.org/media/2211/recommendations-for-a-convention-on-healthy-diets-low-res-for-web.pdf/.

Cordain, Loren, S. Boyd Eaton, Anthony Sebastian, Neil Mann, Staffan Lindeberg, Bruce A. Watkins, James H. O'Keefe, and Janette Brand-Miller. "Origins and Evolution of the Western Diet: Health Implications for the 21st Century." *American Journal of Clinical Nutrition* 81, no. 2 (Feb. 1, 2005): 341–54.

Cortés, Sergio. "Migrants from Puebla in the 1990s." In *Immigrants and Schooling: Mexicans in New York*, edited by Regina Cortina, 183–204. New York: Center for Migration Studies, 2003.

D'Alonzo, K. T., S. Johnson, and D. Fanfan. "A Biobehavioral Approach to Understanding Obesity and the Development of Obesogenic Illnesses among Latino Immigrants in the United States." *Biological Research for Nursing* 14, no. 4 (Oct. 2012): 364–74. doi: 1099800412457017.

Debord, Guy. *The Society of the Spectacle*. Eastbourne, UK: Soul Bay Press, 2011 [1967]. Kindle.

De León, Jason. *The Land of Open Graves: Living and Dying on the Migrant Trail*. Oakland: University of California Press, 2015.

DiMaggio, Paul, and Walter W. Powell. "The Iron Cage Revisited: Collective Rationality and Institutional Isomorphism in Organizational Fields." *American Sociological Review* 48, no. 2 (1983): 147–60.

Douglas, Mary. *Risk Acceptability according to the Social Sciences*. New York: Russell, 1985.

———. *Risk and Blame: Essays in Cultural Theory*. London and New York: Routledge, 1992.

Douglas, Mary, and Aaron Wildavsky. *Risk and Culture: An Essay on the Selection of Environmental and Technological Dangers*. Berkeley: University of California Press, 1982.

Easton, Mark. "How a Mexican Resort Invented Eco-tourism." BBC News. Dec. 5, 2015. www.bbc.com/news/magazine-35004515.

Elizalde, María del Rosario Cárdenas, Fernando Alberto Cortés Cáceres, Agustín Escobar Latapí, Salomón Nahmad Sittón, John Scott Andretta, Graciela María Teruel Belismelis, Gonzalo Hernández Licona, de la Garza Navarrete, Thania Paola, Ricardo C. Aparicio Jiménez, and Edgar A.

Martínez Mendoza. *Estudio exploratorio de los comedores comunitarios SEDESOL*. Mexico City: Consejo Nacional de Evaluación de la Política de Desarrollo Social Investigadores académicos, n.d.

El Poder del Consumidor. "Exigimos a profeco multa y retiro de publicidad engañosa del refresco Sidral Mundet de Coca-Cola." Feb. 23, 2015. http://elpoderdelconsumidor.org/saludnutricional/exigimos-profeco-multa-y-retiro-de-publicidad-enganosa-del-refresco-sidral-mundet-de-coca-cola/.

Environmental Working Group. "Corn Subsidies in the United States Totaled $84.4 Billion from 1995–2012." Accessed April 30, 2015. http://farm.ewg.org/progdetail.php?fips=00000&progcode=corn.

Eschbach, K., and J. M. Hagan. "Deaths during Undocumented Migration: Trends and Policy Implications in the New Era of Homeland Security." In *Defense of the Alien*. Vol. 26. New York: Center for Migration Studies, 2003.

Esteva, Gustavo, and Catherine Marielle, eds. *Sin maíz no hay país*. Mexico City: Consejo Nacional para la Cultura y las Artes, 2007.

Fabian, Johannes. *Time and the Other: How Anthropology Makes Its Object*. New York: Columbia University Press, 1983.

Falcon, Walter P., and Rosamond L. Naylor. "Rethinking Food Security for the Twenty-First Century." *American Journal of Agricultural Economics* 87, no. 5 (2005): 1113–27.

Fanjul, Gonzalo, and Arabella Fraser. "Dumping without Borders: How US Agricultural Policies Are Destroying the Livelihoods of Mexican Corn Farmers." *Oxfam Policy and Practice: Agriculture, Food and Land 3*, no. 1 (2003): 89–121.

Farmer, Paul. *Pathologies of Power*. Berkeley: University of California Press, 2004.

Farmer, Paul E., Bruce Nizeye, Sara Stulac, and Salmaan Keshavjee. "Structural Violence and Clinical Medicine." *PLOS Medicine* 3, no. 10 (2006): 1686–91.e449. doi: 10.1371/journal.pmed.0030449.

Farnsworth, Mary S. "Sex Work, Sickness and Suicide: Argentine Feminist Theater in the 1910s and 1920s." *e-misférica* 6, no 1 (2009). http://hemisphericinstitute.org/hemi/en/e-misferica-61/farnsworth.

Felassi, Alessandro. *Time out of Time*. Albuquerque: University of New Mexico Press, 1987.

Ferdman, Roberto. "The Rise of the Avocado, America's New Favorite Fruit." *Washington Post*, Jan. 22, 2015. Wonkblog sec.

Fernandez Kelly, Patricia. "The Future of Gender in Mexico and the United States: Economic Transformation and Changing Definitions." In *The Shape of Social Inequality: Stratification and Ethnicity in Comparative Perspective*, edited by David Bills, 255–80. New York: Elsevier, 2005.

Finn, S. Margot. *Discriminating Taste: How Class Anxiety Created the American Food Revolution*. New Brunswick, NJ: Rutgers University Press, 2017.

Firth, Jeanne. "Healthy Choices and Heavy Burdens: Race, Citizenship and Gender in the 'Obesity Epidemic.'" *Journal of International Women's Studies* 13, no. 2 (2012): 33.

Fitting, Elizabeth. *The Struggle for Maize: Campesinos, Workers, and Transgenic Corn in the Mexican Countryside.* Durham, NC: Duke University Press, 2011.

Flandrin, Jean-Louis, and Massimo Montanari, eds. *Food: A Culinary History.* New York: Columbia University Press, 2013.

Flores, Linaloe. "TLCAN, 20 Años: Las promesas al olvido." *Sin Embargo,* Jan. 1, 2014.

Foley, Jonathan. "It's Time to Rethink America's Corn System." *Scientific American,* March 5, 2013.

Fort, Ellen. "The Cost of Avocado Toast, Explained by a Restaurateur." *Eater, San Francisco* (blog). May 23, 2017. https://sf.eater.com/2017/5/23/15677684/avocado-toast-prices-menu-costs-san-francisco.

Fox, Jonathan. *The Politics of Food in Mexico: State Power and Social Mobilization.* Ithaca, NY: Cornell University Press, 1993.

Fox, Jonathan, and Libby Haight, eds. *Subsidizing Inequality: Mexican Corn Policy since NAFTA.* Woodrow Wilson International Center for Scholars, Centro de Investigación y Docencia Económicas, University of California, Santa Cruz, 2010.

Francino, M. Pilar. "Early Development of the Gut Microbiota and Immune Health." *Pathogens* 3, no. 3 (2014): 769–90.

Free Library, The. "Tortilla Consumption Continues to Decline in Mexico but Grows Steadily Overseas." Latin American Data Base/Latin American Institute. June 23, 2004. www.thefreelibrary.com/TORTILLA+CONSUMPTION+CONTINUES+TO+DECLINE+IN+MEXICO+BUT+GROWS. . . -a0118555829.

Frellick, Marcia. "AMA Declares Obesity a Disease." 2013 www.medscape.com/viewarticle/806566.

Freudenberg, Nicholas. *Legal but Lethal: Corporations, Consumption and Protecting Public Health.* New York: Oxford University Press, 2014. Kindle.

———. "Is 'Free' Trade Making Us Sick?" Panel at Sobremesa Conference. Jaime Lucero Mexican Studies Institute, City College of New York, May 11, 2016.

Fried, Linda. "Symposium on Childhood Obesity." Columbia University Mailman School of Public Health, April 16, 2015.

Frieden, Thomas. "A Framework for Public Health Action: The Health Impact Pyramid." *American Journal of Public Health* 100, no. 4 (April 2010): 590–95.

Friel, Sharon. "The Politics, Policies, and Processes of 21st Century Trade and Investment: Challenges for Food and Nutrition across the Pacific Rim."

Keynote address at Food Studies at Oxy, Occidental College, Los Angeles, June 15, 2017.

Friel, Sharon, Deborah Gleeson, Anne-Marie Thow, Ronald Labonte, David Stuckler, Adrian Kay, and Wendy Snowdon. "A New Generation of Trade Policy: Potential Risks to Diet-Related Health from the Trans Pacific Partnership Agreement." *Globalization and Health* 9 (2013): 46.

Friel, Sharon, Libby Hattersley, and Ruth Townsend. *Trade Policy and Public Health* 36 (2015). doi: 10.1146/annurev-publhealth-031914-122739.

Gálvez, Alyshia. "Rising Body Counts on the Border: Reflections on the Construction of Social Distance." *e-misférica* 3, no. 2 (Nov. 2006). http://hemisphericinstitute.org/journal/3.2/eng/en32_pg_galvez.html.

———. *Guadalupe in New York: Devotion and the Struggle for Citizenship Rights among Mexican Immigrants.* New York: New York University Press, 2009.

———. "Resolviendo: How September 11 Tested and Transformed a New York City Mexican Immigrant Organization." In *Politics and Partnerships: The Role of Voluntary Associations in America's Political Past and Present,* edited by Elisabeth Stephanie Clemens and Doug Guthrie, 297–326. Chicago: University of Chicago Press, 2010.

———. *Patient Citizens, Immigrant Mothers: Mexican Women, Public Prenatal Care, and the Birth Weight Paradox.* Critical Issues in Health and Medicine. New Brunswick, NJ: Rutgers University Press, 2011.

Gálvez, Alyshia, and Amalia Pallares. "Mothering in the Struggle: Undocumented Youth Activism in a Family Context." Manuscript in preparation, n.d.

Gamio, Manuel. *Hacia un México nuevo.* Mexico City: Instituto Nacional Indigenista, 1935.

———. "Calificación de características culturales de los grupos indígenas." *América Indígena* 4, no. 2 (1942): 17–22.

Geronimus, A. T. "The Weathering Hypothesis and the Health of African-American Women and Infants: Evidence and Speculations." *Ethnicity and Disease* 2, no. 3 (1992): 207–21.

Gil, Beatriz, Obed Méndez, and Armando Sobrino. "Food Policy and Local Participation: A Case Study of 'Cruzada Nacional Contra El Hambre.'" 2014. http://hdl.handle.net/10535/9396.

Gleijeses, Piero. *Shattered Hope: The Guatemalan Revolution and the United States, 1944–1954.* Princeton University Press, 1992.

Godoy, Emilio. "Mexico Ignores Warnings about Bisphenol A." *TierraAmérica: Environment and Development,* Dec. 20, 2011. www.ipsnews.net/2011/12/mexico-ignores-warnings-about-bisphenol-a/.

Goldman, Francisco. "Crisis in Mexico: The Disappearance of the 43." *New Yorker,* Oct. 24, 2014.

Gómez-Dantés, H., N. Fullman, H. Lamadrid-Figueroa, L. Cahuana-Hurtado, B. Darney, L. Avila-Burgos, R. Correa-Rotter, et al. "Dissonant Health Transition in the States of Mexico, 1990–2013: A Systematic Analysis for the Global Burden of Disease Study 2013." *Lancet* 388, no. 10058 (Nov. 12, 2016): 2386–2402. doi: S0140-6736(16)31773-1.

Gonzales, Roberto. *Lives in Limbo: Undocumented and Coming of Age in America.* Berkeley: University of California Press. 2015.

Gonzalez, Juan. *Harvest of Empire: A History of Latinos in America.* Rev. ed. New York: Penguin Group, 2011.

González, Roberto J. *Zapotec Science: Farming and Food in the Northern Sierra of Oaxaca.* Austin: University of Texas Press, 2001. Kindle.

González Alejo, Ana Laura. "Evolution of the Food Supply in Mexico City: From Traditional Supply to Current Modernization." Sixth International Conference on Food Studies, University of California at Berkeley, Oct. 13, 2016.

Gonzalez-Barrera, Ana. "More Mexicans Leaving than Coming to the US." Pew Research Center. Nov. 19, 2015. www.pewhispanic.org/2015/11/19/more-mexicans-leaving-than-coming-to-the-u-s/.

González-Castro, M., M. Olea-Serrano, A. Rivas-Velasco, E. Medina-Rivero, Leandro Ordoñez-Acevedo, and A. De León-Rodríguez. "Phthalates and Bisphenols Migration in Mexican Food Cans and Plastic Food Containers." *Bulletin of Environmental Contamination and Toxicology* 86, no. 6 (2011): 627–31. doi: 10.1007/s00128-011-0266-3.

Gordinier, Jeff. "In Search of the Perfect Taco." *New York Times,* Sept. 20, 2014. T Magazine sec. www.nytimes.com/interactive/2014/09/10/style/tmagazine/redzepi-searches-for-the-perfect-taco.html?_r=0.

GRAIN. "Free Trade and Mexico's Junk Food Epidemic." March 2, 2015. www.globalresearch.ca/free-trade-and-mexicos-junk-food-epidemic/5434350.

Grandin, Greg. *Empire's Workshop: Latin America, the United States, and the Rise of the New Imperialism.* New York: Metropolitan Books, 2006.

Gray, Margaret. *Labor and the Locavore: The Making of a Comprehensive Food Ethic.* Berkeley: University of California Press, 2013.

Grayson, George W. *The Mexico-U.S. Business Committee: Catalyst for the North American Free Trade Agreement.* Rockville, MD: Montrose Press, 2007.

Greder, Kimberly, Flor Romero Slowing, and Kimberly Doudna. "Latina Immigrant Mothers: Negotiating New Food Environments to Preserve Cultural Food Practices and Healthy Child Eating." *Family and Consumer Sciences Research Journal* 41, no. 2 (2012): 145–60. doi:10.1111/fcsr.12004.

Green, Linda. "The Nobodies: Neoliberalism, Violence, and Migration." *Medical Anthropology* 30, no. 4 (July 1, 2011): 366–85. doi: 10.1080/01459740.2011.576726.

Greenhalgh, Susan. *Fat-Talk Nation: The Human Costs of America's War on Fat.* Ithaca, NY: Cornell University Press, 2015.

Greenhalgh, Susan, and Megan Carney. "Bad Biocitizens? Latinos and the US 'Obesity Epidemic.'" *Human Organization* 73, no. 3 (2014): 267–76.

Guarnaccia, Peter J., Teresa Vivar, Anne C. Bellows, and Gabriela V. Alcaraz. "'We Eat Meat Every Day': Ecology and Economy of Dietary Change among Oaxacan Migrants from Mexico to New Jersey." *Ethnic and Racial Studies* 35, no. 1 (2012): 104–19.

Guthman, Julie. "Neoliberalism and the Constitution of Contemporary Bodies." In *Fat Studies Reader*, edited by Esther D. Rothblum and Sondra Solovay, 187–206. New York: New York University Press, 2009.

———. *Weighing In: Obesity, Food Justice, and the Limits of Capitalism.* Oakland: University of California Press, 2011.

Hacking, Ian. "Making Up People." In *Reconstructing Individualism: Autonomy, Individuality, and the Self in Western Thought*, edited by T. C. Heller, M. Sosna, and D. E. Wellbery. Palo Alto, CA: Stanford University Press, 1986.

———. "Where Did the BMI Come from?" In *Bodies of Evidence: Fat across Disciplines.* Cambridge: Cambridge University Press, 2007.

Hallal, Pedro C., Lars Bo Andersen, Fiona C. Bull, Regina Guthold, William Haskell, Ulf Ekelund, and Lancet Physical Activity Series Working Group. "Global Physical Activity Levels: Surveillance Progress, Pitfalls, and Prospects." *Lancet* 380, no. 9838 (2012): 247–57.

Hamblin, James. "How Oreos Work Like Cocaine." *Atlantic*, July 8, 2014.

Hamdy, Sherine F. "When the State and Your Kidneys Fail: Political Etiologies in an Egyptian Dialysis Ward." *American Ethnologist* 35, no. 4 (2008): 553–69. doi: 10.1111/j.1548-1425.2008.00098.

Handley, Margareta, Marisela Robles, Eric Sanford, Natalie Collins, Hilary Seligman, Triveni Defries, Ramona Perez, and Jim Grieshop. "Navigating Changing Food Environments—Transnational Perspectives on Dietary Behaviours and Implications for Nutrition Counselling." *Global Public Health* 8, no. 3 (2013): 245–57. doi: 10.1080/17441692.2012.729218.

Harrup, Anthony. "Remittances to Mexico Reach Seven-Year High." *Wall Street Journal*, Feb. 2, 2016. www.wsj.com/articles/remittances-to-mexico-reach-seven-year-high-1454438518.

Harvey, David. "The Body as an Accumulation Strategy." *Environment and Planning D: Society and Space* 16, no. 4 (1998): 401–21.

———. *A Brief History* of *Neoliberalism.* New York: Oxford University Press, 2005.

Hatch, E. E., J. W. Nelson, R. W. Stahlhut, and T. F. Webster. "Association of Endocrine Disruptors and Obesity: Perspectives from Epidemiological Studies." *International Journal of Andrology* 33, no. 2 (2010): 324–32. doi: 10.1111/j.1365-2605.2009.01035.x.

Hawkes, Corinna. "Uneven Dietary Development: Linking the Policies and Processes of Globalization with the Nutrition Transition, Obesity and

Diet-Related Chronic Diseases." *Globalization and Health* 2, no. 4 (2006). doi: 10.1186/1744-8603-2-4.

Hayes-Bautista, David E. "The Latino Health Research Agenda for the Twenty-First Century." *Latinos: Remaking America*, edited by M. Suárez-Orozco and M. Páez, 215–35. Berkeley: University of California Press, 2002.

Hectors, T.L., C. Vanparys, L.F. Van Gaal, P.G. Jorens, A. Covaci, and R. Blust. "Insulin Resistance and Environmental Pollutants: Experimental Evidence and Future Perspectives." *Environmental Health Perspectives* 121, no. 11–12 (Nov.–Dec. 2013): 1273–81. doi: 10.1289/ehp.1307082.

Heffernan, W.D., D.H. Constance, L. Gouveia, and E. Mingione. "Transnational Corporations and the Globalization of the Food System." In *From Columbus to Conagra: The Globalization of Agriculture and Food*, edited by A. Bonanno, L. Busch, and W.H. Friedland, 29–51. Lawrence: University Press of Kansas, 1994.

Hellman, Judith Adler. *Mexico in Crisis*. New York: Holmes and Meier, 1978.

———. *Mexican Lives*. New York: New Press, 1995.

Hernández López, Ernesto. "Law, Food, and Culture: Mexican Corn's National Identity Cooked in 'Tortilla Discourses' Post-TLC/NAFTA." *St. Thomas Law Review* 20 (2008): 573–93.

Hernandez-Cordero, S., S. Barquera, S. Rodriguez-Ramirez, M.A. Villanueva-Borbolla, T. González de Cossio, J.R. Dommarco, and B. Popkin. "Substituting Water for Sugar-Sweetened Beverages Reduces Circulating Triglycerides and the Prevalence of Metabolic Syndrome in Obese but not in Overweight Mexican Women in a Randomized Controlled Trial." *Journal of Nutrition* 144, no. 11 (Nov. 2014): 1742–52. doi: 10.3945/jn.114.193490.

Hershfield, Joanne. *Imagining la Chica Moderna: Women, Nation, and Visual Culture in Mexico, 1917–1936*. Durham, NC: Duke University Press, 2008.

Hewitt de Alcántara, Cynthia. *Modernizing Mexican Agriculture: Socioeconomic Implications of Technological Change, 1940–1970*. Vol. 75. Geneva: United Nations Research Institute for Social Development, 1976.

Hirsch, J.M. "Tortillas and Salsa Are Outselling Burger Buns and Ketchup in the United States." *Business Insider*, July 8, 2014.

Hoffman, Daniel J. "Obesity in Developing Countries: Causes and Implications." *Food, Nutrition and Agriculture* 28 (2001). www.fao.org/docrep/003/y0600m/y0600m05.htm.

Hollingsworth, J. Rogers, Philippe C. Schmitter, and Wolfgang Streeck. *Governing Capitalist Economies: Performance and Control of Economic Sectors*. New York: Oxford University Press, 1994.

Holt-Giménez, Eric. "From Food Crisis to Food Sovereignty: The Challenge of Social Movements." *Monthly Review* 61, no. 3 (July–Aug. 2009). https://monthlyreview.org/2009/07/01/from-food-crisis-to-food-sovereignty-the-challenge-of-social-movements/.

INEGI (Instituto Nacional de Estadística, Geografía e Informática). "Causas de defunción, defunciones generales totales por principales causas de mortalidad." 2015. www3.inegi.org.mx/sistemas/temas/default.aspx?s=est&c=17484.

Jayawardena, Eranga. "Medical Mystery: Kidney Disease Killing Farm Workers in Sri Lanka." Accessed Jan. 13, 2017. www.cbsnews.com/news/medical-mystery-rare-kidney-disease-killing-sri-lanka-farmers/.

Jhamnani, Rekha D., and Pamela Frischmeyer-Guerrerio. "Desensitization for Peanut Allergies in Children." *Current Treatment Options in Allergy* 3, no. 3 (2016): 282–91.

Jordan, Mary, and Kevin Sullivan. "Trade Brings Riches, but not to Mexico's Poor." *Washington Post,* March 22, 2003.

Kagan, Richard L., and Fernando Marías. *Urban Images of the Hispanic World, 1493–1793.* New Haven, CT: Yale University Press, 2000.

Kelly, James J. "Article 27 and Mexican Land Reform: The Legacy of Zapata's Dream." Scholarly Works Paper 668. 1994. http://scholarship.law.nd.edu/law_faculty_scholarship/668.

Kennedy, G., G. Nantel, and P. Shetty. *Globalization of Food Systems in Developing Countries.* FAO Food and Nutrition Paper. Vol. 83. Food and Agriculture Organization of the United Nations. 2004. www.columbia.edu/cgi-bin/cul/resolve?clio5972865.

Kennedy, Pagan. "The Fat Drug." *New York Times,* March 8, 2014.

Keshavjee, Salmaan. *Blind Spot: How Neoliberalism Infiltrated Global Health.* Oakland: University of California Press, 2014.

Khazan, Olga. "Exercise in Futility." *Atlantic,* April 2016. www.theatlantic.com/magazine/archive/2016/04/exercise-in-futility/471492/.

Kilpatrick, Kate. "The Amaranth Solution: The Aztec Superfood Fighting Mexican Obesity." Aljazeera America. Aug. 17, 2015. http://projects.aljazeera.com/2015/08/mexico-obesity/amaranth.html?utm_medium=referral&utm_source=pulsenews.

Klein, Naomi. *The Shock Doctrine.* New York: Knopf, 2007.

Kroker-Lobos, M. F., A. Pedroza-Tobias, L. S. Pedraza, and J. A. Rivera. "The Double Burden of Undernutrition and Excess Body Weight in Mexico." *American Journal of Clinical Nutrition* 100, no. 6 (Dec. 2014): 1652S-58S. doi: 10.3945/ajcn.114.083832.

Kulick, Don, and Anne Meneley, eds. *Fat: The Anthropology of an Obsession.* New York: Jeremy P. Tarcher/Penguin, 2005.

Kurland, Jennifer. "McDonald's Profits by Targeting Low-Income Consumers, Minorities." *Northern Star,* Feb. 2, 2009. Opinion sec.

Labonté, Ronald, Katia S. Mohindra, and Raphael Lencucha. "Framing International Trade and Chronic Disease." *Globalization and Health* 7, no. 21 (2011): 1–15. doi: 10.1186/1744–8603–7–21.

Laudan, Rachel. "A Plea for Culinary Modernism: Why We Should Love New, Fast, Processed Food." *Gastronomica: The Journal of Food and Culture* 1, no. 1 (2001): 36–44.

Laws, R. L., D. R. Brooks, J. J. Amador, D. E. Weiner, J. S. Kaufman, O. Ramirez-Rubio, A. Riefkohl, et al. "Changes in Kidney Function among Nicaraguan Sugarcane Workers." *International Journal of Occupational and Environmental Health* 21, no. 3 (July–Sept. 2015): 241–50. doi: 10.1179/2049396714Y.0000000102.

Leatherman, Thomas, and Alan Goodman. "Coca-Colonization of Diets in the Yucatan." *Social Science and Medicine* 61(2005): 833–46.

Lender, N., N. J. Talley, P. Enck, S. Haag, S. Zipfel, M. Morrison, and G. J. Holtmann. "Review Article: Associations between Helicobacter Pylori and Obesity—An Ecological Study." *Alimentary Pharmacology and Therapeutics* 40, no. 1 (2014): 24–31. doi: 10.1111/apt.12790.

Leroy, J. L., P. Gadsden, T. González de Cossio, and P. Gertler. "Cash and In-Kind Transfers Lead to Excess Weight Gain in a Population of Women with a High Prevalence of Overweight in Rural Mexico." *Journal of Nutrition* 143, no. 3 (March 2013): 378–83. doi: 10.3945/jn.112.167627.

Lewis, Oscar. *Five Families: Mexican Case Studies in the Culture of Poverty.* New York: Basic Books, 1975 [1959].

Lind, David, and Elizabeth Barham. "The Social Life of the Tortilla: Food, Cultural Politics, and Contested Commodification." *Agriculture and Human Values: Journal of the Agriculture, Food, and Human Values Society* 21, no. 1 (2004): 47–60. doi: 10.1023/B:AHUM.0000014018.76118.06.

Lomnitz, Claudio, and Clarissa Adler-Lomnitz. "Planeación y tradición: La cultura de la alimentación en México." In *La alimentación del futuro.* Vol. 2, edited by R. Carvajal and R. Vergara, 167–84. Mexico City: UNAM, 1987.

López Obrador, Manuel. "La crisis en México." Lecture delivered at Columbia University, Oct. 14, 2014.

Macari, Marisa. "Contextualizing Food Practices and Change among Mexican Migrants in West Queens, New York City." PhD diss., Oxford University, 2013.

MacNeish, Richard S. "Summary of the Cultural Sequence and Its Implications in the Tehuacán Valley." *Prehistory of the Tehuacán Valley* 5 (1972): 496–504.

Magaña, Rocío. "Bodies on the Line: Life, Death, and Authority on the Arizona-Mexico Border." PhD diss., University of Chicago, 2008.

Maldonado, Andrea. "Yoga's Dis/Union: Class Relations, Social Mobility, and Self-Care in Mexico City." PhD diss., Brown University, 2014.

Manheimer, Eric. *Twelve Patients: Life and Death at Bellevue Hospital.* New York: Grand Central Publishing, 2012.

Mann, Traci, A. Janet Tomiyama, and Andrew Ward. "Promoting Public Health in the Context of the 'Obesity Epidemic': False Starts and Promising

New Directions." *Perspectives on Psychological Science* 10, no. 6 (2015): 706–10.

Maraesa, Aminata, and Lauren Fordyce. *Risk, Reproduction and Narratives of Experience.* Nashville, TN: Vanderbilt University Press, 2012.

Marcus, George E. "Ethnography in/of the World System: The Emergence of Multi-Sited Ethnography." *Annual Review of Anthropology* (1995): 95–117.

Marosi, Richard. "Hardship on Mexico's Farms, a Bounty for U.S. Tables." *Los Angeles Times,* Dec. 7, 2014.

Martin, Emily. *The Woman in the* Body. 2nd ed. Boston: Beacon, 1992 [1987].

Martínez, Stephen. *Vertical Coordination of Marketing Systems: Lessons from the Poultry, Egg and Pork Industries.* USDA Agricultural Economic Report no. AER-807. 2002.

Marx, Karl. "The Working Day." In *Capital: A Critique of Political Economy.* Vol. 1, 257. Moscow: Progress Publishers, 1887.

Marx de Salcedo, Anastacia. *Combat-Ready Kitchen: How the U.S. Military Shapes the Way You Eat.* New York: Penguin, 2015.

Maté, Gabor. *When the Body Says No: Exploring the Stress-Disease Connection.* Hoboken, NJ: Wiley, 2011.

Maynard, Ronald J. "Controlling Death-Compromising Life: Chronic Disease, Prognostication, and the New Biotechnologies." *Medical Anthropology Quarterly: International Journal for the Analysis of Health* 20, no. 2 (2006): 212–34. doi: 10.1525/maq.2006.20.2.212.

Mazzocchi, Mario, Bhavani Shankar, and Bruce Traill. *The Development of Global Diets since ICN 1992: Influences of Agrifood Sector Trends and Policies.* FAO Commodity and Trade Policy Research Working Paper no. 34 (2012).

McDonald's Mexico. "Los tamales son del pasado." Facebook post. Feb. 5, 2015.

McEwen, B. S. "Allostasis and Allostatic Load: Implications for Neuropsychopharmacology." *Neuropsychopharmacology: Official Publication of the American College of Neuropsychopharmacology* 22, no. 2 (Feb. 2000): 108–24. doi: S0893-133X(99)00129-3.

McEwen, B. S., and J. C. Wingfield. "The Concept of Allostasis in Biology and Biomedicine." *Hormones and Behavior* 43, no. 1 (Jan. 2003): 2–15. doi: S0018506X02000247.

McGowan, Emily C., Gordon R. Bloomberg, Peter J. Gergen, Cynthia M. Visness, Katy F. Jaffee, Megan Sandel, George O'Connor, Meyer Kattan, James Gern, and Robert A. Wood. "Influence of Early-Life Exposures on Food Sensitization and Food Allergy in an Inner-City Birth Cohort." *Journal of Allergy and Clinical Immunology* 135, no. 1 (2015): 171–78.

McMillan, Tracie. *The American Way of Eating: Undercover at Walmart, Applebee's, Farm Fields and the Dinner Table.* New York: Scribner, 2012.

Medina, Daniela. "En Zinacantán, Chiapas, se busca recuperar la autonomía alimentaria." *Sin Embargo,* June 7, 2015.

Mendenhall, Emily. *Syndemic Suffering: Social Distress, Depression, and Diabetes among Mexican Immigrant Women.* Walnut Creek, CA: Left Coast Press, 2012.

———. "Syndemics: A New Path for Global Health Research." *Lancet* 389, no. 10072 (2017): 889–91.

Méndez Cota, Gabriela. *Disrupting Maize: Food, Biotechnology and Nationalism in Contemporary Mexico.* London: Pickering and Chatto, 2016.

Mexico Ministry of the Economy. "Analysis of the Corn Tortilla Value Chain: Current Situation and Local Competition Factors." 2012. www.economia.gob.mx/files/en/data_and_research/corn-tortilla_value_chain.pdf.

Ministry of Health of Brazil. *Dietary Guidelines for the Brazilian Population.* Brasilia, DF, 2014.

Mintz, Sidney. *Sweetness and Power: The Place of Sugar in Modern History.* New York: Penguin, 1986.

———. *Tasting Food, Tasting Culture: Excursions into Eating, Power and the Past.* New York: Beacon Press, 1996.

Molyneux, Maxine. "Mothers at the Service of the New Poverty Agenda: Progresa/oportunidades, Mexico's Conditional Transfer Programme." *Social Policy and Administration* 40, no. 4 (2006): 425–49.

Montalvo, Tania. "Huevo en polvo o carne enlatada: Este es el menú en los Comedores Comunitarios de SEDESOL." *Animal Político,* March 9, 2016.

Montoya, Michael. "Bioethnic Conscription: Genes, Race, and Mexicana/o Ethnicity in Diabetes." *Cultural Anthropology* 22, no. 1 (2007): 94–128.

———. *Making the Mexican Diabetic: Race, Science, and the Genetics of Inequality.* Berkeley: University of California Press, 2011.

Moran-Thomas, Amy. "Breakthroughs for Whom? Global Diabetes Care and Equitable Design." *New England Journal of Medicine* 375, no. 24 (2016): 2317–19.

———. "Research." 2017. https://anthropology.mit.edu/people/faculty/amy-moran-thomas.

Moskin, Julia. "How the Taco Gained in Translation." *New York Times,* May 2, 2012.

Moss, Michael. *Salt, Sugar, Fat: How the Food Giants Hooked Us.* New York: Random House, 2013.

Moynihan, Daniel P. *On Understanding Poverty: Perspectives from the Social Sciences.* New York: Basic Books, 1969.

Naudziunas, Jessica. "Where in the World Are There no McDonald's?" NPR. Aug. 1, 2013. www.npr.org/sections/thesalt/2013/07/25/205547517/where-in-the-world-are-there-no-mcdonalds.

Neel, James V. "Diabetes Mellitus: A 'Thrifty' Genotype Rendered Detrimental by 'Progress'?" *American Journal of Human Genetics* 14 (Dec. 1962): 353–62.

———. "The 'Thrifty Genotype' in 1998." *Nutrition Reviews* 57, no. 5 (1999): 2–9.

Nestle, Marion. "Are Organics More Nutritious? Again? Sigh." *Food Politics* (blog). Sept. 5, 2012. www.foodpolitics.com.

———. *Food Politics: How the Food Industry Influences Nutrition and Health.* Vol. 3. Berkeley: University of California Press, 2013.

———. *Soda Politics: Taking on Big Soda (and Winning!).* Oxford: Oxford University Press, 2015.

Noma. "Noma Mexico Booking Page." Accessed Jan. 10, 2017. http://noma.dk/mexico/.

Novotny, J. A., S. K. Gebauer, and D. J. Baer. "Discrepancy between the Atwater Factor Predicted and Empirically Measured Energy Values of Almonds in Human Diets." *American Journal of Clinical Nutrition* 96, no. 2 (Aug. 2012): 296–301. doi: 10.3945/ajcn.112.035782.

Ochoa, Enrique. *Feeding Mexico: The Political Uses of Food since 1910.* Wilmington, DE: Scholarly Resources, 2000.

O'Connor, A. "Coca-Cola Funds Scientists Who Shift Blame for Obesity Away from Bad Diets." *New York Times* 9, 2015.

OECD (Organisation for Economic Co-operation and Development). *Obesity Update 2012.* 2012. www.oecd.org/health/49716427.pdf.

Office of the US Trade Representative. "U.S.-Mexico Trade Facts." Oct. 20, 2017. https://ustr.gov/countries-regions/americas/mexico.

O'Neill, Shannon K. *Two Nations Indivisible: Mexico, the United States, and the Road Ahead.* New York: Oxford University Press, 2013.

———. "NAFTA at 20." Council on Foreign Relations Educators' Conference Call, 2014. www.cfr.org/conference-calls/nafta-twenty.

Osterweil, Willie. "Weight Gains." *New Inquiry* (blog). Dec. 15, 2014.

Ostry, Jonathan D., Prakash Loungani, and Davide Furceri. "Neoliberalism: Oversold?" *Finance and Development* 53, no. 2 (June 2016): 38–41.

Paley, Dawn. *Drug War Capitalism.* Oakland, CA: AK Press, 2014.

Pallares, Miguel, and Pierre Marc René. "Sed de plástico: México lidera consumo de agua embotellada." *El Universal,* June 13, 2015.

Palou, Pedro Angel. "The Walls of Puebla." *New York Times,* Oct. 16, 2010. Opinion sec.

Park, Lisa Sun-Hee. *Entitled to Nothing: The Struggle for Immigrant Health Care in the Age of Welfare Reform.* New York: New York University Press, 2011.

Passel, Jeffrey S., D'vera Cohn, and Ana González-Barrera. *Net Migration from Mexico Falls to Zero—and Perhaps Less.* Pew Research Center. April 23, 2012. www.pewhispanic.org/2012/04/23/net-migration-from-mexico-falls-to-zero-and-perhaps-less/.

Patel, Raj, and Gisele Henriques. *NAFTA, Corn, and Mexico's Agricultural Trade Liberalization.* Interhemispheric Resource Center. Feb. 13, 2004.

https://is.cuni.cz/studium/predmety/index.php?do=download&did=113952&kod=JMM591.

Peretz, J., R. K. Gupta, J. Singh, I. Hernandez-Ochoa, and J. A. Flaws. "Bisphenol A Impairs Follicle Growth, Inhibits Steroidogenesis, and Downregulates Rate-Limiting Enzymes in the Estradiol Biosynthesis Pathway." *Toxicological Sciences* 119, no. 1 (Jan. 2011): 209–17. doi: 10.1093/toxsci/kfq319.

Pérez, Ramona Lee. "Las fronteras del sabor: Taste as Consciousness, Kinship, and Space in the Mexico–U.S. Borderlands." *Journal of Latin American and Caribbean Anthropology* 19, no. 2 (2014): 310–30. doi: 10.1111/jlca.12094.

Perkins, John H. "The Rockefeller Foundation and the Green Revolution, 1941–1956." *Agriculture and Human Values* 7, no. 3 (1990): 6–18. http://dx.doi.org/10.1007/BF01557305.

Perot, H. Ross, and Pat Choate. *Save Your Job, Save Our Country: Why NAFTA Must Be Stopped—Now!* New York: Hyperion Books, 1993.

Perro, Michelle, and Vincanne Adams. *What's Making Our Children Sick?: How Industrial Food Is Causing an Epidemic of Chronic Illness, and What Parents (and Doctors) Can Do about It.* White River Junction, VT: Chelsea Green Publishing, 2017.

Piketty, Thomas. *Capitalism in the Twenty-First Century.* Cambridge, MA: Belknap Press, 2014.

Pilcher, Jeffrey. *¡Que vivan los tamales!* Albuquerque: University of New Mexico Press, 1998.

———. "Taco Bell, Maseca and Slow Food: A Postmodern Apocalypse for Mexico's Peasant Cuisine?" In *Fast Food/Slow Food: The Cultural Economy of the Global Food System,* edited by Richard Wilk, 426–37. New York: Rowman Altamira, 2006.

———. *Planet Taco: A Global History of Mexican Food.* New York: Oxford University Press, 2012.

Polaski, Sandra. "Mexican Employment, Productivity and Income a Decade after NAFTA." Testimony submitted to the Canadian Standing Senate Committee on Foreign Affairs. Carnegie Endowment for International Peace. Feb. 25, 2004. http://carnegieendowment.org/2004/02/25/mexican-employment-productivity-and-income-decade-after-nafta-pub-1473.

Pollan, Michael. *The Omnivore's Dilemma: A Natural History of Four Meals.* New York: Penguin, 2007.

———. *In Defense* of *Food: An Eater's Manifesto.* New York: Penguin Press, 2008. www.loc.gov/catdir/toc/ecip0727/2007037552.html.

Pontzer, Herman, Ramon Durazo-Arvizu, Lara R. Dugas, Jacob Plange-Rhule, Pascal Bovet, Terrence E. Forrester, Estelle V. Lambert, Richard S. Cooper, Dale A. Schoeller, and Amy Luke. "Constrained Total Energy Expenditure and Metabolic Adaptation to Physical Activity in Adult Humans." *Current Biology* 26, no. 3 (2016): 410–17.

Popkin, Barry M. "The Nutrition Transition and Its Health Implications in Lower-Income Countries." *Public Health Nutrition* 1, no. 1 (1998): 5–21.

Prebisch, Raúl. *Towards a Dynamic Development Policy for Latin America* [Document]. E/CN.12/680/rev.1. New York: United Nations, 1963.

PRI (Institutional Revolutionary Party). "Declaración de principios." Accessed Jan. 15, 2016. http://pri.org.mx/JuntosHacemosMas/Documentos/DeclaracionDePrincipios2013.pdf.

Proust, Marcel, Harold Pinter, and Di Trevis. *Remembrance of Things Past.* London: Faber and Faber, 2000.

Public Citizen. "NAFTA's Legacy for Mexico: Economic Displacement, Lower Wages for Most, Increased Immigration, Report by Public Citizen." Public Citizen. 2014. www.citizen.org/sites/default/files/impactsonmexicomemoonepager.pdf.

Rabinow, Paul. "Artificiality and Enlightenment: From Sociobiology to Biosociality." In *Zone 6: Incorporations,* edited by Jonathan Crary and Sanford Kwinter, 234–53. New York: Zone Books, 1992.

Rabo Research. "The Mexican 1982 Debt Crisis." Sept. 2013. https://economics.rabobank.com/publications/2013/september/the-mexican-1982-debt-crisis/.

Rapp, Rayna. *Testing Women, Testing the Fetus.* New York: Routledge, 2000.

Reardon, Thomas, and Julio Berdegué. "The Rapid Rise of Supermarkets in Latin America: Challenges and Opportunities for Development." *Development Policy Review* 20, no. 2 (2000): 371–88.

René Redzepi on Tortillas. Directed by *New York Times.* Sept. 14, 2014. www.nytimes.com/video/t-magazine/100000003089989/rene-redzepi-makes-tortillas.html. Video.

Ricardo, David. *On the Principles of Political Economy and Taxation.* 3rd ed. London: J. Murray, 1821.

Ridaura, V. K., J. J. Faith, F. E. Rey, J. Cheng, A. E. Duncan, A. L. Kau, N. W. Griffin, et al. "Gut Microbiota from Twins Discordant for Obesity Modulate Metabolism in Mice." *Science* 341, no. 6150 (Sept. 6, 2013): 1241214. doi: 10.1126/science.1241214.

Ritzer, George. *The McDonaldization of Society.* Thousand Oaks, CA: Pine Forge Press, 2008.

Roberts, Elizabeth F. S. "Food Is Love: And So, What Then?" *Biosocieties* 10, no. 2 (2015): 247–52. doi: 10.1057/biosoc.2015.18.

Rojas-Suarez, Liliana. *Growing Pains in Latin America: An Economic Growth Framework as Applied to Brazil, Colombia, Costa Rica, Mexico and Peru.* Washington, DC: Center for Global Development, 2009.

Rook, G. A., and Laura Rosa Brunet. "Give Us This Day Our Daily Germs." *Biologist* (London) 49, no. 4 (2002): 145–49.

Rosaldo, Renato. *Culture and Truth: The Remaking of Social Analysis.* New York: Beacon Press, 1993.

Roseberry, William. "The Rise of Yuppie Coffees and the Reimagination of Class in the United States." *American Anthropologist* 98, no. 4 (1996): 762–75.

Rosen, Sharon. "Ingredients Derived from Corn: What to Avoid." *Live Corn Free* (blog). 2010. www.livecornfree.com/2010/04/ingredients-derived-from-corn-what-to.html.

Rosenbaum, Emily. "Social and Economic Well-being of Mexicans and Other Latinos in New York." In *Immigrants and Schooling: Mexicans in New York,* edited by Regina Cortina, 21–58. New York: Center for Migration Studies, 2003.

Rosenberg, Tina. "How One of the Most Obese Countries on Earth Took on the Soda Giants." *Guardian,* Nov. 3, 2015.

Rothblum, Esther D., and Sondra Solovay. *The Fat Studies Reader.* New York: New York University Press, 2009.

Rowe, Nicholas. *Mexico's Oportunidades: Conditional Cash Transfers as the Solution to Global Poverty?* Keck Center for International and Strategic Studies. 2010–2011. www.cmc.edu/sites/default/files/keck/student/RoweN%20Fellowship%20REP%2010-11.pdf.

Sadikot, S., and M. Hermans. "Here We Go Again . . . The Metabolic Syndrome Revisited!" *Diabetes and Metabolic Syndrome: Clinical Research and Reviews* 4, no. 2 (2010): 111–20.

Saldaña Tejeda, Abril. "Mitochondrial Mothers of a Fat Nation: Race, Gender and Epigenetics in Obesity Research on Mexican Mestizos." *BioSocieties* (2017): 1–19. doi: org/10.1057/s41292-017-0078-8.

Samb, Badara, Nina Desai, Sania Nishtar, Shanti Mendis, Henk Bekedam, Anna Wright, Justine Hsu, Alexandra Martiniuk, Francesca Celletti, and Kiran Patel. "Prevention and Management of Chronic Disease: A Litmus Test for Health-Systems Strengthening in Low-Income and Middle-Income Countries." *Lancet* 376, no. 9754 (2010): 1785–97.

Sanabria, Emilia. "Circulating Ignorance: Complexity and Agnogenesis in the Obesity 'Epidemic.'" *Cultural Anthropology* 31, no. 1 (2016): 131–58.

Sánchez-Tranquilino, Marcos, and John Tagg. "The Pachuco's Flayed Hide: Mobility, Identity and Buenas Garras." In *Chicano Art: Resistance and Affirmation, 1965–1985,* edited by Richard Griswold de Castillo, Teresa McKenna, and Yvonne Yabro-Bejarano, 97–106. Los Angeles: Wight Gallery, University of California at Los Angeles, 1992.

Schanbacher, William D. *The Politics of Food: The Global Conflict between Food Security and Food Sovereignty.* Santa Barbara, CA: ABC-CLIO, 2010.

Scheper-Hughes, Nancy, and Margaret M. Lock. "The Mindful Body: A Prolegomenon to Future Work in Medical Anthropology." *Medical Anthropology Quarterly* 1, no. 1 (1987): 6–41.

Schlosser, Eric. *Fast Food Nation: The Dark Side of the All-American Meal.* Boston: Houghton Mifflin Harcourt, 2012.

Schmitt, Mark. "The Legend of the Powell Memo." *The American Prospect* (blog). April 27, 2005. http://prospect.org/article/legend-powell-memo.

Schulze, Matthias B., and Frank B. Hu. "Primary Prevention of Diabetes: What Can Be Done and How Much Can Be Prevented?" *Annual Review of Public Health* 26, no. 1 (2005): 445–67. doi: 10.1146/annurev.publhealth.26.021304.144532.

Schwittek, David, and Alyshia Gálvez. *¡Salud! Myths and Realities of Mexican Immigrant Health.* 2017. https://filmfreeway.com/1314729. Video.

Secretaría de la Salud. *Estrategia nacional para la prevención del sobrepeso, la obesidad y la diabetes.* Mexico City: Impresora y Encuadernadora Progreso, 2013.

———. "Resultados preliminares de la ingesta dietética de la población mexicana (ENSANUT 2012)." *ITESO: Licenciatura en Nutrición y Ciencias de los Alimentos* (blog). Oct. 1, 2014. https://blogs.iteso.mx/nutricion/2014/10/01/analisis-de-la-ensanut-2012/.

Sesia, P. M. "'Women Come Here on Their Own When They Need to': Prenatal Care, Authoritative Knowledge, and Maternal Health in Oaxaca." *Medical Anthropology Quarterly* 10, no. 2 (June 1996): 121–40.

Shah, Sonia. "*The Diet Myth: Why the Secret to Health and Weight Loss Is Already in Your Gut; The Good Gut: Taking Control of Your Weight, Your Mood, and Your Long-Term Health;* and *The Hidden Half of Nature: The Microbial Roots of Life and Health.*" *New York Times Book Review,* Dec. 28, 2015.

Sibley, Barbara. "Round Table at Sobremesa Conference." Jaime Lucero Mexican Studies Institute, City College of New York, May 11, 2016.

Siegel, Alana D. "NAFTA Largely Responsible for the Obesity Epidemic in Mexico." *Washington University Journal of Law and Policy* 50 (2016): 195–226. https://openscholarship.wustl.edu/law_journal_law_policy/vol50/iss1/9.

Singer, Merrill. *Introduction to Syndemics: A Critical Systems Approach to Public and Community Health.* New York: Wiley, 2009.

Singh, G. M., R. Micha, S. Khatibzadeh, S. Lim, M. Ezzati, D. Mozaffarian, and Global Burden of Diseases Nutrition and Chronic Diseases Expert Group (NutriCoDE). "Estimated Global, Regional, and National Disease Burdens Related to Sugar-Sweetened Beverage Consumption in 2010." *Circulation* 132, no. 8 (Aug. 25, 2015): 639–66. doi: 10.1161/CIRCULATIONAHA.114.010636.

Skoufias, Emmanuel, and Vincenzo Di Maro. "Conditional Cash Transfers, Adult Work Incentive, and Poverty." *Journal of Development Studies* 44, no. 7 (2008): 935–60.

Small, Ernest. "42. Quinoa—Is the United Nations' Featured Crop of 2013 Bad for Biodiversity?" *Biodiversity* 14, no. 3 (2013): 169–79. doi: org/10.1080/14888386.2013.835551.

Smith, Robert C. *Mexican New York*. Berkeley: University of California, 2005.

Smith Oka, Vania. *Shaping the Motherhood of Indigenous Mexico*. Nashville, TN: Vanderbilt University Press, 2013.

Socolow, Susan Migden. *Women of Colonial Latin America*. Cambridge: Cambridge University Press, 2000.

Sorvino, Chloe. "The Newcomers to America's Richest Families 2015: Clans behind OxyContin, Tootsie Roll, Grey Goose." *Forbes*, July 1, 2015. www.forbes.com/sites/chloesorvino/2015/07/01/the-newcomers-to-americas-richest-families-2015-clans-behind-oxycontin-tootsie-roll-grey-goose/;.

Statistics Canada. "The 10 Leading Causes of Death, 2011." 2015. www.statcan.gc.ca/pub/82–625-x/2014001/article/11896-eng.htm.

Stevenson, Seth. "Cocktail Creationist." *New York Magazine*, Jan. 10, 2005.

Striffler, Steve. *In the Shadows of State and Capital: The United Fruit Company, Popular Struggle, and Agrarian Restructuring in Ecuador, 1900–1995*. Durham, NC: Duke University Press, 2001.

Stryker, Rachael, and Roberto González. *Up, Down, and Sideways: Anthropologists Trace the Pathways of Power*. New York: Berghahn Books, 2014.

Stuckler, David, Martin McKee, Shah Ebrahim, and Sanjay Basu. "Manufacturing Epidemics: The Role of Global Producers in Increased Consumption of Unhealthy Commodities including Processed Foods, Alcohol, and Tobacco." *PLOS Medicine* 9, no. 6 (2012): e1001235.

Stupak, Alex, and Jordana Rothman. *Tacos: Recipes and Provocations*. New York: Clarkson Potter, 2015.

Suárez-Orozco, Marcelo, and Carola Suárez-Orozco. "Children of Immigration." *Phi Delta Kappan* 97, no. 4 (2015): 8–14.

Suárez Vélez, Jorge. *Ahora o nunca: La gran oportunidad de México para crecer debate*. Mexico City: Random House, 2011.

Susser, Merwyn. *Causal Thinking in the Social Sciences: Concepts and Strategies of Epidemiology*. New York: Oxford University Press, 1973.

Sutton, Ryan. "Six Reasons Why Cosme Is One of New York City's Most Relevant Restaurants." *Eater, New York* (blog). Dec. 16, 2014. http://ny.eater.com/2014/12/16/7397631/cosme-restaurant-review-enrique-olvera.

Swinburn, Boyd A., Gary Sacks, Kevin D. Hall, Klim McPherson, Diane T. Finegood, Marjory L. Moodie, and Steven L. Gortmaker. "The Global Obesity Pandemic: Shaped by Global Drivers and Local Environments." *Lancet* 378, no. 9793 (2011): 804–14.

Tomiyama, A. Janet, Britt Ahlstrom, and Traci Mann. "Long-Term Effects of Dieting: Is Weight Loss Related to Health?" *Social and Personality Psychology Compass* 7, no. 12 (2013): 861–77.

Torres, Craig. "Saving Globalization: Two Decades into Nafta, Mexico's Wins Range from Tacos to Engineers." *Bloomberg Markets*, July 12, 2016. www

.bloomberg.com/news/articles/2016-07-12/saving-globalization-two-decades-into-nafta-mexico-s-wins-range-from-tacos-to-engineers.

Traill, Bruce. "The Rapid Rise of Supermarkets." *Development Policy Review* 24, no. 2 (2006): 163–74.

Tsing, Anna Lowenhaupt. *The Mushroom at the End of the World: On the Possibility of Life in Capitalist Ruins.* Princeton, NJ: Princeton University Press, 2015.

Tuñón-Pablos, Esperanza, and Joanna Dreby. "Risk Factors for Overweight and Obesity among Mexican Children in New York." *International Journal of Population Research* (2016): 1–8. www.hindawi.com/journals/ijpr/2016/2420167/cta/.

UNESCO (United Nations Educational, Scientific and Cultural Organization). "Traditional Mexican Cuisine—Ancestral, Ongoing Community Culture, the Michoacán Paradigm." UNESCO/Intangible Cultural Heritage. 2010. www.unesco.org/culture/ich/en/RL/traditional-mexican-cuisine-ancestral-ongoing-community-culture-the-michoacan-paradigm-00400.

United Nations. *Report of the World Food Conference.* Nov. 5–16, 1974, Rome.

US Census Bureau. "US Census 2000." Accessed Jan. 27, 2005. www.census.gov/main/www/cen2000.html.

———. "Census 2000 and American Community Survey 2004, PCT 20." 2006. www.census.gov.

USAID (United States Agency for International Development). "US Foreign Aid by Country." Accessed Jan. 6, 2016. https://explorer.usaid.gov/country-detail.html#Mexico.

USDA (United States Department of Agriculture). *Mexico's Retail Food Sector 2005: GAIN Report Number MX5303.* Washington, DC: USDA Foreign Agricultural Service, 2005.

US Department of Commerce, International Trade Administration. *NAFTA 10 Years Later: Chemicals.* June 2004. www.trade.gov/mas/ian/build/groups/public/@tg_ian/documents/webcontent/tg_ian_001989.pdf.

Vasconcelos, José. *La raza cósmica.* Mexico City: Espasa Calpe, 1948.

Vaughan, Mary K. *Cultural Politics in Revolution: Teachers, Peasants, and Schools in Mexico, 1930–1940.* Tucson: University of Arizona Press, 1997.

Vaughan, Megan. *Curing Their Ills: Colonial Power and African Illness.* Palo Alto, CA: Stanford University Press, 1991.

Viladrich, Anahí. "Understanding 'Nostalgic Inequality': A Critical Analysis of Barriers to Latinos' Healthy Eating Practices in the United States." *International Journal of Healthcare* 3, no. 1 (2017): 58.

Viladrich, Anahí, and Barbara Tagliaferro. "Picking Fruit from Our Backyard's Trees: The Meaning of Nostalgia in Shaping Latinas' Eating Practices in the United States." *Appetite* 97 (2016): 101–10.

Villeneuve, D. C., M. J. Van Logten, E. M. Den Tonkelaar, P. A. Greve, J. G. Vos, G. J. A. Speijers, and G. J. Van Esch. "Effect of Food Deprivation on Low Level Hexachlorobenzene Exposure in Rats." *Science of the Total Environment* 8, no. 2 (1977): 179–86.

Vines, Richard. "These are the World's 50 Best Restaurants." Bloomberg. April 5, 2017. www.bloomberg.com/news/articles/2017-04-05/xxx-tops-2017-world-s-50-best-restaurants-list.

Viruell-Fuentes, E. A. "'It's a Lot of Work': Racialization Processes, Ethnic Identity Formations, and Their Health Implications." *Du Bois Review: Social Science Research on Race* 8, no. 1 (2011): 37–52.

Viruell-Fuentes, E. A., Miranda, P. Y., and S. Abdulrahim. "More than Culture: Structural Racism, Intersectionality Theory, and Immigrant Health." *Social Science and Medicine* 75, no. 12 (2012): 2099–2106.

Vivas, Esther. "Food Crisis: Causes, Consequences and Alternatives." *International Viewpoint,* Dec. 14, 2009.

Wallerstein, Immanuel Maurice. *The Modern World-System: Studies in Social Discontinuity.* New York: Academic Press, 1974.

Wann, Marilyn. "Fat Studies: An Invitation to Revolution." In *Fat Studies Reader,* edited by Esther D. Rothblum and Sondra Solovay, ix–xxvii. New York: New York University Press, 2009.

Warman, Arturo. *Corn and Capitalism: How a Botanical Bastard Grew to Global Domination,* translated by Nancy Westrate. Chapel Hill: University of North Carolina Press, 2003.

Weis, Robert. *Bakers and Basques: A Social History of Bread in Mexico.* Albuquerque: University of New Mexico Press, 2012.

Weisbrot, Mark, Lara Merling, Vitor Mello, Stephan Lefebvre, and Joseph Sammut. *Did NAFTA Help Mexico? An Update after 23 Years.* Center for Economic and Policy Research. March 2017. http://cepr.net/images/stories/reports/nafta-mexico-update-2017-03.pdf?v=2.

Weismantel, Mary. "White." In *Fat: The Anthropology of an Obsession,* edited by Don Kulick and Ann Meneley, 45–62. New York: Tarcher Penguin, 2005.

Wells, Pete. "When He Dined, the Stars Came Out." *New York Times,* May 8, 2012.

———. "Curious, Seductive Breezes from Mexico: Cosme in the Flatiron District." *New York Times,* Feb. 4, 2015.

———. "Top New York Restaurants of 2015." *New York Times,* Dec. 15, 2015.

———. "Slips and Stumbles at an Elite Perch." *New York Times,* Jan. 12, 2016.

Williamson, John. "What Washington Means by Policy Reform." *Latin American Adjustment: How Much Has Happened* 1 (1990): 90–120.

———. "Democracy and the "Washington Consensus." *World Development* 21, no. 8 (1993): 1329–36.

———. “What Should the World Bank Think about the Washington Consensus?” *World Bank Research Observer*, 15, no. 2 (2000): 251–64.

Wills-Karp, Marsha, Joanna Santeliz, and Christopher L. Karp. “The Germless Theory of Allergic Disease: Revisiting the Hygiene Hypothesis.” *Nature Reviews Immunology* 1, no. 1 (2001): 69–75.

Wilson, Christopher, and Gerardo Silva. *Mexico's Latest Poverty Stats*. Wilson Center, Mexico Institute. 2013. www.wilsoncenter.org/sites/default/files/Poverty_Statistics_Mexico_2013.pdf.

Wise, Timothy. *Agricultural Dumping under NAFTA: Estimating the Costs of U.S. Agricultural Policies to Mexican Producers*. Washington, DC: Woodrow Wilson International Center for Scholars, 2010.

———. “The Cost to Mexico of US Corn Ethanol Expansion.” Global Development and Environment Institute Working Paper no. 12–01. Tufts University, Medford, MA, 2012.

———. “How Beer Explains 20 Years of NAFTA's Devastating Effects on Mexico.” *PRI Global Post* (blog). Jan. 2, 2014. www.pri.org/stories/2014-01-02/how-beer-explains-20-years-nafta-s-devastating-effects-mexico.

Wolf, Eric R. *Europe and the People without History*. Berkeley: University of California Press, 2010 [1982].

Woolf, Aaron, dir. *King Corn*. 2007. DVD.

World Bank. “International Diabetes Atlas.” Accessed Oct. 2, 2017. https://data.worldbank.org/indicator/SH.STA.DIAB.ZS.

World Health Organization. “Diabetes Country Profiles, 2016.” 2016. www.who.int/diabetes/country-profiles/en/.

Yang, Joshua S., Patricia A. McDaniel, and Ruth E. Malone. “‘A Question of Balance’: Addressing the Public Health Impacts of Multinational Enterprises in the OECD Guidelines for Multinational Enterprises.” *Global Public Health* 7, no. 10 (Dec. 2012): 1045–61.

Yates-Doerr, Emily. “The Weight of the Self: Care and Compassion in Guatemalan Dietary Choices.” *Medical Anthropology Quarterly* 26, no. 1 (2012): 136–58.

———. *The Weight of Obesity: Hunger and Global Health in Postwar Guatemala*. Oakland: University of California Press, 2015.

Ybarra-Frausto, Tomás. “Rasquachismo: A Chicano Sensibility.” In *Chicano Aesthetics: Rasquachismo*, 5–8. Phoenix, AZ: MARS (Movimiento Artístico del Rio Salado), 1989.

Yoshikawa, Hirokazu. *Immigrants Raising Citizens: Undocumented Parents and Their Young Children*. New York: Russell Sage Foundation, 2011.

Yuñez-Naude, Antonio. “The Dismantling of CONASUPO, a Mexican State Trader in Agriculture.” *World Economy* 26 (2003): 97–122.

Zahniser, Steven, Sahar Angadjivand, Tom Hertz, Lindsay Kuberka, and Alexandra Santos. *NAFTA at 20: North American Free-Trade Area and Its*

Impact on Agriculture. USDA, Economic Research Service, 2015. www.ers.usda.gov/publications/pub-details/?pubid=40486.

Zepeda, Eduardo, Timothy A. Wise, and Kevin Gallagher. *Rethinking Trade Policy for Development: Lessons from Mexico under NAFTA*. Carnegie Endowment for International Peace. 2009. http://carnegieendowment.org/2009/12/07/rethinking-trade-policy-for-development-lessons-from-mexico-under-nafta-pub-24271.

Zimmet, Paul. "The Challenge of Diabetes: Diagnosis, Classification, 'Coca-Colonization,' and the Diabetes Epidemic." In *The Medical Challenge*, edited by Ernst Fischer and Gerald Möller, 55–112. Munich: Piper Verlag, 1997.

Index

Made in the USA
Middletown, DE
18 January 2024